BONNIE KAYE'S STRAIGHT TALK

A COLLECTION OF HER BEST NEWSLETTERS ABOUT GAY HUSBANDS

BY

BONNIE KAYE, M.Ed.

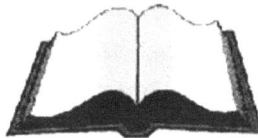

CCB Publishing
British Columbia, Canada

Bonnie Kaye's Straight Talk: A Collection of Her Best Newsletters About Gay Husbands

Copyright © 2008 by Bonnie Kaye, M.Ed.
ISBN-13: 978-1-926585-04-8
First Edition

Library and Archives Canada Cataloguing in Publication

Kaye, Bonnie, 1951-
Bonnie Kaye's Straight Talk: A Collection of Her Best Newsletters About Gay
Husbands / by Bonnie Kaye. – 1st ed.
ISBN 978-1-926585-04-8
Also available in electronic format.
1. Bisexuality in marriage. 2. Closeted gays--Family relationships.
3. Gay men--Family relationships. 4. Gay men--Relations with heterosexual
women. 5. Marital conflict. 6. Self-help techniques. I. Title.
HQ1035.K37 2008   306.872   C2008-905823-2

Publisher: CCB Publishing
               British Columbia, Canada
               www.ccbpublishing.com

Dedication

This book is dedicated to the thousands
of women who come to me to heal.

It is also dedicated to my wonderful family and friends
who give me unconditional support.

I also dedicate this compilation to my soul mate of nearly 15 years.
He has inspired my greatest of writing through his constant
encouragement and love.

Part One

Bonnie Kaye's Straight Talk

INTRODUCTION

In June of 1999, my first book, now republished as "The Gay Husband Checklist for Women Who Wonder" was published. To help promote the book, I developed my website at **www.Gayhusbands.com** offering to help women who suspect or find that they are married to gay men.

Within that year, after receiving so many positive responses to the book, I decided to write a monthly newsletter that I named "Straight Talk." A dozen years earlier, after the end of my own marriage to a gay man, I started writing a column for a local gay newspaper which was later syndicated for eight other national gay newspapers by that same title discussing how a straight woman views the gay community. The newspaper column lasted approximately a year, and then I decided to stop because it was thwarting my own healing process by being immersed in the gay community week in and week out.

After healing, I was ready once again to help others. I believed that a newsletter addressing the issues that we all face would be valuable. And as my monthly letters from my readers continually say after seven years, the newsletter is their "lifeline."

Each month, I addressed issues that affect straight wives and girlfriends who find themselves in a situation that is similar to Alice in Wonderland—a world of topsy turvy upside down mirrors where what is real because false and what is false becomes reality. I keep it real—I tell it as I see it—which is the only way I can explain it.

Sometimes my views have been accused of being biased. I'm told that I'm not flexible and that I only see things in black and white. I suppose I'm guilty of that. But guess what? I stand by my views. One thing you can say for me—I am consistent! That is because I refuse to give in to people who want to compromise their lives and happiness. I am not about compromise—I'm about living a happy life free of additional emotional burdens that weigh women down.

My newsletters reveal my heart and soul. They tell of my personal triumphs and defeats. I reveal my personal thoughts and personal weaknesses. I am the first to share what so many of my women feel. I try to give encouragement as they walk through the path of gay husband recovery.

Our women, now over 7,000 worldwide, love to read these newsletters not only because of what I have to say, but equally as much because they learn so much from my readers who write in every month with their experiences. I have included some of those letters in the second part of the book knowing that they will also inspire you. I thank my readers for sharing their innermost thoughts with my other readers.

I hope this book will be your guide in the days, months, and years ahead. This is a book to help you heal and to validate all of your thinking and suffering. I like to always add stories of hope because we need to keep that word HOPE focused in front of us in order to heal.

If you would like to be added to my future newsletters, just drop me a line at **Bonkaye@aol.com**. I will be happy to add you to help you in your journey.

BONNIE KAYE'S STRAIGHT TALK

PROFOUND AND REVEALING WORDS FROM A GAY EX-HUSBAND

I receive several letters each week from men who are struggling to come out to their wives. I respond quickly to these men in hopes that my support and encouragement will give them the courage to be honest with their spouses. I also receive several letters each month from gay men who find my website or see my book who commend me for the work I am doing in helping people understand the complexities of straight/gay marriages.

Two months ago, I received a letter from a man who was about to become an important part of my life. Jay is an attorney in Pennsylvania. He is the first man I have ever met who can write words in a manner that clarified all of my own thoughts and feelings allowing me to conceptualize a key to the problem of straight/gay marriages that I will share with you. Jay's sensitivity and honesty reflects what most of us would like our husbands or ex-husbands to tell us. Too few of us ever get to hear these words. I asked Jay if I could reprint some of his thoughts because I believe it validates so much of what all of us feel and need to hear. After reading his words, I am sure you will appreciate not only what he says, but also the beauty of how he says it.

Jay's first communication to me in early February stated:
I am a gay man who was married for 23 years. My ex-wife and I have two children. I am writing to encourage you to continue the important work you are doing. I only wish that in 1996 when I finally began to come out that there had been resources such as yours to support our family through our transition.

3

I thanked him for his kind words, and his response was this:
I think that both men and women in these circumstances must recognize that there are no winners but there are survivors who create new ways to relate, maintain, support and redefine their family. In the process of ending my marriage, I lost my best friend and the dream we had of growing old together. Slowly, we have worked to continue to parent our children in accordance with the many values that we continue to share. There are many things I would, in retrospect have done and handled differently, but my single largest regret is that I did not deal with the secret of my sexuality while still in my marriage and in the years of counseling before divorce. So to those men who you counsel, I would urge them to give the woman they chose to love and bear children the earliest chance to deal with the truth. They probably will not have a marriage together, but they will at least have a chance of preserving the love that once brought them together with hopes and plans for a lifetime.

More words of insight kept coming as the weeks progressed. I will highlight just a few of these pearls that will lead to my conclusion:
I keep reminding myself of the shame that fueled my own 'denial' and kept me closeted for most of my life, however I also know the damage that secrets do to those who keep them and would like to teach that lesson to my kids as well.

...my kids have always been a priority. I can recall vividly, my own frustration at seeking advice on how to come out to my kids and finding little support from the gay or straight communities. Of course, I was looking for the right way to do it and assure that the kids would not go off the deep end or reject me. No one could have given me the surefire approach. However, I think there is a real void. God knows there are self help books out there on everything else.

No woman deserves to be in this situation. In the past, I spent a lot of time searching my own soul, trying to figure out how much of the failure of my marriage was attributable to homosexuality and how much was the struggle for control, neediness and other dynamics extant in any couple relationship. My ex-wife and I hurt each other a lot. There are still things about her that I dislike, but I have concluded that the presence of my secret in that relationship was the primary poison. Much of the rest of our conflicts flowed from it....the absence of trust, the neediness, possessiveness, the anger and ultimately the conflict that I both created (even if it was not by premeditated design) and used to find the impetus despair and courage to leave. Accordingly, as painful as it is to admit, I know that the secret and immutability of my homosexuality is inextricably bound up in all that was wrong in our relationship. Yes, I had difficult issues to confront. As with any person facing difficult times, some of them I handled quite poorly. I could empathize with your own horror and dismay at how you thought and acted at various points.

I share your belief that bisexuality is often a transitional label and crutch used by homosexuals unable or unwilling to come to terms with their natural orientation. I lived that myself. After my separation from my wife, I woke one morning after a date with a woman and was appalled by the self discovery that I might do this to another woman because I hated who and how I was.

And the most profound words were yet to come:
I was much more demanding about the order around me when I was married to my ex-wife. While I still like a nice home, I find I am less compulsive about cleaning and demanding that those around me keep things tidy and neat. I believe that my need for external order in my prior life was a way of coping with my own internal chaos (and tension created by my attempts to compartmentalize my being.) Of course, my discomfort with disorder at home also served to legitimize my disappointment in my ex-wife as a homemaker. "If only she were a better wife.......we would be happy" was my mantra. Indeed, she was disorganized and sloppy, but as it turned out, I have realized that IF ONLY SHE HAD BEEN A MAN, I WOULD HAVE BEEN MORE TOLERANT. Ouch.

All of Jay's words allowed me come to a great realization. For those of us who have or had gay husbands who complained actively or passively about our inadequacies and faults as wives, I have another thought:

Who would we be today if we had a straight husband? How would our destiny have changed if we were loved, nurtured, sexually desired with passion and tenderness, given emotional support and encouragement, and made to feel like we were part of a real couple in tune with each other's needs, wants, and aspirations? What if we didn't have to spend countless hours each day wondering why we were failures as wives, women, and lovers—ripping away our self-esteem layer by layer until we became strangers unto ourselves and others? What if our husbands' dishonesty and cheating didn't change us to become untrusting, suspicious, and doubting wives, forcing us to question our ability to make rational decisions? How many of us were sidetracked through those "detours of deceit" that diverted us from the direction that life might have taken otherwise?

Bottom line—no matter how much a gay man loves a straight woman, it is not the kind of love that fulfills the basic human need that all of us have. It can never be the kind of love that inspires the music that becomes classics or the poetry that makes the heart flutter. It is not the kind of love that can ever be returned to the degree that you are giving it. Even the best of relationships are barely more than great friendships—not the passion and excitement that make us thrive and look forward to waking up each day. And even these relationships are woven with dishonesty, distrust, infidelity, resentment, and frustration. Life was not meant to be this complicated.

What Jay has done for me personally is say what I am still waiting for my ex-husband to say after 20 years. Occasionally, a word of wisdom will float out from my ex-husband expressing how "screwed up" he was through the years. Does it change anything? Not really. But yes, knowing the truth does help validate who we are, what we became because of our gay husbands, and how we can change and now move forward. It's the first step towards healing the scars, bridging the understanding, and bringing closure to a chapter in our lives.

Thank you, Jay, for sharing your thoughtful insights with all of us. Jay has also graciously volunteered to help men who are going through the struggle of coming out. He has been very valuable in this role over the past few weeks. If you know of anyone who may need guidance, direction, and a supportive voice, let me know and I will forward your information to Jay. If you have any personal questions you would like to ask him, he is happy to respond. Just let me know.

MAY 2001

GAMES PEOPLE PLAY –THE "IF ONLY" AND THE "BLAME" GAMES

I have worked with too many women who at first assume that the reason for their husbands' homosexuality is due to something they did wrong. For those of us who have had time to work through this problem over a longer period, it is easy for us to react by saying that this thinking is ludicrous. But try to remember when you first suspected or discovered your husband's interest in men. Then it doesn't seem quite as ridiculous.

When I reflect on my own inner feelings of shame during those early years, I remember feeling a great sense of responsibility. I used to play a game that most of us fall prey to. I call it the "If Only Game." It goes like this. "If only I could be a better wife….if only I was more attractive…if only I was better as a lover…if only I was a better housekeeper, if only I wasn't so demanding…if only I could lose more weight….if only I was smarter…if only, if only, if only…then maybe he could love me enough not to think of men.

My ex-husband, Michael, was excellent at playing the other mind-twister game, which I call the "Blame Game." After I questioned him for the first time about his sexuality two years into our marriage, he used this as an opening to play this game as his new weapon of mental torture. This is where he would come closest to revealing the truth by throwing in my face, "If I were gay, who could blame me? After all, you are always making too many sexual demands… complaining about something…gaining weight…acting jealous… being possessive …much too demanding….all consuming…and the list went on. Then he would end the conversation with the words I desperately wanted and needed to hear—"It's a wonder that I'm not gay." Whew, what a relief. I was a failure as a wife, but at least not failure enough to make him gay.

A young woman who visits my on-line support sessions on Thursday evenings recently told us that on an intellectual level she

7

knows she didn't make her husband gay, but emotionally she still feels that she is responsible. I often hear this in the beginning of a marriage separation. During the early stages of disclosure, it is easy to believe that we are somehow at fault for our husbands' decisions to enter the gay world. Even when we can accept the news, we still can't grasp all of the implications. We can't figure out how our husbands were "straight enough" to marry us, make love to us (even if it wasn't frequently or passionately), have children with us, have married lives with us, but chuck it all for sex with a man. When we pass through the denial stage and accept that our husbands are gay, we still have a difficult time believing that it wasn't something we did that drove them over the borderline and into the twilight zone of homosexuality.

What takes time for us to fully comprehend is that we had no part whatsoever in our husbands' homosexuality. This was who they were long before we ever knew them. Some of them knew it and fought it hoping that marriage to a woman would miraculously make them straight. It can't…and it didn't. Others claim they honestly didn't know it because it didn't surface until years later. But even the late bloomers almost always felt that something was not quite right—they just didn't think it was a sexual thing.

Playing the "If Only Game" is a very natural part of self-questioning that all of us initially go through. The problem is that some of us keep playing, sometimes for months and even for years. This is a dangerous game if played for too long because it indicates that you have not been able to put things into perspective. It also stops you from moving ahead and trying to rebuild your life. Prolonged questioning of your failures in the marriage serves no purpose at all. If you failed at the marriage, it's because you were in a no-win situation. You were set up for failure, not for success. Success was not an option.

If you had been in a marriage with an emotionally healthy straight man, all of your efforts of being a supportive and loving wife would have been appreciated and in fact, cherished. So don't use your marriage with a gay husband as a map for your future relationships. If you try again with a straight man, you'll see how different and better it can be.

LIVING LA VIDA LIMBO

Let's discuss married gay men who won't leave the marriage or for that matter, won't leave the closet. This is a subject that can never be talked about enough because it seems to be a stumbling block for so many of us who can't get our husbands to "come clean" with the truth about their homosexuality. I receive so many letters each month from women who are sure about their husbands but fear confronting them. But I also get letters from women who do confront their husbands with evidence in hand and get denials with distorted truths giving excuses such as "Those pictures belonged to a co-worker," or "I have no clue how those websites got on our computer."

For those women whose husbands eventually tell you the truth, count yourselves as lucky even though you may not feel that way at the time. No doubt hearing the word gay is devastating, but not hearing it is even worse. This month alone, I have received 32 letters from women who asked me for advice because their husbands or ex-husbands will not admit to their homosexuality. These women know the truth. They have stumbled on it one way or another. It has smacked them in the face through hidden websites, email, pornography, letters, hotel receipts, phone bills, etc. And yet, their husbands just keep lying or denying. They are not ready to be honest--and may never be ready. Some men will never be ready to accept their homosexuality because it is too painful or embarrassing.

These are the men whom I call the "Limbo Men." Their whole lives are lived in limbo. They are emotionally straight, but physically gay. They never feel totally comfortable in either world, but they are much more comfortable "passing" in the straight world where they are accepted as part of mainstream society.

All married gay men go through "limbo" for a period of time. In other words, they are stuck in between both worlds hoping that by wanting the straight world badly enough they will be able to "cross over" into it. They keep thinking that if they play the role long enough, they will become transformed into the part, not just play the part as an actor. But the Limbo Men I place in this category are different from other gay men who eventually come to terms with themselves. They are even different than the gay men who are staying in their marriages but who acknowledge they are gay, at least on some level.

The real Limbo Men have no sense of remorse for what they are doing to their wives. In fact, they often feel as if they are the victims and strike back at their wives in an emotional or physically abusive manner. They blame their wives for their unhappiness and never have a clue about the damage they are doing to these women, whom they promised to love, cherish, and respect. They place the blame of their unhappiness on their wives, when in fact, there is nothing that their wives could possibly do to make them feel happy or fulfilled. Their wives are women, and they are gay men.

These are the men who will never leave their marriages. They will stay there until the day they die, leading a painful existence and sharing that pain with their wives. More specifically, pouring that pain upon their wives. We all know that misery loves company, and these men are happy to make you as miserable as they are.

So often, these "Limbo Men" husbands luck out. They have wives who are much kinder and more understanding than average. These are the women who will keep trying every little trick in the book thinking someday they will get their husbands hooked. The women live an accepted existence, looking for the crumbs in the marriage while trying to turn those crumbs into a cake. It is truly a tragedy and waste of human life.

JUNE 2001

A TRIBUTE TO VIVIEN LEIGH AND ALL THE OTHER NYMPHOMANIACS OUT THERE

A few years ago, I was watching a television special on Vivien Leigh, deceased mega-movie star best known for her role as Scarlet O'Hara in the 1939 movie saga "Gone with the Wind." As the story went on about her life, there was mention of the word "nymphomaniac." The story continued about the years of depression and mental illness she endured and her tragic death after losing her battle to tuberculosis.

When I heard the word "nymphomaniac," it grabbed my attention and brought back some very troubling emotions. The word is derogatory for certain. When people call others this name, it is a name

10

of shame, not admiration. I know this because I had heard this word too many times through my marriage to my gay husband. And yes, it took its toll on my self-confidence as a woman. No woman likes to be accused of being a sexually demanding partner. It is degrading to think that there is something wrong with you when you think that your sexual needs are normal.

Through the years, I heard many other women express their feelings of shame over this accusation. Of course, by then I knew the deal. I knew this was a way for some gay husbands to make their wives feel abnormal enough that they would stop asking for sex. This accusation usually came when they were running out of headache excuses to avoid the physical interaction that was being increasingly difficult to pull off.

When I investigated further about Vivien Leigh's life, I learned that the love of her life was Sir Lawrence Olivier. Olivier was gay or as some men like to call themselves, "Bisexual." Was I surprised to find this? No not at all. It was so much easier to label Leigh a "nymphomaniac than to understand the real problem—her husband's homosexuality.

I understand this. I know what it's like to be told that the fault for bad sex in a marriage is my fault. My husband used to say that I was too demanding or too pushy when it came to wanting sex. I remember what it feels like to be told that wanting sex as much as I wanted it was "abnormal." I couldn't understand why once or twice a week was "excessive" for a newly married couple. I would voice this concern only to be shot down with more insults. When my husband saw that I wasn't backing off, he resorted to calling me the worst name of all...nymphomaniac. That quickly put to rest any thoughts for a night of passion. It belittled me enough not to ask again. So sex (not lovemaking) deteriorated quickly within that first year and I became too ashamed to suggest or approach it.

I learned through conditioning that I was much too "aggressive" in that area, so I stepped back and retreated.

Yep, it hurt like hell. I think this is one of the worst parts of being a wife of a gay man. It slowly strips away from you one of the most important parts of being a woman. You start to believe that you are inadequate as a lover. After all, if you were a good lover, your husband would want you, right? Well, we know in these cases, wrong, but while we're living this way, it's hard to keep it in perspective.

Getting back to Vivien Leigh, the more I researched her life, the angrier I became. It is common knowledge that she suffered from mental depression. She went through a series of shock treatments and was labeled manic/depressive. Sir Lawrence Olivier finally left her twenty plus years into their marriage saying he could no longer deal with her mental state. It seems to fit the prototype of so many of our own marriages. Some biographers attribute her depression to her tuberculosis, as explained away by some medical practitioners. I guess back in the 1950's and 1960's, the medical field wasn't aware of the mentally debilitating state of straight wives married to gay men. I'm sure there were not any support groups around for women in this position.

It is interesting that so many of the women I hear from and work with are also taking medication for depression. Even more interesting is the fact that none of them are suffering from tuberculosis. Rather, they are depressed because they feel like they are failures in their lives and marriages. They cannot please their husbands no matter how hard they try, and they place the blame on themselves. Even after they know the real problem in their marriage, they continue to be depressed internalizing the blame. We may rationalize intellectually it is not our fault, but on some level, our intellect is clouded by irrational emotional feelings of responsibility.

If Vivien Leigh were alive today, no doubt she would have much greater support in her struggle to understand why her marriage failed, why she was depressed, and why she was a normal woman with normal sexual desires. The love of her life went on to marry some other love in his life after the marriage ended. How that marriage worked out is a mystery.

So the next time you see a movie with Vivien Leigh, realize that we hold a common bond with her. Let her serve as an example of what can happen to a woman when she lives her life in a maze of distortion. And let us also learn from her tragedy and seek professional help to put our lives on track lest we end up spending wasted years on medications that don't change the source of our unhappiness.

"AND TALKING ABOUT SEXUALITY"...

I won't tiptoe around the subject. I know that sometimes it takes a while before women are able to discuss this sensitive issue.

Eventually it comes to the forefront, but sometimes it is too painful or embarrassing an issue to discuss one on one or even in a group. Therefore, I will write this to the many of you who think about it, but are too afraid to talk about it.

In my book, "The Gay Husband Checklist for Women Who Wonder," I have a checklist for the prototype of woman that gay men seek out. Sometimes it is a conscious search; other times it is an unconscious choice. But there does seem to be a list that most of us fit in to.

The majority of women whom I hear from fit into the category of "women with limited sexual experience." I can usually spot these women quickly because they send me similar letters. They write that they thought their sexual relationship with their gay husband was satisfactory or satisfying. Usually they add in that is fine when they have "sex"---it just doesn't happen very often. It makes me so sad that women think that the sexual acts they have had with their gay husbands is, well, for lack of a better term, "REAL SEX." Gay husband egos aside, it is satisfactory sex, or perhaps functionary sex. But real true passion—well, it's just not.

Truth be told—I know the difference. Not only did I have a gay husband, I also had a couple of gay boyfriends in my younger years. We did "it," but "it" always left something to be desired. My ex-husband Michael wasn't bad on those occasions when we had sex. But it always seemed like he had to try so hard—almost forced—after the honeymoon was over. And there's nothing to deflate your ego more than thinking that a man is doing you a favor by making love to you—especially a man who loves you.

I called Michael last week and asked him if he could think back to the days when we were sexually involved prior to and shortly after the marriage. I told him that I needed his honest, objective opinion about our sex life together. Did he really enjoy it? Did he look forward to it? Was it a hardship for him? He told me that in the beginning, he actually did enjoy it. Having sex with me was working toward his goal of getting married and having a family. He was hoping that I would be the solution to his fantasy of the American dream.

He still did not consider himself gay at that point although he had already had numerous gay sexual encounters. But he felt that he was straight because he never had an emotional entanglement with these guys. There was no kissing, hugging or intimacy—it was just sex. I hear that from many gay men who cross over the line to the straight side for a while. They are not trying to fool us—they are trying to fool Mother Nature. Or they are hoping that Mother Nature has been playing a joke on them because they are able to perform with a woman to some degree. Michael was certainly adequate enough as a lover to fool me. It was never a great sex life, but it was a good sex life for the first few months. There was nothing that out of whack that would make me suspicious that he was gay.

Now, all these years later, I am happy to say that I could definitely tell the difference. This is due to the love of an exceptional man who entered my life seven and a half years ago. It wasn't love at first sight on his part, but it was on mine. After chasing him for 16 months, he gave in and we began what I define as the love affair of my life. We've had some bumpy moments in our relationship, but this is due to the fact that he is a man and I am a woman. You know how men are from Mars, and women are from Venus. One road that has never been bumpy is our sex life. After seven and a half years, it is still top of the line. He is playful and passionate. He aims to please because he gets satisfaction out of pleasing me—and it turns him on instead of off. Every encounter is an adventure. We don't have sex—we make love. This is perhaps the real difference. Making love to someone is an important way of expressing love. Wanting to please your partner before pleasing yourself is the most unselfish form of showing love. Making sure that your partner is satisfied shows the real nature of giving love. I have come to enjoy new aspects of lovemaking that I never dreamt existed. And I don't have to scheme about how I can have him make love to me. He is always ready, able, and willing to go. We are a middle-aged couple whose sex life is continually peaking.

This man makes me feel as if I am the most desirable woman in the world.

He hasn't noticed that I am fat yet because his love for me blinds him to my imperfections. I haven't noticed that he's not Steven Segal yet because in my eyes, that's whom he looks like. Maybe our lives are like the movie "The Enchanted Cottage", where two people appear physically to each other only to be what they see in each other, even if no one else can see it. But isn't that what true love really is?

They say that sex is the part of the relationship that takes the least amount of time. Maybe that's so. But it is such an important part of a relationship because it creates intimacy, closeness, and trust. A healthy sexual relationship builds a sense of self-esteem in a woman because the woman feels desirable. For me, it gives us an added treasure to look forward to and cherish several times a week. In between, it brings us closer with holding, touching, and caressing as a sort of after-math. This keeps our love alive and flourishing.

Am I bragging? Well, sort of. But I am not doing it to make anyone jealous—but rather to make a point. There is hope for every woman whose sexual esteem has been broken and battered much like mine was. It took me 11 years to open my heart to love or sex after my marriage. I felt so deflated as a woman and as a sex partner. I was content living in a state of celibacy and suppressing that side of my human need.

I was out there looking for a while before my soul mate came floating into my life. During that period, I met lots of men while looking for love. I had some short-term relationships and even a few shorter encounters. I was ready to awaken the side of me that had died years before during my marriage. I was awkward at first because it had been so long. But when the right moment came, I took advantage of it. I know I wasn't at my best at first because I was so nervous, but I certainly enjoyed the passion of a straight man. It felt so nice to have someone want to fulfill that need and do it happily instead of feeling like I was forcing him. It wasn't perfect the first time or even the tenth time, but it kept getting better as I started gaining back my sexual confidence. Yes, it is scary starting this side of life over again, but it is so worth it. All women are born with sexuality. Women who are married to gay men have had that side suppressed or deadened by their spouse. We just learn to give up on that part of us and to bury it thinking that this is the natural course of marriage or a relationship. Please know that it can be revived and brought back to life.

My soul mate has never called me a "nymphomaniac." That's because I'm not. I never was. I am just a normal woman with very normal sexual needs. Over the past seven and a half years, he has cultivated my sexuality and taught me that I can reach new heights of enjoyment. It is easy to keep me sexually interested because my partner never allows our sex life to become boring or mundane. He is a straight man—a straight man who appreciates a straight woman. Let this be a lesson for all of you. Never give up the part of you that helps maintain your identity as a woman. Give yourself a chance to be loved again. Look for your soul mate because chances are, he is out there looking for you.

"GET OVER IT"

Another problem that many women write to me about is the pressure they get from family members or friends to "get over it" when it comes to recovery from their marriages. They can't understand why they are having such trouble doing this, and they feel even more inadequate (as if we need more to feel worse about) because it just isn't happening as quickly as other people.

I get upset when I hear this pressure expressed from women who are really trying to move past their anger and hurt but not at the pace that others expect of them. After all, marriages fall apart all of the time. In fact, almost 50% of marriages in this country end in divorce. People start over again and find new relationships. Why are you having such a hard time?

What other people don't realize is that there are numerous issues that we have to deal with after a marriage to a gay spouse ends. Some of these issues are unique and unlike those that women with straight husbands face. We have to figure out what to say to the children and when to tell them; we also have to decide what to tell family, friends, and co-workers. We live in a world where people still don't understand about a gay husband and fear the ridicule we will face from them. There are many very ignorant people out there. Even in this day and age, people say, "What did you do to make him gay? After all, he wasn't gay when he married you."

We have to rebuild our own self-esteem, which has been sorely damaged through these marriages by not only feeling the failure of a marriage, but also wondering how much of a lie we were living. We have to rebuild our sense of trust within our own decision-making processes knowing that we walked blindly into a situation where we were so misled. Most of us have lost or never had the feeling of what real intimacy means in a relationship. We have difficulty trusting men again and trusting our own ability not to walk into this situation one more time. And this is a genuine fear that many women express—"It happened to me once. How do I know the next man I get involved with won't be gay?" After all, why couldn't we tell the first time around? This is confirmed by the ignorance of others who insist that we "must have known but married him anyway because we thought we could change him."

There are other complications as well. There are those women who still feel some sense of responsibility for their husbands' homosexuality. They are convinced that they played some part in their husbands turning to men.

That's because some gay husbands are cruel enough to say that to them rather than take the responsibility for the truth.

We have to deal with our own feelings of homophobia. Even if we understood homosexuality in general terms, it took a whole new meaning when it entered our marriages and ruined our hopes and dreams for our futures with our husbands. We have to deal with our own feelings about our husbands bringing lovers into the lives of our children and how that will affect our children emotionally. We have to fear how other people will treat our children if they find out. And of course, we now have to contend with the possibility that our children will be gay because this is a new reality.

Certainly straight marriages that end go through emotional upset and turmoil. We have to go through those same problems, such as single parenthood, financial problems, selling the home, and legal tangles. But in addition, we are forced to deal with all the additional issues stated above. This is a double whammy that just doesn't end when a marriage ends.

So, the next time someone tells you to "Get over it," don't feel that there's something wrong with you. Just smile and say, "Someday I will." Take the time that you need to rebuild your strength. Gay Spouse Recovery takes time. Sometimes it takes a lot of time. Eventually things will equal out, but some scars are bound to remain. And that's okay. We are not machines that can just wipe away the emotional impact, nor should anyone tell you how you should feel after this disaster.

OCTOBER 2001

FACING OUR FEARS OF DEALING WITH A GAY HUSBAND

In my last newsletter, I promised that I would address the most common fears women have when they are finally able to accept that they are married to a gay man. These are the same fears I had when I learned about my husband. I think that the fear of the unknown is much more difficult to deal with than the truth. These questions are painful, but they need to be discussed to alleviate some of your irrational worries and help you understand your rational ones.

Q. If my husband is gay, will my children be gay?
A. It's possible. I was scared for years. I believe that gay is genetic, not a choice or learned behavior, and I know that genes can be passed on to children. In the 1980's as I met a greater number of families and started calculating multiple homosexual members of the immediate or extended family, I began to see a pattern that really alarmed me. No one wants to have a homosexual child. That is not a homophobic statement at all, but rather one based on a mother's love for her child. We all know how difficult it is to be gay in our society, and we don't want our children to have to face those hardships. However, recognizing that this was possible, I raised my children in an environment of positive feelings about homosexuality from a young age.

I corrected them when they would repeat derogatory statements they heard from friends, classmates, teachers, neighbors, and even television. I was honest about my friends who were openly gay and allowed them to serve as role models long before they knew about their father's homosexuality. I emphasized that people had no choice in their sexuality any more than they had a choice in their color, height, or eye color. Just because people were different, it didn't make them wrong or bad. I did this because I knew there was a greater chance of one or both of my children being gay because their father was gay. And, I later learned that my ex-husband's father was "bisexual," even though Michael had never met him because he was adopted by extended family members at birth.

As things turned out, our daughter, now 21, is a lesbian. When I discovered this two-and-a-half years ago, I cried. No matter how much you prepare yourself for this possibility, you still cry when it becomes a reality. And when I finished crying, I hugged her and told her that I didn't care—and I don't. My daughter told me that thanks to my attitude, she was able to accept who she was without running away from it and hiding like her father felt he had to do. She was comfortable with her sexuality. For that, I am grateful. I know all of the confusion and pain her father lived with for years trying to accepting himself. I assure you that my daughter will not be marrying some unsuspecting man to prove that she is straight. I feel good about that. Ironically, it was much easier for me to accept my daughter's homosexuality than it was for her father to accept it. And, her father is extremely defensive and angry if I bring up the fact that this is genetic, as if I am blaming him. There is no blame here, nor do I hold him responsible. But I know there is a part of him that feels responsible even though there is no blame intended.

I have spoken to so many women who have experienced one or more of their children being gay or struggling with accepting their homosexuality. I know that it is heartbreaking, but don't let this be a barrier between you and your child. By now you should understand that homosexuality is not a choice that anyone would consciously make. There are no choices when it comes to this. Love your child without letting this become an issue; otherwise you will both lose out. And in case this is a fear that becomes your reality as it did mine, stop the negative gay talk in front of your children lest they get the message that there is something wrong with them that will stop you from loving them if they are gay.

Q. Can my child's sexuality be influenced if she/he spends time with his/her father and sees his lifestyle?
A. Absolutely not. Gay is not something that can be influenced when it comes to a person's sexuality. No one can "become" gay by hanging around gay people. Sexuality does not "rub off" on children. It can influence their opinions in either a positive or negative way about homosexuality, but it doesn't "turn them gay." I find it so sad when I receive letters from time to time from women who have this terrible fear and for that reason, do their best to keep their children out of the reach of the fathers. This certainly can't help the situation and in fact, only worsens it. A child needs a father, and sexuality shouldn't be the issue. Responsible parenting should be the only concern. That being said, a gay father also has the responsibility to be sensitive to a child's feelings. If a child is uncomfortable being in a gay environment such as parties, picnics, social gatherings, etc., that should be the first consideration. Also, it isn't surprising that a child will feel uncomfortable with the father's lifestyle, especially during adolescence. No matter how much a child loves a father, it doesn't

mean he or she is going to be comfortable with homosexuality through those difficult years. .

Q. Do I have to worry about my gay husband being around my son? I read stories about some gay men liking younger boys and it scares me. And what about his gay friends? Will they go after my son?
A. I understand this fear. It comes from the darkest side of the horror stories that we tend to hear when learning about homosexuality. I think a lot of this fear comes from the fact that our own husbands or ex-husbands are fixated on younger men. But it's ironic how we don't fear for our daughters when we are married to straight men. The thought of incest would never cross our minds, even though there is a far greater number of a father-daughter incestuous relationship than there are gay father-son concerns. I won't say that this doesn't happen or can't happen, but I certainly wouldn't worry about this happening. This is a very irrational fear. Just because a person is gay doesn't mean that he is a child molester. It is so important to be able to differentiate between homosexuals and pedophiles.

Homosexuals often get the bum rap of being pedophiles, which is very disturbing to me. Pedophiles prey on innocent children, male and female, without much differentiation on whom they victimize. Even within the realm of pedophilia, there are many different kinds of child molesters, which make the situation even more complex. However, it is not unusual for gay men to like guys who are much younger than they are. We feel this sense of discomfort when we find many of our husbands going after or out with younger men once they come out. This certainly does seem to be the natural trend with gay men, especially when they come out at a later age. I have no concrete answer on why this happens, just numerous theories formed from the answers I've received from the gay men that I discuss this with, including my own ex-husband. Some say it's because they are recapturing their own youth; others say they are finally being able to act on the attraction they've had since they were that age but never had the chance to act on it.

Although the following statement will offend the sensitivities of some of my gay friends, I'll risk it. The value system of gay men differs from the value system of straight women when it comes to acceptance of having sexual relations with younger men in their teenage years. What would be totally unacceptable for us to accept as proper conduct is quite acceptable within the gay way of thinking. I am not sure where gay men draw the line of acceptable ages for pursing young men. However, I don't think that many gay men would object to a man at any age having sexual encounters with teenagers who are 17 or 18. The concern we all have is where does the line stop? Is 16 okay? Is 15 or 14? 13? There are some very shaky grounds when we speak about this.

As wives or ex-wives, the thought of our husbands being with young men whom we see as teenagers is a repulsive thought. We would feel a similar sense of repulsion if our husbands were straight and pursing 17 year old girls, so it's not just a gay issue. However, we are so devastated by the imagery of our husbands with other men, that the thought of them being with younger men still in their teens is far more discomforting to us. This added to the fact that this is not only acceptable but also common behavior within the gay community is what is so upsetting to us. The explanation that these teenage boys are seeking older men because it represents a sense of security, experience, and stability doesn't comfort us at all. We are still sickened at the visualization.

We are also worried about our own sons. It's a common fear that most of us have on some level. Will our husbands' friends be pursing our sons as they go through their adolescent years? I worried about it. Is it a rational fear? I don't know, but it doesn't stop me from feeling that way.

Q. Now that I know that my husband is gay, do I have to be worried that I have AIDS?
A. I think this is the first thing that comes to the minds of women once the words of "gay" are spoken. They are petrified that they might be infected with AIDS. Obviously, there are still a lot of misconceptions about AIDS or else they wouldn't be so worried. Ironically, most of the women who write to me about this fear haven't had sexual relations with their husbands for years. They have nothing to worry about. Is it possible to get AIDS without sex? Well, I won't say no but the chances of it happening are so remote. AIDS is not airborne, nor can you get it from drinking from the same glass, using the same towel, or sharing the same bed. It is transmitted through blood or semen, so if you and your gay mate have been sharing needles it is possible.

Once blood reaches the air, the virus dies within a matter of seconds. So unless your husband has been bleeding on you after he is cut and you have an open wound, I wouldn't worry about it. I tell women that if it will give you peace of mind to be tested, than do it. But there is no reason to have this irrational fear if you haven't had sexual relations with your husband for over a year.

But, if your husband has had recent sexual relations with you, then definitely get tested. Even if he tells you that he hasn't acted on his homosexuality, get tested anyway. Gay men coming out to their wives often lie about their sexual experiences because it is too difficult to tell the truth. Sometimes the truth comes out weeks, months, or years later. Sometimes it never comes out. So you do need to protect yourself and get tested.

If you have had recent sexual relations with your husband, it is good to check out all sexually transmitted diseases—not just AIDS. Numerous women have had complications because they had STDs and were not aware of it until complications prevailed. STDs can fester for a while before they appear so you may think you're safe when you're not.

HEY BONNIE KAYE, I'M GOING TO BE THE EXCEPTION TO YOUR RULE

Each week, I received dozens of letters from women who are looking for advice and help. Some of them are asking for hope in their marriages, explaining that they are able to accept their husbands' indiscretions and confessions because their husbands are filled with remorse and promises that it won't happen again. I answer them gently, but honestly, explaining that the best of intentions at the moment of confession will not be the way it will stay indefinitely. I go on to state that when a husband is finally ready to reveal his sexuality, it is not unusual for him to try desperately to find a way to keep his marriage together if he is not ready to leave it. Most men don't confess the truth until they are ready to leave the marriage, but some reveal the information in an effort to "cleanse their guilt" and hope that this will absolve them from their homosexuality. After all, isn't confession good for the soul?

A few of these women get angry with me claiming that I don't understand. Their husbands are good men who have been wonderful husbands and fathers except in this one instance. They can't understand why I would want to break up a perfectly good marriage when they could get help to resolve this one problem. And their husbands chime in. "I can change. I will go for help and be able to keep my marriage together." And they begin to go for family counseling together, finding out ways to work around this problem that will make the couple live happily ever after forever. They will show me that my jaded views on straight/gay marriages are not true in every case.

So, let me reiterate this again. I know that there are exceptions to every rule. I am sure that there must be a marriage out there that is working out well, even though I haven't found it yet. It all depends on what you consider to be a marriage that is working.

Recently, an angry woman refuted the information that I sent to her, calling me on numerous quotes from the newsletters. She claimed that her marriage was wonderful in most ways. In fact, in one of her correspondences to me she stated,

"I think because of his gay tendencies, he has been more attentive, more loving, more sensitive, more compassionate....His gay side has been an attribute to his personality."

I don't doubt these words. Most of us fell in love with our gay husbands because they were attentive, sensitive and compassionate.

Another statement she made was:

"I was a confident, fulfilled, happily married woman, wife and mother. He did have a secret life going on but it did not affect me, or how I was living. Not until he "came out" did our lives begin to change, and I sense that they will turn for the better, not for the worse, or the dissolving of our marriage."

I am not quite sure what this means. To me, if a husband is having a secret life, how can it not affect you when the news comes out? I personally believe that this information means that the life you think you were living with someone is a lie. And not just a little fib, but a totally big lie. If a husband is having a secret life apart from you, regardless of the sexuality issue, how does this equate to something that will make your marriage turn for the better? If any of you understand this, please educate me—I'm a willing learner.

She then continues:

"I take it from this that you believe that there is simply NO WAY that you will support those trying to keep their marriages intact, you even say that you will REFUSE to support anyone, like us, who is determined to keep our marriage together, and that you will only give support and understanding to those that are dissolving their marriages. It seems as if you are an advocate for divorce instead of restoration. We are looking for restoration, not devastation."

Well, yes, that is true. I just don't know how in good conscience to give support to couples who want to keep these marriages together. I don't know how to tell any woman that she has to try to understand that her husband will always on some level be attracted to other men. I don't know how to advise women that no matter how hard they try to be good wives that this will never be enough to stop their husbands from wanting to have sex with men. I don't know how to get women to erase from their minds and memories the information that they have come to learn, nor do I know why I should expect them to accept this as acceptable in a marriage based on trust between two people.

And I'm okay with this. I'll take my chances keeping my points of view. I know that there are marriages that are coping through this situation for various reasons. They are staying together because it fits whatever needs are there. They can be for financial reasons, family reasons, or emotional reasons. And I am willing to give support to anyone who is in a marriage like this as long as they understand that I am not supporting the marriage—but rather her.

The women that I work with are in all different phases of their lives. Although the majority of women are divorced, some are still in their marriages. But those who are in them have no false illusions or hopes. They are there physically because of circumstances, but they are not there mentally or emotionally. I give them support so they do not get lost in an emotional blitz of unreality and denial. Some women just can't make the break at the moment, but they don't delude themselves into thinking that their marriages are working. They are working the marriage because at the moment, they need to for various reasons. They are wise to the fact that their marriages will never be what they need them to be, and they don't try to make them into something that they can't be. They know that when the right time arises, they will be able to physically leave as well.

Chances are, if you are married and part of my support network, you know exactly what I mean. Sometimes women are stuck in relationships due to various predicaments. I have a number of you whom I correspond with regularly who are there out of obligation because your husbands are ill and you can't walk away. You are good women who have made a conscious decision to do what you have to for the time being until the opportunity comes when you can break free and live with your own conscience. But to encourage you to stay in your marriages by telling you to forgive your husband for marrying you knowing he was gay or to understand that he later came to terms with his homosexuality and it's not a big deal, would be ludicrous. I won't do it. I can't do it.

As I advised this woman, there are people you can find who can accept this way of life. The Internet affords people the opportunity to search for magical answers and solutions that fit everyone's needs if you search long and hard enough that I don't give. There are couples who are living with homosexuality in their marriages and somehow coping with it and even accepting it. And there are all kinds of well meaning and professional people out there who will tell them they are doing the right thing. I am sure that Dr. Laura would advise couples to make their marriages work by telling the gay husband to hold off on acting on his sexual impulses until the children are grown. After all, it's much better for children to be raised by two parents than one, which is not the way I feel when a marriage is just a functional marriage. I don't know how gay men put aside their feelings for twenty years or so and not act on them, but if they can, more power to them. I'm sure there are men out there who are doing this even though I haven't met them. And in all fairness, is this right thing to do to the wife? Give her a sense of false security that the marriage is workable until the children are grown and then say, "Well honey, the kids are grown and now it's time for me to pursue my own life?" Now that the wife has invested years of her time building a marriage, she is faced with the same nightmare only at a later time when she has to start over and it's more difficult because years of her life have been wasted in a relationship that is ending.

And one last comment that I'd like to share with you that offended this woman:

25

I resent being told that "Gay men do not belong married to straight women. Period." How can you say that with such absoluteness, without knowing individual situations? This implies ALL, every single one. That none should be married. Period. How can you make such a definite, 100% claim?"

All I can say here is that I stand by my words. Gay men do not belong in marriages to straight women. Period. 100%.

NOVEMBER 2001

WHEN THERE'S JUST NO PROOF

Every week, I receive numerous letters from women who are desperate to find "proof" that their husbands are "bisexual" or gay. On my website at www.Gayhusbands.com, I have a section called, "Catch Him." It gives women the directions to check their computer's temporary Internet files on line to see if there are any gay sites that their husbands are visiting. I also advise them to install inexpensive spyware to monitor all of their husbands' activities. Some of these women write back to me after finding the evidence that they were so afraid of finding. At the same time, there is a great sense of relief because their suspicions were finally confirmed.

It's interesting to see the various emotional reactions after women confront their husbands with their discoveries. Some rethink their immediate fears and write back to me saying that after questioning their husbands with the information, and they were made to second-guess their suspicions when their husbands give them a perfectly logical explanation as to how these websites appeared. Here are some of the most common explanations:

1. "He claims he has no clue how they got there. Someone else must have been using the computer." In other words, there are gay men sneaking into your home and using your computer to go to gay pornographic websites right under your nose but you don't notice it.

26

2. "A friend of his at work is having sexual identity problems. He asked my husband to do some research for him because he's too embarrassed to do it himself." This means that your husband must be an exceptional man if he is willing to help a gay man come to terms with his homosexuality by visiting numerous gay porno sites. Does this educate your husband so he can be an effective helper?
3. "My husband said that it is normal for men to look at all kinds of sexual sites. It doesn't mean anything just because the sites are gay. It's normal curiosity." I still haven't met the straight man yet who is sexually turned on by the site of men having sex. Curiosity may account for a one-time look, but not repeated visits.
4. "My husband said that just because he is looking at gay sites doesn't mean that he is going to have sex with men." So why isn't he looking at sites where women are having sex with men? Why doesn't that turn him on instead?"

Well, I stand by my words. Straight men don't view gay porno sites. Consider this the confirmation you are looking for. You don't have to look any further. You definitely have a problem, or shall I say, your husband and your marriage definitely have a problem.

As hurtful as this confirmation may be, these are the lucky women because they have something concrete to back up their suspicions. I hurt for the women who just can't get any proof. Their husbands don't use a home computer or have a computer at work that can't be accessed. They are experts at covering their trails and leave no hard evidence around.

For those of you who write to me and are perplexed and confused about how to find proof about your husbands, let me say this. Some of you will never find what you are looking for no matter how hard you look. I know women who have spent countless thousands of dollars hiring private detectives to track their husbands and they still didn't get the proof they needed. That's because you would literally have to shadow someone day in and day out for long periods of time before you could sometimes find that proof. Some of these men are very clever and very cautious. They carefully cover their tracks so no information can be found. Unless you have tens of thousands of dollars to spend on this, it's virtually undoable. I give a lot of credit to the ingenuity of some of the women who write to me who go to such lengths to find any slipup. This includes going through cell phone bills, putting taps on the phones at home, and carefully scrutinizing credit card bills and receipts. Sometimes there is an answer by doing all of this. But sometimes there are no answers and more often, no way to access this information.

So let me give this word of encouragement. Most often, a woman's best proof is her own sense of intuition. I trust that more than I trust other findings. Women have a sixth sense when it comes to these matters. I often ask women who write to me why they suspect their husbands are gay as opposed to having an affair with another woman. And the reasons usually fall into line. Every blue moon I am able to comfort a woman and tell her that her suspicions don't seem to indicate homosexuality, but that is the rarity. And believe me, I'm thrilled when I am able to relieve someone's fears. But in almost all cases, I know there is a problem.

Most women who write to me for help are not women who are in happy marriages. I'm still at a loss to understand why people are willing to stay in a marriage that is not rewarding, lacks affection and passion, and gives little if any emotional encouragement or self-esteem building. I say this to women who are in marriages with straight men, not just gay men. I believe that life is short—unless, of course, you are saddled in a bad relationship. Then it becomes very long and grueling. I never quite understand why women are willing to throw away years of their life that could be rewarding and fulfilling to stay in a relationship that is debilitating and at best, existing. People marry with good intentions, but that doesn't mean it is going to work out. Ironically, women married to gay men try to stick out their marriages much longer than women in unhappy straight marriages. I understand why, but it's not a pleasant picture.

Women who are married to gay men feel this need to keep trying to make something work that is not workable. They internalize that the failure of the marriage is their failure, when in fact there is nothing they can do to make these marriages successful. It's beyond their control, but they can't accept that internally. They go back to the "if only" game—"if only I can be a better wife, my husband will love me more and be happy with me." As I've discussed in earlier newsletters, this just doesn't happen. We are not the cause of our husbands' unhappiness in the marriage. Homosexuality is the cause. We just look like the cause to them because we are what are standing in the way of them acting on their needs, so we become the "whipping girls" so to speak.

So, for the record, let me say this. If your marriage is failing and you have tried every reasonable thing to make it better and it still isn't working, cut your losses. Stop looking for proof and wasting more days, months, and years. Look for a way to get out of the marriage. Start making a plan to find a way to move on. You don't have to feel guilty or like a failure. The longer you stay in a destructive marriage, the worse you will feel. There's a whole world out there waiting for you. You'll never have the chance to find out what you could have if you hold yourself back just waiting for it to happen. You have to take action. You have control of your future even if you can't control the present.

DESTRUCTIVE COUNSELING

I get requests from women all over the country asking me if I can refer them to a counselor or psychologist for help. This is a major responsibility, and I never refer anyone if I don't personally know a therapist.

But this raises an important issue. I want to warn you about is finding incompetent or misguided counseling. This is something that disturbs me deeply because I receive letters from women who are investing hard earned money but obviously getting very poor and counterproductive advice which leaves them more confused and doubting of themselves. Most people are not familiar with the world of therapy and depend heavily on the feedback they receive from the counselor. I have learned over the years from women who tell me about the direction of their therapy that this can only add more problems to an already problematic situation.

The majority of women who write to me don't need therapy—they need support. And once they learn that the problems they are facing in their marriage are not their problems but rather the problems of their husbands, they are able to find resolvable solutions just through the support of others who have experienced the same problem.

Recently, I have spoken to several women whose therapists are definitely giving them destructive information. These therapists don't understand the dynamics of a straight/gay marriage. One woman this month told me about a therapist who doesn't believe that her husband is gay. In this case the husband is fixated on gay pornography, but the therapist is saying that he's a sex addict and not gay. She has him attending Sexual Addiction meetings and is encouraging the wife to stay focused on the marriage and not give up. The wife feels very discouraged because her husband continues to watch these gay videos on the computer while she is there, claiming that it excites him to do so because it is like "forbidden fruit." She also knows from her own minimal sex life that her husband has sexual problems. And yet, she has been told to hang in with him because he is not gay. This is ludicrous. Watching gay pornography does not sexually arouse straight men. Trust me on this.

There are some women are going to marriage counseling with their husbands where the counselor is treating the couple as if it were any other couple with straight-couple problems. Let me assure all of you that going for marriage counseling together is not going to be the answer to fixing the marriage. Any therapist who tells you that the problems can be worked on in these marriages is really clueless. These are not marriages that have the traditional problems that other marriages face. These are a unique set of problems that need to be viewed in their own rite. And all of the counseling in the world is not going to make your husband's desire for men magically disappear.

Another important problem that I want to mention is about counselors who hold their own personal beliefs as the truth in their therapy approach. These are therapists who have religious convictions that cloud their objectivity. In just this month alone, I spoke with five women who went to Christian based counseling. Their therapists advised them to stay in their marriages while their husbands found their way back to heterosexuality. Their train of thought is that homosexuality is chosen, not in-born. They believe that if these husbands understand the consequences of their actions, they will "choose" to be straight if given enough time and encouragement. Obviously, these women are having doubts about this kind of help being effective because they are writing to me out of frustration and despair. Although I do understand and respect religious personal convictions, I haven't found any happy results from people who have to spend years of time trying to make something work based on someone's ability to change into something that is not his nature. I know that people can change behaviors when forced to do so, but it doesn't change what someone's sexual orientation is. It's somewhat like what they call "dry alcoholics." There are people who stop drinking, but inwardly, they can't change what they are. They are never happy, and they resent those around them who have "forced" the change.

If there is counseling to be had, it needs to be counseling to build up self-esteem and independence of the wife so that she can make the right decision to leave the marriage. Women in these marriages are often emotionally broken and lack the ability to believe in themselves. In these cases, finding a good therapist to help you regain your confidence and courage can be very important. But the direction of the counseling needs to be one of moving ahead, not staying stuck in an unhealthy situation and seeing how you can make it work.

Another word of caution—if you are not connecting to a therapist, end it early and keep seeking someone that you find to be helpful and encouraging. Just because someone is practicing doesn't mean that he/she is competent for helping you. Keep seeking help until you find someone that you feel comfortable with. I remember when I was 22 years old, MANY YEARS AGO, I was having some personal problems and decided to seek professional help to guide me through this period. I had no understanding of counseling or therapy. I went to a local hospital and they assigned a therapist to me. I went to him for six sessions, and after each session, found myself more and more depressed. He was practicing a form of therapy that was totally ineffective for my problems, but I was too inexperienced to understand this. Rather than switch to a different therapist, I stopped going thinking there was something wrong with me because I wasn't benefiting from the treatment. It took me many years and lots of schooling to understand what this man was doing. He was a new therapist and practicing his style of therapy that was not suitable for the type of problem that I had. I wasn't smart or savvy enough to understand that I could have asked for someone else who could have been more effective for me.

Many times when we seek out help because we are in vulnerable positions, we put all our faith in professionals who may not have the expertise we need to resolve our problems. This doesn't just happen in counseling, but many other situations such as legal or medical problems. That's why it is so important to recognize when something is not working for you and to keep pursuing the professional help that will work best for your needs.

RECURRING ANGER

I've had several requests to address the issue of returning anger. Just when you thought you were past that stage in your recovery minus your gay husband, it's back. Women have written to me asking me what's wrong with them when this happens. They are afraid they are backsliding because they feel so angry all over again.

There are different kinds of anger when a marriage ends. The anger that you have when you find out that your husband is gay is different than the anger you will face in future years when you are raising children as a single parent. Then we face the anger that all women face when they are left with raising the family as the primary caretaker. Sometimes we confuse this anger with our gay husband issues, and in all fairness, this is not a gay issues, but rather a universal one of irresponsible men. You don't have to be gay to be irresponsible.

My own father abandoned my mother and left her with five children. He went on to have a happy, prosperous life 3,000 miles away, taking everything we owned. We ended up virtually homeless. My mother became the primary caretaker and supporter of us, and at the time, my younger sisters were only 1, 3, and 5. My mother had never worked before, and with virtually no workforce skills, went out and started building a career for herself. She never had an easy life after that point, but continued to be there for all of us emotionally and financially until her death a year and a half ago. Ironically, my father, who moved to California 34 years ago, is a millionaire. He has chosen to abandon his children, claiming that we should be able to make it on our own like he did.

My father is not gay. He went on to remarry and had a different family. He was very willing to take care of them financially, but not us. My story is not unique. I know many men who move on after marriage to new families and have new children and never look back. I don't understand it and I never will. It would be inconceivable for me to think of a mother doing that to a child, but it seems more common in men. All men, just not gay men.

I share this information with you because we do have our own issues to heal from as wives of gay men. But we also have other issues to deal with that are universal to all women. It's important to understand the difference in the problems because if not, we will always be angry and bitter about the gay issues. It is important for our own state of mental health to distinguish between the two. It is also important for our healing process to understand the difference so that we are able to move ahead in life and not be held back by our own insecurities.

As I've stated in earlier newsletters, wives of gay men go through an additional set of recovery issues than women who have straight husbands. We need to rebuild our shattered sense of self-belief and self-esteem. If we are continually pulled back into the gay spectrum, we will never be able to find happiness and fulfillment with a future mate. We will start confusing issues, which will start the self-doubt process all over again.

Anger needs to be channeled into positive responses, or else it turns into bitterness. I have seen this happen too many times. Bitterness affects our own sense of happiness and the happiness of our children. It stagnates us from moving ahead in our own lives, so who ends up losing here? You have lost so much already, why continue to keep being on the losing end?

When you are angry due to circumstances that seem totally out of your control or because of your ex-husband's actions, learn to confront the anger by taking positive action. If you feel that talking to your ex-husband will only result in a yelling match with no resolve, sit down and write him a letter explaining to him why you are hurting. Sometimes when he sees it in writing, it makes him actually think and act rather than just react. It helps you feel better too because too often in the course of a conversation or argument, you lose sight of the issues that you want to discuss because your anger takes you to other places that don't need to be revisited. A letter gives you a chance to express your anger and make sure that the important points are covered. If you have forgotten any, you can always add a P.S. or write the letter over—or even rip it up if you don't feel like sending it. Sometimes just writing the letter is enough of an outlet.

Understand that after a marriage is over, there are lots of "normal" hardship issues that we face as single parents. Raising children is exhausting, and not having a back up for some relief can be overwhelming. It hurts when we are tired at the end of the day and feel so trapped while our husbands are out with their new gay mates or gay friends. But if our husbands were straight, chances are they'd be doing the same thing. It's not a gay thing, just a male thing. The fact that he's out with a man may make it more emotionally uncomfortable, but we have to be able to once again separate those feelings from the feelings that most single mothers experience of abandonment and lack of financial security.

So, if you feel anger creeping up in your life again, know that it's okay. You probably have a lot to be angry about. Just don't let it take over your life. Work through it so it doesn't turn to bitterness. Find support or call a friend and talk it out. Don't let it fester in you, because unresolved anger turns into bitterness, and the only one who really hurts is you.

Remember, you are never alone. There is a great amount of support for anyone who needs it. Write to me or join our Thursday evening support chat sessions for group comfort and help. Have a pleasant Thanksgiving holiday and realize that life can always get better as long as there is hope.

DECEMBER 2001

THERE'S NO PLACE LIKE HOME FOR THE HOLIDAYS

Let me first wish all of my readers a happy holiday season. Well, how about a peaceful holiday season? I think that expecting a "happy holiday" may make you start to think that you are supposed to be happy, when in fact, many of you reading this are going through your own heavy-duty pain.

When I was married to my gay husband, I usually found holidays to be very depressing. People appeared so happy wherever I went, all wrapped up in a mystical holiday spirit. Inwardly, I felt like a knife was cutting me because I so desperately wanted what I thought everyone else had—namely, a loving spouse and happy family. I went through the holidays very mechanically doing all the right things, but somehow, I always felt disappointed when they were over. My husband made sure to surround us with lots of people in order to take the focus off of "us" as a couple. Holidays meant that we were home—alone—a definite no-no. My husband did his best to make sure that his numerous friends and family members would spill into our home. He called as many as possible to invite them over with promises of good food (that I would have to prepare) and great conversation (that he would monopolize) There was too much danger in having a long period of quiet time together. That would mean that I might make the "demand" (in his head) or "suggestion" (in my head) for intimacy.

It became an all too familiar holiday pattern. Surround us with lots of people I couldn't care less about, and in fact feel irritated by, to avoid my desperate pleas for affection, intimacy, and .....sex. And on those rare days when people just couldn't make it over due to snow blizzards or other plans, you can be sure that was a day when an argument would ensue. The fight didn't have to be over anything of importance—it just had to start and then build itself into a mountain. I'm sure that my husband realized that a molehill would have never stopped me from making a suggestion. But once things escalated into a mountain, they were too high to climb and usually left me sleeping on a couch or not sleeping at all while I cried.

Overdramatic? I don't think so. When I recall some of the absurdities that went on in our marriage that I couldn't understand, it finally makes sense. After speaking with thousands of women, this is often an emerging pattern. After it happens enough times, you retreat and take a giant step backwards. You know the drill. Ask for something that your husband doesn't want you to ask for long enough, and you'll just stop asking. It beats a fight or argument over nothing of importance, as well as the humiliation of being turned down again for wanting a normal, human need—namely intimacy. .

Somehow, the fantasies that had played over and over again in my head throughout my youth, adolescence, and early adulthood about home and the holidays just never happened. That's why I became conditioned after the first few holidays not to get excited, not to see the beauty, not to feel the spirit, and most importantly, not to get my hopes up. That went for every holiday. I had to reshuffle my way of thinking about the song "No Place like Home for the Holidays." I definitely knew that they were not talking about my home.

And so, my friends, if your holidays don't meet up to your expectations of what they are supposed to be, don't feel that it's you.

It's not. It's your situation. And if you are not in your marriage, don't think that those feelings go away quickly—the memories of when you were in your marriage can linger on for many years to come. The good news is the feeling of excitement can return in time. If you meet your soul mate at a future point, you will understand the joy of watching the Big Apple fall down at midnight while he holds you close to him and starts the fireworks at midnight to celebrate your future year together. You'll be able to turn off the television after the third verse of Auld Lang Syne and make your own music.

And even if you spend the night alone until you meet your soul mate, or if you never meet him, it won't hurt nearly as much as spending it with someone who makes you feel as if you are the person who takes the joy out of the holiday because you are always hoping for something that he is just not willing or able to give you.

AND SPEAKING ABOUT THE HOLIDAYS...

Speaking about the New Year.....I love the thought of a New Year coming in while an Old Year is going out. It's a time to make resolutions for change. It's a reminder that there is no time like the present to make some new resolutions that can resolve some of your problems. Most women are busily making plans to start a new diet or to stop smoking. Women with gay husbands can commit to making a new start free of the mental pressure that is wearing you down.

I always say that when you finally find the emotional and mental freedom, you are more than halfway to your goal. This is an excellent time to start planning your physical escape from your unhappy marriage. It's not something that has to happen today or this month, but it is an opportunity to think about a better place that you can be in before another year passes by without any movement to happiness.

This is an opportunity to reflect back on your past years of marriage to your gay husband. If you are one of the nearly thousand of women receiving this newsletter, chances are you are living with conflict in your life. This is the best time of the year to start making a plan that will help you to reach your goal. For some of you, that may mean going back to school to learn skills that will make you financially independent. For others, it may mean joining a support group or finding a women's group that will help you rebuild your self-esteem to give you the strength to do what you need to do. As long as you plan positive actions in your personal life, you will start to gain the strength that you need to make permanent positive changes in your life.

So, even though New Year's Eve may normally be a painful night for you, look at it differently this year. Make a conscientious effort to stay up late and watch the Big Apple descend for the countdown. This year will be for you. View it with the optimism and hope that it is supposed to bring. Vow to make this a year of change—a better year for you and your children. Make a mental plan on how you are going to get there—and like with all resolutions, try to stick to it!

THE HONEYMOON REVISITED

I love happy endings to stories. With straight/gay marriages, some of you also have the advantage of having some happy middles of stories even if the endings are sad. Of course, these middle stories don't last very long, but while they happen, it's like having a second honeymoon.

I hear it from many women. The story is usually the same, so here goes a typical one that I received this week:

"Dear Bonnie,

It's a miracle! After I confronted my husband with my suspicions about his being gay, he admitted to me that he had passing thoughts about men but would never act on them. And now, things are better than they've ever been. Now it's just like when we were on our honeymoon—but even better. My husband is being very attentive to me and very considerate. For the first time in years, he is being affectionate to me. He is holding my hand in public and kissing me goodnight every night.

And now for the best part—my husband realizes that he is not gay.

He has approached me for sex for the first time in years. He is really doing everything to be the kind of husband that I knew he could be if he could just get those homosexual thoughts out of his head. Now I realize that we can move forward in our marriage with all of the bad times behind us."

Most of the time, the letters end with, "You were wrong, Bonnie." Sometimes, I'll hear a more insightful thought from a woman saying, "I know that this is just a temporary stage, but I'll take it for the moment!"

I do want to tell you that these honeymoons don't last for long. Sometimes they'll last a few weeks or even a few months. But as letters that come in later with humble apologies to me say, the "honeymoon revisited phase" is usually over within a short amount of time. You see, after the husbands lulls you into a false sense of security once again, he feels he has you back where he wants you and so his "Normal," or shall we say, "Abnormal" patterns creep back slowly or sometimes quickly. But they always come back. I tell these women there is no need to apologize. I know how I used to hang on to any false hope that came my way no matter how quickly it whizzed past my eyes.

Why do our gay husbands revisit the honeymoon phase? Quite simple. They fear that you now suspect or know the truth about their homosexuality and they are determined to throw you off track and start doubting yourself. They are not ready to be honest, and so they buy time. They become affectionate, attentive, and start to give you unexpected gifts. They say they are willing to work on their "sexual dysfunction." The claim they will go for marriage counseling, and in some cases, give it a try for a few weeks or months.

And you feel good. You start believing that your suspicion about the worst possible scenario is untrue. And all those little signs that you thought were leading you in that direction were really something else. Maybe it was just a curiosity phase. Maybe your husband was having problems from medications. Maybe he does have some gay tendencies, but maybe that's from an extra chromosome or two that has been misplaced. Maybe he's learned his lesson by realizing that you are going to leave your marriage if you find out that he's doing his thing.

Then you think you are so "stupid" when the second honeymoon is over and reality hits again. Please don't apologize or feel stupid. I was lulled endless times into what I wanted to be a functioning marriage. I grasped for any sign of rebuttal from my husband and swore I could make things better if only he would work with me on it. Yes, I even had a couple of extra sexual encounters that he initiated in good faith to prove to me that our marriage would be A-okay. But how long could he fool me? He couldn't even fool himself. He couldn't carry out this lie indefinitely, and within a short time, things reverted to where they were—or shall I say deteriorated back to where they were—when I threw out my suspicions.

So, next time you see things changing, be aware that it is just a temporary ploy. Don't get your hopes up—enjoy the peace and quiet for whatever time it lasts. Use this time to strengthen yourself mentally because this is not the time that your husband will be battering you down mentally. Recognize it for what it is and take advantage of the quiet time to make a plan to protect yourself and your future. And rest assured—the honeymoon will be over before you know it. Once you understand this, your chances of being disappointed will become one of expectation and much easier to handle.

JANUARY 2002

THE EXCUSE FOR ABUSE

My friend Gayle wrote me a note a few weeks ago. She stated:

Bonnie, have you ever covered the topic of "abusive behaviors" with women (and men) in "our situations?" I know that you've discussed it, but is it worth giving more attention to this subject? I know so many of us continue to struggle with not only "the situation," but also the continued abuse that goes along with it and how to effectively deal with it. Your thoughts are appreciated whenever on this.

This is a common cry from many women who have gay husbands and who remain in their marriages for long periods of time. The try so hard to be "good wives," and yet, no matter what they do, they are still the brunt of their husbands' emotional abuse. I will try to explain why this happens.

Let me preface this by saying that for the New Year, I have coined a new term for another classification of gay husbands. It is "Straight Gay Husbands." I hope you like it. It is my new reference to gay men who are permanently living the straight life, sort of like wolves in sheep's clothing. They are the husbands who will not acknowledge their homosexuality privately or publicly--ever. Some of them know

39

that you know, but try to confuse you enough to put enough doubt in your mind to make you think that you are the crazy one. It's the best defense to your "offensive" questions. These are the men that shut you up or shut you down the moment you think about making mention of the possibility of homosexuality. They know what they are, and they know what you suspect; but keep your mouth shut because they don't want to hear about it--especially from you.

These men are different than the gay husbands that admit they are gay/bisexual but promise not to act on those needs while they remain married to you. (Like we really believe that story!) They are also different than the gay husbands who are leading very secret lives and not leaving a trail of crumbs for you to follow. They are not even quite like the Limbo Men I have described who are caught in between two worlds. These are men who are definitely not stuck. They are identifying strictly as straight. There is no way they are entering the gay world through the front or back door, or even through the closet. They detest the gay world and what it stands for which gives them even greater reassurance, at least to themselves, that they are not gay.

The Straight Gay Men are the ones who have to remain in total control of all of their physical motions lest someone should suspect they are not quite as straight as they claim. It's funny how many women tell me how their husbands' physical appearances, gestures, and movements change once they come out. I can't even fathom how difficult it must be to have to go through life calculating every breath and step you take. It's sort of like walking down a sidewalk and having to make sure that you "don't step on a crack or you'll break your mother's back" as the game use to say. My balance and coordination never let me win that game.

These husbands are quick to use you and the children as their proof that they are not gay to the outside world just in case they let their guard down and anyone might accuse them of the "unthinkable." They honestly don't identify as gay even though they have sex with men. They don't get themselves involved emotionally with men, just sexually. That helps them justify the fact that they are straight, not gay.

Some women can't understand this. If you look like a duck, walk like a duck, act like a duck, but have sex with a goose, are you still a duck or are you a goose? I say you're a goose. I don't care what you act like to the outside world; I only look at who satisfies you sexually. And if you're a duck making love to a goose, your feathers have to ruffle in a different direction when you stand up and straighten them out. But this does make things that much more confusing and complicated. So, to simplify your confusion, let me say this— STRAIGHT MEN DON'T HAVE GAY SEX. You can call it whatever makes you feel better, but I still call it gay—all the way.

Women who live with Straight Gay Men and Limbo Men are often the most commonly emotionally abused women. They would have to be. Their husbands are truly living in a complex world that makes little or any sense. They are living unfilled lives because they don't have any emotional connections. They don't connect emotionally with their wives because they aren't really straight. They don't connect emotionally with men because they refuse to be gay. And so they function but don't connect. This lack of emotional connection creates a sense of insensitivity when it comes to your feelings and your emotions.

It also closes them up as human beings. They are unable to connect with a wife because they are living an internal, and what seems like an eternal, lie. This lie keeps overtaking any sense of good feelings towards the person whom they believe is responsible for this state of living—namely you. Now we know it is ridiculous to think that you should be their reason for living this lie, but subconsciously, this is how they feel.

As much as they love to have you as their "cover" is as much as they hate to have you sharing under their covers. They resent your nagging demands for sexual intimacy because it "isn't their thing." It's your thing. And why do you have to try to make them feel inadequate just because they are? Even when you stop asking for it, you are still thinking about it and they can tell. It means they have to come up with a continuous string of stories to account for their lack of sexual behavior with you. This puts pressure on these guys who feel you are being unreasonable. Why do you have to make such a big deal out of sex?

They feel that in all other ways, they are ideal husbands. They are there raising the family with you. They are helping to support your financial needs or at least sharing in them. They are taking part in the social activities that you have decided are important. They are doing lots for you—and how do you show your appreciation? By badgering them with little innuendos and questioning looks.

This really shows a lack of appreciation on your part and so they get pissed.

The Straight Gay Men think they are Supermen. And to a degree, they are. They juggle, manipulate, calculate, and carefully plan out all of their actions. It takes a lot of energy to do this, and they marvel at their ability to pull it off. It gives them an air of smugness that shows in their personality. I'm not quite sure what they think they're pulling off because they know that you are doubtful of their explanations. There are only so many headaches, backaches, depressions, and side effects from medication that you can keep relying on. But they feel confident if they use these excuses enough, you'll give up. Most women do. As I've said before numerous times, no woman wants to feel like she has to beg her husband to make love to her. It's degrading and demeaning. We get the hint after enough sexual rejection and stop asking. But it doesn't mean that we stop thinking—and wanting.

Every time we see other couples holding and caressing lovingly together, this is a reminder. It's a reminder of what we thought we should have had but never were able to achieve. It's a reminder of what our hopes and dreams were for married life when we took that life-altering step and said, "I do." We are momentarily reminded of what marriage was supposed to be, but never became. And this sadness shows in our faces, in our eyes, and in our hearts. When our husbands glimpse at us, they know what we are thinking. They know what we are wishing. They know that the words they don't want to hear may possibly be coming out of our mouths at any moment. Rather than take a chance and have to come up with one more excuse, they find some way to knock us down and put us back into the non-assertive mental state that they so easily know how to do.

We are women who have been conditioned. Remember, Straight Gay Men remain in the marriages indefinitely and have years to erode your sense of self-worth. They are not going anywhere, and they want to make sure that you feel inadequate enough so that you won't go anywhere either. I don't know who could have taught these men about the facts of life and marriage, but obviously, they weren't listening or didn't have a teacher. Didn't anyone ever tell them that sex is part of marriage? Didn't they ever hear that intimacy grows from making love to the person who loves you? Do they really believe that they can sit for years in a marriage and overlook that little detail? Yes, they do. And we become their silent partners because we have been silenced on the issue of sex.

The irony is that even if you leave these men, as some women do, they will remarry again. Yes, they will remarry another woman. They will still do their occasional gay sex thing to satisfy their sexual need, but that goes with the territory. It is amazing to me how these men can live such a delusional existence until the day they die. And they will drag other women into their web of deceit. The next victim (and men who do this more than once are victimizers) will fall for it just like you did—but even better. Your Straight Gay Husband has a track record. He will still use you as his shield by telling his next conquest that he was married before, ergo, he is straight. And the woman who is in a subsequent marriage with this man has no reason to question his sexuality at all. He married before; he's marrying again. Chances are his next wife will feel even more inadequate than you feel. He'll make sure to tell her that the two of you never had problems in the bedroom before. And if she does meet you, she'll be too embarrassed to ask you the truth. And you'll probably keep protecting him.

So if you are in a long-term marriage to a Straight Gay Man, don't plan on things ever getting better. There may be temporary second honeymoon periods, only to prove to you once again that you are crazy for even suspecting there is something wrong with your wonder man. But it's guaranteed that things will resort back to the "normal" pattern of digs, harsh words, and put-downs. Count on it. Then decide if this is the most that you want out of life because as long as you are in this marriage, this is all you can expect.

FEBRUARY 2002

HAPPY VALENTINE'S DAY--NOT

In the past, I have written about the difficulty that straight wives have during the holiday season. It is not uncommon for depression to set in somewhere around Thanksgiving and continue right through the New Year. During that six-week period, there are three holidays that revolve around family happiness and unity, something most of us are missing.

While we get caught up in the preparation for these holidays, we can't help but to feel an emotional letdown when they actually take place. We know what they represent, and yet, we never feel the wonder and joy of what the holidays represent that others are feeling. We go through the motions waiting for the emotional impact to kick in, but when it doesn't, that's when the depression sets in.

And now, just as we start to get back to our "normal" existence state of mind to cope in our relationships, we are once again brought down by the most hurtful holiday of all—Valentine's Day. This is the day that exemplifies love and romance. It's hearts and flowers all the way. It's the day that symbolizes what being in love is all about. It's a day where two people who love each other take the time to stop and think about that love and to remember how it feels to be "in love" even if some of the passion has faded through the years.

If you are the wife of a gay man, this is a day that really hurts. This day, more so than all of the other holidays, is a slap of reality about your marriage. You see, on the other holidays you can cover yourself with a veil of illusion because they are family holidays. Whatever you are lacking in your marriage can be compensated for through your children and other family members. But Valentine's Day is different. It's about the two of you. And no matter how you justify it by thinking it's a day of love in general, it's not. Yes, you can buy Valentine's Day cards for your son or daughter, mother and father, co-workers and friends to try to make it better. But there's really no escaping what it really is—a holiday for lovers.

The reason why this holiday in so painful is because it is upfront and personal and right in your face. No matter how you try to avoid dealing with the reality of living with a gay husband on a day-to-day basis and lull yourself into a false sense of security, Valentine's Day reminds you of the lie you are living with the man whom you fell in love with and married in good faith. It's a reminder of everything that you were supposed to have but were cheated from having. And the man who robbed you of your dreams is still lying in bed next to you. Each morning when you wake up with him next to you, it's one more day of living a lie.

Now the lie wasn't your lie to start with—it's his lie. But it has become your lie because you're living it with him. You're going through the motions of what marriage is supposed to be, but it's falling way short of what your intentions were when you made that commitment at the altar Your husband, who promised to love and cherish you through sickness and health 'til death do you part, never mentioned that he would never be able to love you the way you needed to be loved. In fairness, maybe he didn't know that he wouldn't be able to do it. No doubt, he was hoping that he could pull it off. And I'll even go so far as to say that maybe he didn't come to terms with the fact that he was gay on that life-changing day. But in almost all cases he knew he was having conflicting feelings. He knew something was off even if he couldn't figure out that it was homosexuality.

Even when I speak to gay men who tell me that they honestly didn't believe that they were gay, or hadn't acted on those impulses prior to marriage, they still knew looking or thinking about men sexually aroused them. And even if they still couldn't come to terms with that, they knew when they stopped making love to you early in the marriage that they were not attracted to you because you were a woman. But they kept quiet because they were afraid if they told you their secret, you may blow it for them. You might pull away their security blanket leaving them vulnerable and feeling naked. It wasn't always an easy choice for them to keep lying to you, but it was easier than telling the truth.

So to those of you who are living in one of the many situations that bring us all together under this umbrella of commonality, let me personally wish you a Happy Future Valentine's Day. Believe me, it can happen to you just like it happened to me. This is a day I celebrate in a big way. It's a day that makes me happy because I have a man whom I am in love with. He makes my heart flutter and my knees still get shaky when we touch—and that's after eight years. I don't say that to brag, but rather to let you know how life was meant to be. You were meant to have a man who can love you and make love to you. You were meant to meet someone who would cherish you and treat you as if you were the most important part of his life. The fact that you were sidetracked doesn't mean that you are doomed forever. It is never too late to find the happiness you are seeking as long as you don't give up hope. And even if you don't want to think about falling in love, at least think about not living in an abusive situation. Work on loving yourself enough to move away from a man who is not your soul mate but who is destroying your soul instead, one layer at a time.

Go out and buy yourself a giant box of chocolates. Enjoy each one of them as you remember how sweet life is supposed to be and how wonderful it will be once you remove yourself from a disastrous situation.

A GIFT FROM MY EX-HUSBAND

Since Valentine's Day symbolizes love, allow me to tell all of you the wonderful gift that I received from my ex-husband several weeks ago. We finally had the conversation I had been waiting for and wanting to have for nearly twenty years. It was the conversation of honesty, understanding, and apology. Even though we had skirted around these issues numerous times throughout the post-marriage years, he never came up with the words I was waiting to hear until now. It felt so good to hear him say, "Honey, I was an asshole and I'm sorry." Wow, these were very powerful words. Now some of you may laugh and wonder why I even cared after all of these years, but I did care. I wanted to hear those words come out of his mouth. I wanted him to understand the pain that I had suffered from his abuse. I wanted to know that he understood the impact of what he had done to me. And after I heard those words, I was finally able to forgive him—for real.

It's so odd that my ex just couldn't understand that I didn't blame him for being gay. He knows my point of view because we've discussed it hundreds of times. He doesn't even necessarily agree with me. I say that gay is not a choice—people are born gay. He tells me that maybe in most cases that is true, but not in all cases—like his. He doesn't believe he was born gay—he was "made" gay due to family circumstances. I am not sure why he feels the need to think that he was "made" gay. Maybe he feels better because this way he doesn't have to take any responsibility for his irresponsible behavior. Or, maybe it's because he doesn't have to feel any remorse for what he's done as a gay man in straight man's clothing. Anyway, regardless of this, he really opened up to me and he also listened to my feelings for the first time.

Here's his story. Michael claims that when he married me, he honestly didn't know that he was gay. He had gay sex with guys, but

46

there was nothing emotional about it—only sexual. He never kissed these guys or held them passionately. He just "did it" to get some sexual satisfaction. That didn't mean he was gay, or at least in his early 20's, he didn't think that way. He knew he enjoyed having sexual encounters with males, but he still had a strong desire to find a wife and have children. He was sure that's what made him straight, not gay. He was also not like those "swishy" guys portrayed on television. They made him sick. They were the real gays. He was macho and athletic. No way he was gay.

When we met, he did fall in love with me. And why not? I was interesting, very nice, caring, attractive, and bright. I was kind of exciting back in those days. I was the leader of an activist group back in the 1970's so I was sort of a semi-celebrity. We had an intense courtship and a quick marriage. When Michael claims that he loved me then, I do believe him. He loved me as much as he was capable of loving a woman. I was the first woman he ever loved so he believed this was going to be the miracle he was looking for to change him. And for a while, he did change—his sexuality that is. He became for all intents and purposes—STRAIGHT.

He was able to perform straight sex. And he didn't hate it. He didn't mind it. He didn't love it, but he could do it. I asked him if he fantasized about men when he made love to me and he was very clear that the answer was "NO." He did remember calling me a man's name during one of our sexual encounters, but he insists that was a true mistake. He was not thinking about a man at the moment. Okay, I guess. He did explain that when we were in our mid-twenties, sex was still sex. It could still feel good even if it didn't feel right. He could still have an orgasm sometimes and feel a sense of sexual relief and enjoyment. But he never felt it was fulfilling. After a while, it became more of a chore than a pleasure. And those nagging feelings of male attractions started resurfacing no matter how hard he tried to push them away.

Then our conversation went into some dangerous territories, namely the number of times he cheated on me during those four years. He has continued to claim through the years that there were hardly any times. One thing about me—I have a very sharp memory when it comes to remembering when someone hurts me. Maybe I forgive, but I never forget. Even my current boyfriend who is my soul mate knows that any mistake that unintentionally hurts me is cleanly tucked away in my memory bank for future reference at my discretion. So when Michael and I started pulling rabbits out of a hat of his slip-ups during our marriage, even he was shocked at the number I kept reaching in and grabbing long after he had forgotten them. And when we finished dredging up each and every one that we could remember, we had quite a list. In fact, he was not very proud of his record. He apologized very sincerely. He said he was an immature jerk back then who didn't give a damn about me—only himself. Then he asked me if I could finally forgive him and stop being angry about it. Guess what I said? I said NO. I said no because he still didn't get it.

See, what Michael never understood until that conversation was that I did forgive him for being gay. I even forgave him for cheating on me during our marriage because he was gay. What I didn't forgive him for were the many years that followed that he continued to be a jerk. I couldn't forgive him for leaving me stranded for years to raise the children virtually on my own. While he was out with his numerous male partners living la vida loca, I was in taking care of all of the children's day-to-day needs. He was just so into him that he didn't have time to be into them. I was literally left holding the bag and stuck with the responsibility of being a single mother. Yes, I say stuck. There were nights I cried myself to sleep because I was so physically and mentally exhausted from juggling all ends. I didn't have the emotional, physical, or financial support I needed from him. He just wasn't there for the children or me. He thought he was at the time, but now he knows that he wasn't.

He claims that when he left, his world came tumbling down. He was crushed and miserable. He loved his family and couldn't stand the thought of not being with his children. And maybe that was the case for a while. But like so many of the other men that I hear about from my support group members and women who write to me in crisis, those feelings of loss seem to fade mighty quickly as our gay husbands entrench themselves tightly into the gay lifestyle. There just doesn't seem to be a balance for a long time to come. This leaves us with the burden of everything. And this was the part that was so hard for me to forgive.

You see, lots of marriages fail for lots of reasons. In fact, probably half of all marriages end in divorce today. But that doesn't mean that most of the fathers walk away from their responsibilities. Some do, and plenty of straight men are jerks. But see, they don't claim to love their wives when the marriages end like our husbands do. Even when our husbands are leaving us, they still claim they are "loving" us. They just can't help themselves for being gay. And unlike straight marriages that fail, most of us still love our gay husbands when our marriages are over. We didn't choose for the marriages to end—they did. Most of us were blindsided until the end with no clue why our husbands didn't love us enough to stay. Some of you still don't understand because your husbands are still being dishonest and living in a state of denial—even though you are sure of the truth.

When our husbands leave, they promise that things won't change between them and the children, but in almost all cases, they do. Maybe not the first few weeks, but shortly thereafter. We were counting on their promises to come through for the children and be there as responsible, participating fathers. That's what made the separation a little more palatable. But inevitably, their lives change dramatically and everything else is secondary. As we often say in our support chats, "It's all about them." And for most of them, it is.

Now that doesn't mean they don't change back. I definitely see that in time, so many of these fathers try to be fathers again. Maybe it comes with age; maybe it comes with maturity. Maybe it's just because they have their fill of themselves and now they are ready to pick up where they left off. Unfortunately, many years are missing and can't be returned. And the hardships that we, the mothers, have gone through can't be undone. And that's what my ex needed to know. That's what he had to understand what I needed to forgive him for— not being gay. He needed to understand that he was not just a stupid, selfish jerk during our marriage, but also for many of the years that followed when he stranded the children and me.

The best news is that he finally does understand. He finally understands that I wasn't angry that he is gay. I got over that fact years ago. I was angry that he was always looking out for his own needs before our needs. He finally admitted I was right and asked me to forgive him. I did. There was something very heart lifting about this forgiveness because it was real. It didn't change the past, but at least he finally understood what it did to me. He could finally feel my pain, my fears, my frustrations, and his part in causing them. It gave me the closure that I was seeking for so long. Hopefully, your ex-husbands and husbands will give you this same gift—the gift of truth, understanding, and apology for their actions during and after the marriage. It took me nearly 20 years, but better late than never.

MARCH 2002

ANOTHER EXPLANATION TO THE SEX THING

In the last issue, I spoke about the recent healing conversation that I had with my ex-husband. In that article, I asked my ex about our sex life when we first met and how he was able to "pull it off" in the beginning. He explained how in his 20's, when we met and married, he could become sexually aroused because sex under any circumstances was something that could "feel good." Add into it a mix of emotional attachment and determination to be straight, and all things were possible, at least for a short time.

A friend of mine, Dina, sent me a much better and detailed explanation that she had discovered a few years ago. I asked her for her permission to share it with you because I think it sheds the best insight that I have found to date:

In late adolescence, young adulthood up to about 30's, a guy is driven by raging hormones and need for release - basically he could "do it" with anything or anyone just to get off. As time goes on, and they are not as driven biologically, they have to supplement the drive with some fantasy thrown in - that's the time when the male fantasies become prevalent. In turn it becomes harder and harder to get turned on "normally" and eventually even the male fantasies are no longer able to make him perform.

That is usually the "crisis" that leads them to actively fool around and/or eventually come out and leave. I think this is a good point to make to those straights who rationalize that if husbands can perform or could at some time that is an indication that they were not "totally" gay blah, blah, blah. Bottom line folks is that they could perform at a point in time when they did no discrimination at all....we were just one step better than taking matters into one's own hands!

Thanks, Dina, for that insightful explanation. I think this clarifies the situation for so many women who can't understand how their gay husbands are able to have sex with them in the beginning, but not sustain it throughout the marriage.

Some women wrote to me asking me to discuss the "Psychological Sexual Warfare Games" that their husbands play with them. That's my coined terminology to these demoralizing situations. Some gay men keep the games going in order to divert the thoughts of confirmed suspicions. This happens usually once the wife accuses her husband of being gay, or when he knows that she is barking up the right tree, as the saying goes. By this time, the wife is usually totally turned off to the thought of having a sexual encounter with her husband. This is when he turns on the charm and amorous moves.

Now, the gay husband knows that his wife knows, at least on some level. He also knows that it has been a long road of unfulfilling sexual experiences over a number of years. And he also knows at this point that the last thing his wife wants is sex—at least with him. That's when he starts to touch her knee, her shoulder, hold her close, make the overtures, and goes for the gold. He is now an Olympiad in wimps clothing. He knows that it is a safe bet that he is going to be running a solo act here, because there's no way his wife is going to respond to his tainted touch.

The worst part is that now he claims the victor's spoils. Now he starts throwing those accusations around like a Herculean master yelling, "Whenever I want to have sex you reject me," or "Don't ever say I didn't try. It's not my fault that we don't have a sex life." And that's how he weaves the web of self-doubt again. Just when you are so sure that he is gay, well, maybe he's not. Maybe he's changing. Maybe it's your fault. Maybe if you had been more receptive to him through the years. Maybe you were reading him wrong. Maybe all of that evidence that you compiled really did belong to someone else, right?

Wrong. It's a game. It's a game of desperation because you have gotten too close to the truth and he knows it. Some of these guys just love to catch you off-guard. It gives them great pleasure to keep you confused while they are trying to figure themselves out. Or, if they have figured themselves out, they want to make sure that you don't because it leads to the potential disaster of hurting them. And that's why they do it.

I always tell women that if your husband tries this, don't get too spooked out. Expect it, but don't sweat it. By the point in the marriage that this happens, it's almost guaranteed that if you would turn around and say, "Let's do it dear," he would develop a sudden crippling backache or migraine headache. He is making a calculated guess that you will say no. By this time, you've already been stripped of your sexual esteem, and one calculated shot in the dark isn't going to restore it. You know that, and so does he. That's why he feels confident in "offering" you something that he thinks you want so badly emotionally but knows you will reject physically. .

And feel free to laugh when he throws up in your face, "I was always the one who wanted sex. You're the one who is cold blooded." Ha ha. You don't have to laugh a big, boisterous howl, just a little ha-ha will get the point across. Then go back to doing something that would be far more interesting than having sex with your gay husband—like washing the dishes or ironing the clothes. At least you know when you do something like this, it will turn out right!

LOW SELF-ESTEEM ISSUE

I can never talk enough about the issue of self-esteem. When I reflect back now, at the age of 50, I can honestly say that I have spent a lifetime building up my own self-esteem. I can trace this back to my early childhood days when I was always the "chubby" girl. Eventually I transitioned from being a chunky teenager to being an obese adult. I have spent my adult years being fat. There have only been short periods of perhaps several years from time to time when I was heavy instead of obese.

When I met my gay husband, I was physically at the best point of my adult life. I had lost over 100 pounds and I was feeling and looking good. My self-esteem and confidence was at a new height. I was NOT desperate when I met him, so I can't use that as an excuse of why I married a gay man. Like almost all of us, I honestly did not know that he was gay. It's that simple. He made sure to let me know that he wasn't by yelling up a storm when I mentioned a friend of mine suspected that he may be "bisexual." I remember that feeling of total relief when he stood up in the middle of the restaurant and nearly turned the table over in sheer anger. Ah, the man was protesting— and it couldn't be nearly enough--forget too much.

Why would I even think he was gay? He was tall, athletic, very handsome and extremely charming. We had sex in those early days. It wasn't the best sex, but it wasn't that bad either. I had worse in the previous years, and I believe that all of them weren't gay.

My ex-husband married me because he loved me and wanted to have all of the things that straight men had. And in his mind, at that time, he was NOT gay. Yes, he had gay sex. Yes, he had a string of sexual encounters with men before we married. But in his mind, he believed that he was straight because there was no emotional commitment to these men. He enjoyed women and dated his fair share of them. And he believed that sexually he could pull it off as long as he loved someone enough. Through the years, I have come to terms with the fact that most of these gay men really don't believe in their hearts that they are gay when they marry us. They can have gay sex galore, but they are not gay in their minds. They don't even view themselves as Bisexual, just straight men dabbling with same sex encounters. Go figure.

Getting back on track here, I married a man who was mentally abusive to me. Not all gay husbands take this route, but many of them do. They are frustrated with life because they are living a lie, and the one they lash out at is the one responsible for living this lie in their minds—namely, us. Yes, I know it makes no sense at all, but that's just the way it is. Even though my self-esteem was quite high when I got married, it didn't take long for it to get battered back into oblivion within a relatively short amount of time. I was on a temporary high when I met my husband. I was feeling good about myself for the first time in my 28 years of life. I had not even had two solid years of good feelings about myself before this marriage. That means that I had numerous years of personal insecurity, loneliness, poor self-image, and peer-inflicted pain scars from adolescence that carried over into adulthood.

I was the girl who was picked last to be on whatever sports team that gym class played on any given day. I lacked the motor coordination to be an effective sportswoman, and my excess weight slowed down my athletic abilities. It was pretty heartbreaking and humiliating knowing that you would always be the last or almost last person picked. I was the girl who never got asked to dances or proms. I was the girl who didn't have dates on the weekend because the guys I wanted didn't want me. They wanted the pretty cheerleaders or the girls who radiated confidence. I was the girl who fell in love so often but always had her heart broken time after time when some girl who was prettier, thinner, or more graceful crossed my path. Ultimately, I was the girl who got left out. There were so many of us when I was growing up, but that didn't make me feel any better. I wanted so badly to be someone worth loving, but that didn't seem within my reach.

For that reason, I made poor choices in relationships from early in the game. I just wanted to be wanted to badly, that I was willing to "settle" for guys, later men, who were not worthy of having a relationship with anyone. They were men who had value systems that were different than mine, but yet, my desperation kept me moving in their direction because they seemed more obtainable.

In my mid-twenties, I was nearly 270 pounds and at five feet tall, I wasn't long for the world. I began to care about living after having extensive chest pains, and started to lose weight. First I lost it in a healthy manner; then I developed an eating disorder when the healthy way just stopped working very well. Within 18 months, I lost approximately 130 pounds so I was feeling quite good about myself. I was never thin, but I was looking good, feeling good, and doing quite well in life. I was very vain at that point, and that was fine too. It was time for me to finally feel good about myself. Professionally, I was where I wanted to be, and personally, I was testing out the waters and looking for the right somebody to love.

Maybe if I had married a wonderful supportive man, my self-esteem building process would have continued on an upward trend. But instead, I found a man who was downright cruel who used to find great pleasure in knocking me down whenever I dared to stand up to question any of his unusual behaviors. This was his way of fighting back. My ex wasn't really a bad man, he was just a sad man. He was sad because his life was falling apart being married to me. He was lying all over the place to cover his tracks, and every time I would uncover just one little crack, he became so angry. He was trying to tie that web of lies together but I seemed to be untangling them faster than he could tie them.

Rather than accept responsibility for his misactions, my ex would yell and scream about my inadequacies. He would magnify every molehill into a mountain when it came to my imperfections, making me believe that I was the awkward, gawky, overweight teenager all over again. I didn't have enough "self-confidence" time accumulated to make me believe differently. After a while, I bought into all of the lies that my husband kept telling me about me as he shredded away the few good years of feeling good and reverted me back to my original form of feeling inadequate.

And so once again, I found my comfort in food and started putting back my weight, one pound at a time. When I became pregnant, I looked at it as a license to eat all I wanted because the weight would come off after the baby was born. That's what people kept telling me. I did gain 70 pounds during those months feasting on Baskin Robbins ice cream daily by the gallon. When my premature daughter was born and weighed less than five pounds, that's what came off my body. And although in time I was able to take off half that amount gained, I regained it when I was pregnant with my son. I was once again a fat woman.

When my husband told me that he couldn't make love to me because I was too fat, well, that seemed reasonable to me. At that point, I didn't think much of myself so why would I expect a man to think much of me? It sounded so logical and made so much sense.

I say this first of all because I receive letters from so many women who write to me and tell me that they are 20, 40, 60, 80, or 100 pounds overweight. They didn't start out that way in their marriage for the most part, but ended up that way due to frustration. Some of them had childhoods like mine where weight was a factor, but many of them never had a weight problem until during the marriage. They usually throw into their letters that marriage caused them to overeat because there was nothing else giving them much satisfaction on the home front. And as they gained weight,

I am sure that their husbands secretly cheered on the weight gain because now they had a new reason to retreat in the bedroom—namely, fat. Now fat became the natural enemy and justification for lack of passion, as if there was ever much passion to start with. Like my husband told me shortly before we split up, "Who would ever want to sleep with someone who looked like you? Have you looked at yourself lately in a mirror? If I became gay, who could blame me?" OUCH, with all capital letters. There were lots of tears that flowed from my eyes after that conversation. My ex had a wonderful talent for destroying any residual good feelings I had left from days of old. There was nothing left by the time he was done with me except a sense of survival—to find a way to survive without him in my life.

When I first started my local support group, the first two women who joined were also fat. I will not cover up that word and make it into something that it's not. I don't use that word to be insulting, but rather to be honest. I don't need a bunch of "feel good" words about what I am. I feel good about myself now even if I am fat. It's amazing what a wonderful straight man can do for your sense of self-worth. My soul mate hasn't noticed the weight gain I've made over the eight plus years we've been together. He still thinks I'm beautiful and makes me feel that way about myself.

But, getting back to the point, I thought at first it must be a thing that women of weight encounter because my first two group members were big women. But after that, I was shocked to find how many thin women who were beautiful, attractive, and graceful women by society's standards were in the same situation. As many of you know from my book, I still have my theories on the prototype of woman that a gay man seeks out when he wants to get married. One of the prototypes is a woman with low self-esteem. There are so many of us and we are all such easy targets. However, what I learned is that self-esteem is often something that women have within themselves from what's going on inside, not outside.

I recently corresponded with a lovely woman who read my book last year. She thanked me for giving her the key to the problem in her life. She is an airline stewardess who is viewed by men as beautiful. And yet, after nine years with her hands-off husband, she felt as deflated as the rest of us. She has now moved on in her life and feels wonderful about it. I hear from many women just like this-- women who have never had self-esteem issues over their looks. Over this year alone, I have worked with three models, two in New York and one in California who certainly didn't have a problem with their physical appearance. And yet, all of their external physical beauty didn't help them feel beautiful inside. Within this same time frame, I have helped women who were doctors, lawyers, nurses, stockbrokers, professors at universities, a CEO in a Fortune 500 company, and a Broadway actress. Certainly they had accomplished enough in their professional lives to be admired by the masses for their intelligence and status. And yet, they felt just as horrible about themselves as I used to feel about myself. It seems as if having a gay husband is the great equalizer among women of all sizes, shapes, colors, professions, economic situations and societal boundaries.

I guess what I'm getting to is simply this. If the beautiful women who had high self-esteem throughout their lives can fall into this dark and lonely hole, what chance do women like me--who by society's standards have imperfections creating emotional baggage--have? If a woman who held her head high all of her life can have hers chopped off the block, why would I expect mine not to be in the same pile only squashed down a little more?

I talk about this because women write to me constantly looking for excuses of why their gay husbands may have been turned off to them. They write about their torment of how hard they tried to be better wives by dieting which sometimes led to eating disorders, having breast implants, liposuction, plastic surgery, changes in hair color, and so many other things to try to physically change their husbands' desire for them. It's almost as if they are still apologizing or looking for reasons why they were at fault. And their pain becomes my pain. I hurt for every woman who has to spend one extra minute not feeling good about herself because she has failed with her gay husband.

In my last newsletter, I wrote about the long awaited conversation that I had with my ex-husband that brought closure to our misunderstandings. I think that these are the feelings that our gay husbands and ex-husbands have to know and understand. It's not just the superficial damage or the obvious problems that result from these mismarriages. It's the internal damage and scaring that they just don't have a clue about.

I can forgive any gay husband for being gay. That is not a conscientious decision, nor is marriage a calculated move of deceit to punish some loving woman. And I acknowledge how difficult it is for gay men to come to terms with their homosexuality during a marriage. However, what I can't forgive is the cruelty that they display to their wives while going through their own hardships. And even when they are able to be honest and move on in their lives, they somehow lack the understanding of what we are left to deal with. They feel we should just be able to "get over it" as if we can walk away from the damaging years unscathed. Well, we can't and we don't. And perhaps when they can recognize this and try to undo some of the damage that they caused, a better understanding will come about between wives and gay husbands or ex-husbands. There is great comfort in knowing that your gay man understands that the hurt goes much deeper than just superficial cutting. And when he can comprehend that and tell you that he is sorry for the internal damage he has done to you, then you will finally be able to start to heal—and even start to forgive.

DECEMBER 2002

UNHAPPY HOLIDAYS...FOR US

Well, there's no place like home for the holidays, as the song goes. But then again, chances are the person who wrote that song didn't have a gay spouse. This is the time of year that hurts the most when you are living with a gay husband, whether he be in the closet, out of the closet, claiming to be "Bisexual" or promising he'll never act on it. It doesn't matter what the status is when the situation comes down to the same bottom line. There is no way to feel happy when your heart is breaking and your life is always tilting over the wrong way.

The season between Thanksgiving and Christmas is depressing for many people for various reasons. But for us, there is a special sadness because we know the joys that were meant for us just aren't happening—nor will they be happening in the future with the men we married. We have to face a whole new set of hopes and dreams on our own or with someone else. Some of you are still stuck in the same muck as you were last year during this holiday season, and to you, I am sorry. I'm sorry because I know that no matter how much decking up your halls with boughs of holly you do to create an illusion, there's no action happening under the mistletoe with your husband. Or, shall I say there's no action happening for you with your husband under that hanging plant. If you're waiting for some action or some passion, don't bother wasting your time standing paralyzed with hope under a clump of green hanging from your ceiling.

What's even worse is that the start of the holiday season seems to have moved back a month this year. I heard those holiday carols start playing as soon as Halloween was over. That gives us an extra four weeks to have to be reminded of the cheer of the season, which doesn't belong to us.

Why are these days worse than any other time of the year? Because this is a time when you are forced to get together with other family members and friends and "put on a happy face" as the saying goes. It's your time to be on stage with one of your great performances. You need to convince everyone around you that life is really wonderful, just like that movie "It's A Wonderful Life."

You don't want to ruin everyone else's holiday just because yours has been ruined. This wouldn't be fair, would it? This performance has to be of Academy Award caliber because there are lots of people out there that you need to fool, including co-workers, friends, family members, children, and sometimes—most importantly—yourself.

I say "yourself" because sometimes you are the most important person whom you need to fool. If you really had to face your feelings while going through this time of year, you'd be popping those anti-depressants by the handful. In order to survive the holiday season of "joy," we put our emotions into a different psychological "mindset." We suppress our feelings of emptiness and fill our lives with busywork to keep us running and doing, never allowing ourselves the luxury of time to think. Thinking would be counter-productive to the holiday spirit.

We look around us to grab onto anything and everything that will make us feel grateful for what we do have in life instead of what we don't have. We stare at those beautiful creations our gay husbands have helped us create—namely, our children. How many times do I hear women say, "something came out good from my marriage—my children"? Almost all women with children tell me that. And it's true. All of us who have children look at this as the pot of gold at the end of the dark storm where there's really not a rainbow. This is not to negate the fact that you have these treasures, but they certainly aren't growing up with the ideal family that you had envisioned when they were born. But not to be a "humbug" during these happy days, you create a winter wonderland of family unity, or shall I say, family fantasy.

And some of your husbands live up to the fantasy during these heartfelt holidays. They are on good behavior. They know that Santa Claus is coming to town, and there's something magical about this time of year, even if you are a grinch or grouch for the other 11 months. Most of your husbands will step up to the plate for the "holly jolly holidays." They'll do their husbandly duties for the public puttin' on the Ritz so to speak. Everyone will think that you are a happy loving family. Of course, in private, don't expect that role to carry over—the one where they do their "husbandly duties." That would really be pushing your luck.

The most difficult part of the holidays is the illusion of magic that is created. Everyone is on his best behavior. Your gay husbands are trying their best to do the family thing the right way. Those yearly traditions that they grew up with in their own families seem to surface around late November and linger until January 2 or so. It confuses us like hell. Just when we thought there was no hope for the future, this kinder, gentle, more loving husband pops up—reminding you of the days when you thought both of you were in love and your marriage would live happily ever after. And just as you're mentally being dragged into this annual false sense of hope, boom, the New Year arrives and it's over. Things are back to abnormal. Sad, isn't it?

So if you are still stuck in a dark space, namely your marriage to your gay husband, try not to set yourself up for the big drop down. Face the season with reality. Don't let misplaced kindness fool you. Enjoy it while it's there, just to give you some peace in your ongoing storm, but don't delude yourself that this is forever. It's not—not by a long shot. It's only the temporary holiday spirit of love that is floating in the air. It will be blown away with a strong gust before you know it. In spite of it, have a peaceful holiday and surround yourself with the people who love you the most during these difficult days.

ENLARGING THE CLOSET

I find it somewhat remarkable that we often find "men in the closet" the topic of our conversations without mentioning whose keeping them company—namely, US. I would like to discuss this because too many women suffer from this "closetedness," and they need to understand why.

It seems that no matter how rational the explanation is that we are not responsible for our husbands' homosexuality, for some women, there is a part of you that somehow still feels responsible. I know this because I often speak to these women. Here's a typical conversation:

"Bonnie, thanks so much for helping me understand about my husband's homosexuality. Everything finally makes sense to me. It seems like all of those missing pieces of the puzzle are finally in place. Yes, I do understand that my husband was this way before I married him but he didn't even know it himself."

Then comes the next part:

"I can't tell anyone. There's no one I can discuss this with—not my family, not my friends, not my doctor, not my therapist, not my—well, not anyone."

Then I ask, "How come? What's the problem with discussing this with someone who is really close to you?"

The answer that comes:

"People won't understand."

And then I ask the question that hurts so much:

"Do you think they'll blame you?"

Ouch. That's the thought that hurts because I'm getting very close to the truth.

"Yes, people are going to blame me. They are going to think that I am the cause of my husband's homosexuality. I can't tell anyone this terrible secret."

And then I ask the question:

"Do you feel in any way that you're responsible?"

Then I get the answer that makes me wince:

"Not really."

"Well, sometimes."

"Not usually."

In other words, sorta, kinda, like maybe. Ugh. Just when I thought the worst was over, it's still there. Mrs. Superwife is still feeling responsible in one way or another for her husband's "choice" in sexuality.

This is so common in the months that follow the initial news about a husband's homosexuality. No matter how many times a woman hears that it was not her fault, she doesn't quite believe it. She can't understand how the man who loved her, married her, made love to her, had children with her, and vowed to love her forever and ever until death do they part has been able to forget all of those beautiful life memories, commitments, and wedding vows. She still questions what she did wrong to make him turn this way. Somewhere in the part of the brain labeled "Logic," there has been a total eclipse that has blanked out the truth in previously understanding the situation. Just when you think, "By George, I've got it," a rush comes over you and you think "I don't have a clue." How did this happen?

Women have often commented to me that they feel they are hiding in the closets with their husbands. And they go one step beyond that—they are still in the closets when their husbands come out. They continue to feel isolated and alone in this situation no matter how much they know intellectually that there are millions of women in the same situation.

Sometimes being part of a small group is very isolating. But I know rare diseases that have far less membership than our group and they don't seem embarrassed to discuss their problem. They may only have a few hundred people in their group. We have millions—and yet we still feel compelled to keep this information a secret.

I think that we always have a sense of shame or embarrassment that keeps us hidden away long after our husbands have made their disclosure to the outside world. Our husbands are often more willing to take the criticism that society throws at gays than we are. And you know what? I think society is far more ignorant when it comes to the situation of wives of gays than they are of gays.

What do I mean? I mean that society will sooner accept a gay person as gay than a straight woman who married a gay. We are the ones who are really facing the ignorance of society. As if we didn't feel bad enough about ourselves when this whole thing happens, we have to face people's stupidity not only while this is happening, but long after it's over. But this ignorance is easy to understand. Look how many of us blamed ourselves for our husbands' homosexuality until we started to understand that we were not the cause. And look how long it takes women to honestly believe they were not the cause. And as I said earlier, just when I think I have them convinced at least on an intellectual level, the emotions kick in a throw off the thinking ability. That's when I hear the talk of, "I know I'm not responsible for my husband's homosexuality, but I can't stop wondering if maybe he would have suppressed those feelings all together if I had been more understanding…supportive…attractive….etc."

Five steps forward, one giant step back. Add a few external messages from the hubby ("I swear I didn't have these feelings when we married."), the parents ("Why would he turn to a man? Are you sure? Maybe your imagination is over active. Maybe you aren't meeting your wifely duties."), the friends ("You must have known something. Come on, I could tell. Do you mean to tell me you couldn't? Everyone suspects him."), co-workers ("You didn't know your husband was gay? Or is it you didn't want to know? You must have been pretty stupid not to know that."), or well meaning casual acquaintances ("He's such a great guy. I can't believe he's gay. And even if he is, I wouldn't mind having a guy like that anyway. He seems to be such a great husband. I could live with that little flaw.")

How about when we bring it up to future potential dates or partners? First question: "Have you been tested for AIDS or other sexually transmitted diseases?" And if you tell them that you haven't had sex with your husband for 10 years, they still want proof. They still think AIDS can be spread through the air in your house. Some of them will not call back after they learn that your husband was gay as if you are carrying around a disease that can "turn" them gay. Or you feel so afraid of turning someone off whom you are looking to turn on that you leave out that part of the story of the past marriage. You are hoping that the new man will love you enough in time to overlook that part of your past and the news can wait until then. You are still living your husband's lie for him long after he's telling the truth.

It is difficult having to be an activist for a cause, and especially a cause where you are starting off with so much misunderstanding and ignorance. Sometimes it's just less exhausting to keep mum. After all, your husband did it for years. And maybe you've been doing it for years. Thankfully there are others who are able to go out there and say, "My husband is gay, but I'm okay." They share their stories with the newspapers, television, and radio getting the word out. Even I have become semi-closeted to protect the privacy of my son and my ex-husband. I wish I could do as I did in the old days and just show up for national television shows that keep inviting me now to let the world know how it really is. But as I tell others, always put the children first. They had no choice in being here. We have choices. I'll just keep plugging away in the less visible media with hopes that the word will keep spreading.

DISTINGUISHING THE TRUTH

The word "truth" is always controversial to me. You can have two people watching the same exact event, and yet, when they report it, you receive two very different versions of the actual event. Is one being honest while the other is being dishonest? No, not at all. It's all a matter of perception, or how people filter the information in their own minds.

Keeping that in mind, I question a gay married man's perception when it comes to a particular issue. It is not uncommon to hear gay men say that after they leave their marriages, the relationship with their children is estranged because the ex-wife is alienating them by bad mouthing, discouraging, and turning the kids against them.

Although I know that women are angry about losing their marriages to homosexuality, I have rarely met a woman who isn't more than willing to have her ex-husband be part of the family life. Out of thousands of women I hear from yearly, I have maybe heard one or two women who have stated they don't want their children around the father because he is gay. They may not be happy about the gay thing, but they would never let that stand in the way of a father-child relationship.

Personally, I think a lot of gay men use this as an excuse for being irresponsible to their families. It's much easier to blame the wife and children than to accept responsibility for their own actions. And do I think they are making up this story because they are looking to feel better about themselves? Well, sometimes yes, sometimes no. Some men, I give the benefit of the doubt because of what I feel is their distorted perception of the "truth."

We all have truths, but all truths aren't the same. I hear many gay husbands say that they had no idea that they were gay when they got married, and I definitely believe that is the case for the majority of gay married men. But then somewhere in the marriage, there were episodes of infidelity while they went out and had gay sex. And yet, they still claim this isn't "gay" or "cheating." In their minds, they believe this to be the "truth."

Some gay men will tell you that their wives were argumentative and difficult to please. But they are telling you this from the point of view of a gay man. When a woman feels that she is unfulfilled and missing out on life, why should she act happy? But how often do these men say, "I can certainly understand why she was unhappy. I didn't know how to make her happy"? I only occasionally hear that from ex-husbands. It's more often a list of complaints of where their wives fell short.

These marriages are what I call, "A Mutation of Life." All perceptions of what is real versus untrue is a mutation. We are always reacting to our husbands based on what they "think they should do as a straight man." They do their best to play the part, like an actor in a television series. In this case, it's more like a long running soap opera.

It reminds me of the movie, "Imitation of Life," which was made in the 1930's and remade in the early 1960's. It is one of my all time favorite movies. In this story, two very poor women, one white and one black, both single parents of young girls, meet and become instant friends. The black woman is seeking shelter for her and her daughter. Both women are almost penniless, so the white woman agrees to have her move in as her housekeeper. The white woman becomes a famous actress. The black woman runs her home and helps raise her daughter. As the girls grow into their teenage years, their friendship takes a different direction due to the racial differences. The black woman's daughter is very light and tries to pass in the white world as a white woman. She leaves home and starts her life as a white woman. Her mother keeps finding her because she loves her so much, even though the daughter begs her to stay away lest her secret be exposed.

The ending of the story always makes me sob no matter how many times I see the movie. The mother dies and the daughter gets there too late. She is crying for her mother, but she didn't have time to say goodbye and I love you. It's a great movie classic. Anyway, the young woman who "passes" as white lives in constant fear of being discovered, much like our gay husbands. She can act the part of a white woman, and even believe hard enough that she is a white woman, but her background will always come back to haunt her.

I can't imagine having to play a role as someone who I'm not for more than a day. I can't even conceive of living a lie day in and day out for years. But gay husbands do it all the time. And guess what?

Since they are living a lie, we are living their lie with them, even though we may have no idea while it is happening.

Does this mean that our marriages are lies? Well, in a big way, I think so. We are reacting in our own lives to the actions of our husbands. They are acting in their own lives based on what their perceptions of being a "straight" husband should be. So when they get annoyed or irritated, we start looking to please by changing who we are and what we want to accommodate their happiness.

This translates into us doing things that we wouldn't normally do or ways we wouldn't necessarily want to be if we had a husband who loved us just for who we are instead of resenting who we aren't. That's why so many of us feel so betrayed when we learn our husbands are gay. The feeling that hurts so much is that we remolded ourselves to be "better wives" in the hopes that our husbands would love us more. Some of us "tiptoed" through life trying not to step down too hard fearing ridicule and criticism. Some of us gave up our own hopes and wants because we were too busy working at getting our husbands to love us better.

Since our husbands' perceptions of us will never be true ones, their perception of how we are alienating our children from them is also not usually a real one but rather a distortion or justification in their own minds. I have heard from thousands of women who wish their husbands would take a more active part in the co-parenting of the children after the marriage is over. They long for some free time to breathe and wish their husbands would take the children for a while. They feel overwhelmed by their new responsibilities and lack of time to think. And in so many cases, the financial responsibilities that now are thrown our way choke us. Gay never seems to be the issue—responsibility is.

Too often, I have women write to me that their husbands claim there are "turning the kids against them," when in fact, they themselves are turning the children against them. Children need to feel that they are just as important to their fathers after they leave as they were before. And when they start getting ignored because their fathers are into some other world that they have no idea about, the resentment starts taking place. The children do not need to hear a discouraging word from their mothers—they are watching the actions of their fathers and reacting all on their own.

When these fathers decide to find the time to be with their children, they expect the children will be happy just to see them. If they haven't been around or active in the children's lives, the children can become resentful or alienated without any help from their mothers. Children have their own feelings and perceptions that no one has to influence. I have rarely seen a wonderful father who is active in his children's lives banned or alienated because he is gay.

Instead of these men having pity parties bemoaning their "angry, bitter wives" who are brainwashing their children, let them spend the time constructively figuring out what they can do to improve their children's lives and repair the relationship. Being a good father shouldn't have to be a sexuality issue. It's a parenting issue. My children would have never resented their father's sexuality because it was different; what they did resent was being made to feel that they weren't as important as a hot date when their father broke his promises and commitments. These are the realities that we live, not the distortions.

So, the next time you read about a gay father's rejection by his children due to his wife, think twice. Chances are his wife was very similar to us in nature. Chances are she wanted her husband to be more involved with the children than less involved. And chances are he screwed up big enough to make it easier to blame his wife rather than take the responsibility.

FEBRUARY 2003

HAPPY VALENTINE'S DAY TO ALL MY GIRLFRIENDS

It's that painful time of the year again for many women who are presently married to gay men or still recovering from the aftermath of their gay husbands—namely, Valentine's Day. I don't forget the sting of that day that stung me so many times in subsequent years of my life while my heart was frozen in the "void" status. I was always a romantic that thrived on being in love. But through the years of my marriage to my gay husband and the recovery years that followed, it was like that Gershwin tune that goes, "They're writing songs of love, but not for me...."

For those of you who are struggling through your marriages, Valentine's Day always fall short of your expectations. Some of you have not lost your enthusiasm—you've made all the plans in your head for a fantasy that never comes true. You plan a romantic evening with a beautiful home cooked dinner of his favorite food. You psyche yourself up for that yearly hope that the hearts of the day will make your husband's heart change and create an evening of passion. After the anticipation builds throughout the day, the reality becomes a good night peck on the cheek intermingled with the words, "I love you," and off to bed he goes—meaning off to sleep, not sex.

I wish I would have known through those lonely years what I learned later in life. It would have lessened the stabbing pain at the end of the evening and the tears that left my pillowcase soggy. Here's the message: Don't lose your hope for romance or passion. They are both somewhere in you future. That's the good news. That part of you doesn't have to die at all, no matter how much your gay husband wishes it would. You see, to him, it's a major pain in the neck. Every time you get those "touchy feely" urges to go touching and feeling him, it gives him the willies. Yikes! What's the new excuse of the day going to be? How many headaches, toothaches, ulcers, depressions, and exhaustion excuses does he have to come up with? It's such a nuisance.

The other good news is that there is someone out there waiting for your love. It's not going to be your husband, so you can put that thought out of your mind. But your soul mate is out there looking for you. I believe that. I see it happen over and over again. It happened to me when I had written off the possibility. Women whose hearts have been deadened through the lack of nurturing by gay men who are not capable of giving it, one day have their hearts awakened again by straight men who know what it means to love equally and unconditionally. And no one is happier than me when I hear from a woman who is "born again" after being buried under for years. I cheer my girlfriends and applaud their courage in coming alive again. I tell them, "Go for it."

I have watched the transition of some of my wonderful friends in our online support group this year. I have seen women who never felt that love would come their way once again feel their hearts flutter. Even if things didn't work out, they didn't retreat or give up. I tell them keep practicing for the real thing. Practice makes perfect. For most women, it's been so long since they've been around straight men that they've forgotten what to do. That's where the practice comes in.

If any of my readers would like to share their stories of feeling alive again, please send them to me so I can share them with the several thousand readers who need this kind of inspiration. As always, your stories can remain as anonymous as you like. To those of you still waiting to feel those flutters again, Happy Future Valentine's Day to you. It's always within your reach.

MARCH 2003

DENIAL

I'd like to end this month's newsletter with a few thoughts about the subject of "DENIAL." I've been doing some rethinking about my use of this word. I realize that I've been making excuses for some of your gay husbands by suggesting that they are in "denial." When husbands eventually admit to having gay sex but state they didn't think this was "gay," they often say it's because they were in "denial." In fact, I honestly believe that their gay peers also buy into this thinking. But now I think it only serves as another excuse for dishonesty. It kinda sounds good to the unsuspecting mind. "I'm sorry honey, I would have told you years ago, but I didn't know. I didn't understand. I was in a state of DENIAL!!!" And when a gay husband uses this as his excuse, it actually makes a horrible situation seem just a little better. It takes some of the stabbing sting away from our psyche. It generates a sort of "win-win" situation all the way around.

How? Well, let's face it. If your husband says that he was in "DENIAL," that means he wasn't consciously or purposely betraying you. In fact, he wasn't technically cheating on you. He swears he never really enjoyed it. In some cases, he can barely even remember it. He had absolutely no emotional attachments to the stranger that he spent a few quick moments with. His "thinking head" was in such a different place than his "sexual head" that he never even realized that it happened during those weeks, months or in some cases, years. How can you possibly hold this against him? He was almost like, well, for lack of a better word, a VICTIM.

Whew! Don't you feel better? I would. And, there are even some extra bonus points here. You have more peace of mind than before because your gay husband really loves you and those momentary encounters, which only were a few seconds in a vast sea of time were simply that—momentary "BLACK-OUTS" where your honey can't remember what happened. He can't even remember how it started or ended. It is just a blank spot in his subconscious or, hmmm, unconscious, so to speak. He has no recollection of the actual person whom it happened with, and don't even think about a name. There was no name. The face is a blur for sure. And after it happened, it was tucked away, or shall I say thrown away from his mind, never to return.

When gay husbands refer to "DENIAL," I realize it means that they were acting on their needs to sexually fulfill their homosexuality. "DENIAL" really means that they don't dare tell you, their wives, lest you should understand what the real problem is in your marriage. The only one I think they are really in denial to is you. When you ask your husband what the real problem is in the marriage, he will DENY there is a "real" problem. When he stops making love to you and you ask him why, he'll once again deny that there's a problem. In fact, anything you ask him that even alludes to homosexuality—bam! There must be something wrong with you because your husband DENIES he has a problem.

It's really difficult for me to "swallow" the line about DENIAL at this stage of time. I have done things that I'm not proud of in my life, but I never pretended to myself that I hadn't done them. I try to live up to my responsibilities and don't look to peddle them off elsewhere. As horrifying as acting on gay sexual urges may have seemed at any particular moment during a marriage, once the deed is done, it's done. Using DENIAL as a tactic to keep running away from the truth seems pretty lame. I'm not saying you have to shout it from the rooftops, but I do think that you need to you need to tell the person whom you married and promised to be honest with for better or worse. Yes, this is worse, but let's be fair here. Your wife hasn't done anything wrong except try to love you. Why can you love her enough to be truthful? Because you are in denial? No, I don't think so. Let's call it what it is—namely CONSCIENCE FAILURE.

MAY 2003

Distorted Perceptions

I've written about this before, and probably not too long ago. But I could never write about this enough, so I'll talk about it again. It's what I call "Distorted Perceptions." It's an important part of understanding the whole concept your marriage and why it failed.

I think I've gotten most of you on board with understanding that you had no influence on your husband's homosexuality. No matter how easy it is for us to fall into the trap of believing that we were not "good enough" or "smart enough" or "pretty enough" or "sexy enough" for our husbands, I hope after reading my constant reassurances, you finally understand that your husband's homosexuality was there long before you were.

The next concept of why your marriage failed is a little more difficult for you to understand. You are still looking at your marriage as if it takes "two to tango" as the saying goes. I often hear women say, "He made mistakes, and I made mistakes," or "We both had faults," Let's acknowledge that no one is perfect. Yes, we all have faults. But it is not your "faults" that created the problems in the marriage. On the other hand, it is very possible that the problems in the marriage intensified your faults.

Example? Okay. Let's start with me revealing to you some of the problems I had in my marriage. Because of all of the erratic behavior and inconsistencies in my marriage, I was overly suspicious of my husband's actions. Whenever I couldn't account for his missing time, I believed he was out cheating on me. I made an automatic search of all of his belongs when he wasn't looking. This included all of the pockets in his clothes, his little black phone book, and his wallet. I looked in the car at the mileage gauge, looked under the seats for clues of unfamiliar items, and went through the glove compartment for any suspicious papers, matchbook covers, or receipts left behind and haphazardly thrown in there. As soon as I would find a possible incriminating piece of evidence, I would confront my husband. He would get angry and yell at me how I was neurotic and ridiculous. He always had an explanation of whatever evidence I found, and he did his best to convince me that I was the one with a "vivid" imagination that was always in the overactive mode.

From where he was sitting, I looked like the overly nagging wife. Snooping didn't become me. But I became obsessed. Once the trust was gone, there was no way for me to regain it, especially when his patterns of suspicion continued. As much as I tried to ignore what kept hitting me in the face, I was unable to do so. As time progressed, my obsession deepened. Every time he left the house, my imagination took over and images of young men jolted out in my mind. Every guy my husband spoke to became suspect to me. My reactions to people were totally different because of this. No doubt, there were many innocent people who became victims of my unfounded hostility, but I was unable to distinguish fact from fiction because of the ones who were my realities and nightmares.

Now, my husband blamed me for overreacting to almost everything. And maybe in many cases I did. Bottom line: This was not who I was, but who I became because HE WAS GAY AND LIVING A LIE. And that lie infiltrated the darkest part of my soul turning me into someone whom I didn't recognize or even like.

There were days when I woke up and didn't want to live any more. This was NOT ME. The real me had a passion for life that had been temporarily snuffed out. I didn't know it was temporary while I lived it because my life was now on another plane—somewhere between the Twilight Zone and death. I say death because on three different occasions I attempted suicide. It seemed like an excellent alternative during those moments that seemed so inescapable and hopeless. This was NOT ME either. Prior to my marriage, I was so high on life. I was active, sociable, surrounded by high self-esteem, and very independent. I turned into someone who was depressed, scared, insecure, co-dependent, and crying constantly from being hurt.

The decisions and the moves that I made during my marriage were based on the mutated perceptions inside my marriage. Before I suspected that homosexuality was the cause of my unhappiness, I came to believe that it was me who was causing the problems in my marriage. If I told my husband that our marriage had problems, he would reply, "We don't have problems—YOU have the problem. I am happy in the marriage. YOU are the unhappy one." Many of you have written to me that your husbands tell you the same thing. The problem is YOU—not him, not the "marriage." And naturally, my husband, as well as yours, never looks beyond the fact that YOU have a problem, because it's always all about them. I guess I was falling into a darker hole each day so it was easy for me to believe that I was the one with the problems. He wasn't falling into a dark hole. He seemed content, and why not? He had a wife and a life outside his wife.

He was living his lie. And it was a big lie. Not a little white lie. Lying about your sexuality is a really very big lie. VERY BIG. What is a little lie? A little lie is taking money and buying something and not telling your spouse. A little lie is getting a couple of drinks at the bar with some friends while you tell your wife you are working. A little lie is not revealing that you broke your diet, smoked a cigarette after you quit, or paying more for something than you're supposed to but keeping quiet not to start a fight because you've unbalanced the family budget.

It's not like I'm condoning lying, but I certainly do understand it. I've lied myself when the thought of revealing something is going to result in an unnecessary argument that can be avoided and has no real effect on the state of a relationship. To lie is human. To live a lie is different. It's not something that is inconsequential. When you live a lie, there are always consequences for someone. In our cases, it ends up being our consequence.

The basis for a relationship should be one built on give and take. When a man stops having sex with his wife because it's too much of a burden for him because he is gay, he is giving wrong information to his wife. I don't hear too many men take responsibility for their lack of sexual activity other than made up stories about being too tired, too overworked, too depressed, too headachy, too sore from exercising, etc. When those excuses run out, then the tables turn. Then it's— YOU. You are too heavy, YOU are too naggy...YOU are too unsympathetic...YOU are too demanding, and of course.....YOU ARE A NYMPHOMANIAC or something just as insulting. Because YOU now think YOU are the problem in your marriage, YOU are the one who tries to change YOURSELF. So, now you are changing yourself to become the ideal wife of a man who doesn't want to make love to you no matter how good you look, how nice you act, how talented you are, or of course—how devoted you are to your gay husband. Ouch! That hurts.

Eventually, after your husband rejects you enough times, you stop expecting sex, and you also stop asking for it. He breathes a deep sigh of relief. Whew!! "She finally gets it. Stop asking because you're not going to get it." Once your wife stops asking you to have sex, she has resigned herself to living an unhappy life with you. How happy to do you think she's going to be? And when she's not happy, that's her fault too, right? Wrong. It's the husband's fault.

Some gay husbands believe that money is the key to happiness—YOUR happiness. They will try to compensate for their sexual inadequacy by buying you gifts and trinkets, as if that will do it for you. It's the same pattern as the physically abusive husband who beats his wife, begs for forgiveness, tells her that he loves her, and goes out to buy a present to prove it. HYPOCRITS. Like a bracelet is going to make you feel better about yourself. "I don't think you're good enough to make love to, but I think you're good enough for a bracelet." Thanks pal—but no thanks.

I know they say that the failure of a marriage is the fault of both parties, and maybe that's the case in functional marriages. But guess what? I don't think it's that way when you live with a gay man. You aren't happy. He can't be happy. He is saying that you are making him unhappy because of your own unhappiness. But if he would have been a straight husband, maybe you would be happy. Perhaps you could have met life's challenges as a team instead of being on different teams. And not only are you both on different teams, but you're both playing in different ballparks. If the pitcher for the New York Yankees throws the most perfect pitch in NY, the best player in Boston standing hundreds of miles away can't hit it—NO MATTER WHAT. You are in two different cities on two different teams. Two different places in two different spaces.

The same goes for straight wives with gay husbands. If your husband is telling you that the lack of sex in your marriage is YOUR fault, and he is a gay man, no matter what you do to make yourself more physically attractive, and some of you have gone to the extremes of breast implants and liposuction, it's not going to change anything. You are playing in the wrong ballpark. Or shall I say, you have the wrong plumbing.

If you think I'm saying to all of you that you are perfect and without fault, well, I'm not. No one is perfect; we are all human. We all make mistakes. We all have bad days. We all have human traits, and this is fine. And no husband—straight, gay or otherwise is perfect either. I don't think any of us are seeking perfection. We are seeking husbands who are playing in the same ballpark. And although many couples who are STRAIGHT couples grow apart, they do it in a more honest way. They don't always look to place the blame on your lap. They take some responsibility for the marriage unraveling. And you can make sense of those marriages that don't work without feeling that you are responsible for their failure. In a marriage with a gay husband, you don't even know what is real and not real. You are living in a labyrinth that has only twists and turns. There is no way to ever find a way to the end of the maze. The twists and turns go nowhere except in vicious circles.

And so, when you sit back and recount the years that have passed and try to figure out what went wrong in your marriage, do yourself a favor--stop thinking about it. When you live with a gay man who is parading in disguise as a straight man, nothing can change the circumstances. Or shall I say, only you are capable of changing them—by leaving the marriage and moving on to a life that makes sense. What's really so amazing is that life can make sense once your marriage is over. No more mazes to run through, no more Twilight Zones or Outer Limits. No more trying to solve the unsolvable, no more fighting against the unchanging tide. When you live like this, you zap your mental and physical energy because spinning gold out of hay only happens in fairytales.

AUGUST 2003

LET'S HEAR IT FOR THE BOYS

I have had an increasing number of gay men who have been writing to me in recent months. For the most part, they are men who are either in marriages or recently left marriages and are having difficulty dealing with "guilt" for the unhappiness they have brought their wives and families.

I always applaud these men because they are honest—at least at some point. Whenever I read these stories, I feel tremendous compassion for the tragedy that has fallen on the families at all ends.

Perhaps you are wondering why I am writing about this at all. This newsletter is, after all, primarily there to support straight women who are suffering and struggling through this situation. But guess what? I'm there for the men also who are in pain and need support. Maybe misery loves company, but from where I'm sitting, no one has to really be miserable in the long run.

In my heart, I believe that most gay men who marry are hoping against hope that homosexuality will be a thought or thing of the past once marriage comes along to "save" them. And no matter how much most straight wives believe that gay men know they are gay when they get married, I don't believe that at all. I have come to learn that there are many gay married men who haven't acted on their homosexual feelings, or even had homosexual feelings, until years into the marriage.

Am I an apologist? Of course not. I'm just a realist and a humanist. And I'm also honest. I see both sides of this one-sided situation. I can't even begin to imagine the struggle that gay men go through when learning to accept who they are. I understand all of the societal and family pressures that make them try so hard to be who they are not. I've seen all kinds of people trying to change because of fear. And in this time of enlightenment of humankind, some lights just seem to be snuffed out by ignorance. We are still living in a society that tells us that homosexuality is a deviant practice. Millions of vocal people still believe that there are choices to be made, and people can decide to be "straight" if only they try hard enough or are strong enough. It takes great courage and conviction to say, "The hell with what people think—I am what I am." It takes courage because being who you are can result in terrible consequences such as the loss of family members including parents, being outcast in the community, discrimination on the job, and in some cases, physical violence by ignorant people who are looking to pounce on gays just because they are gay.

Until the day comes when gay is viewed no differently than straight, gay men who can "perform" straight sex, even minimally or poorly, will do all that they can to convince themselves that they are straight. Is this what I would call denial? No, this is what I would call illusion. Or delusion. At best, confusion. And how confusing must it be when gay men truly fall in love with straight women because love itself is confusing?

I have rarely met a gay man who has stated that he got married and didn't love his wife. Maybe he wasn't able to love her the way she needed to be loved, but how would he know that? How many straight men marry women who they really don't totally love because they feel pressured or obligated? In a society that has a divorce rate that is nearly 50%, I'd say a lot. And even worse, how many bad straight marriages stay together when they should be ended because people are unhappy? Far too many that I see. People just get "stuck in the muck" and accept that this is what life is about. Yuck.

Now, that being said let me return to my real issue. To summarize so that I am very, very clear:

1. I believe that most gay men who marry do love their wives when they marry them.
2. I believe that most gay men who get married try their best to be the kind of husband they think they're supposed to be.
3. I believe that most gay men who marry really want to be straight.
4. I believe that most gay men who marry don't think they are gay when they get married.

Am I doing well so far?
So let me analyze these statements a little further.

1. I believe that most gay men who marry do love their wives when they marry them. I don't believe that most gay men who marry are looking to "use" their wives at the time of marriage. It is their real intent to pull things together and create a loving family unit. Some of these men have had homosexual sexual encounters, but they believe that this is "normal" for guys. Hey look, I grew up with those reports from knowledgeable doctors like Kinsey who said the majority of men have some kind of homosexual encounter sometime in life. Why shouldn't we believe that it is "normal" to have a few innocent encounters? Also, sexuality is very confusing throughout the teens and 20's. Almost any touch and feel can feel exciting. Plenty of straight women have told me that they had a good sex life in the early years of their marriage. That's why so much confusion sets in. I think another issue here is that other gay men know who they are so much earlier in the game. They say that from the time they were small, they always knew they were attracted to men. This is an important lesson—

not all gay men are the same, at least when it comes to recognizing who they are and what they feel. Acknowledged.

2. I believe that most gay men who get married try their best to be the kind of husband they think they're supposed to be. Some are good husbands, at least for many years. They are good friends, good providers, good fathers, and good partners. They try to live up to the expectations of what married life is supposed to be. I know this because so many women write to me so brokenhearted after telling me that they had a wonderful marriage. I admit I found this hard to believe in the beginning. That's because my own marriage was so miserable. But guess what? My ex had relationships with guys after me and they were just as miserable as my marriage was. He didn't treat his partners with any more kindness than he treated me. It's just who he is. He's a solo act who does not belong in a loving relationship. I also believe, however, that even though they try, they fall short of the expectations. They are gay men living in a straight marriage. They don't belong there because they are gay. They are trying to play a "role" that they can't interpret the right way because it's not who they are.

3. I believe that most gay men who marry really want to be straight. If someone has the opportunity to be straight, believe me he is going to take it. If he can feel love towards a woman, he's going to give the straight thing his very best try. And why not? Why wouldn't he at least try to be straight? Maybe this "marriage thing" will be what he needs to make those nagging feelings or suspicions fade away—FOREVER. I believe that many gay men love their wives so much that they are "Temporarily Straight." I even believe that some men have no clue that they have male attractions when they marry—especially young. NOT EVERY MAN HAS A YEARNING FOR MEN FROM THE TIME THEY ARE YOUNG. Some do, but not all. Time seems to be the great determining factor. The more time that goes by, the less the straight thing seems to work. Everyone's body seems to have a different timer when it comes to sexuality. There isn't a set day, time, or age that every man feels that big pull. Some know it early on, but many really don't know it until later on. There is no

logical answer here or predictor of when these feelings will surface.

4. I believe that most gay men who marry don't think they are gay when they get married. Okay, some men know or strongly suspect. But I believe that most gay men don't know they are gay when they get married, even if they have had sexual encounters with other men. They mistakenly feel that gay sex is not part of being gay. They think that gay means you have to be part of the gay world—and they are not. They may have had gay sexual encounters, but it wasn't personal or emotional—just sex. They didn't love their sexual partners or in many cases, even known their encounter partners, nor had a desire to do so. It was just a sexual act. Big deal. Their "straight side" is far more dominant than that gay sex thing. They love their wives—they make love to their wives. And in most cases, they can enjoy sex with their wives—at least for a while. I also believe that those men who believe they are gay are hoping that with a loving marriage, they will become straight. I don't think most gay men go into a marriage thinking, "I'll be a straight husband for my wife, but a gay lover for my gay relationships." They are really hoping that gay will go away.

I bring up these points for several reasons. I don't want straight wives to think that gay husbands have evil intentions when they get married. I know this is ridiculous. Some marriages have wonderful years together, and these are the marriages that are the most difficult to move past. These are the marriages where women hang in hoping that someday their husbands will wake up and realize what they gave up. Some women get hung up on thinking that their husbands will come to their senses when they realize that they are throwing away their marriages and families over some sex act. They just can't understand. Or in some cases, they just don't want to understand. How can a sexual act mean more than the love of a family?

Ironically, those husbands who eventually tell the truth are the ones who are looking for more than sexual encounters. They are looking for a soul mate who can understand their needs. We are not the soul mates they are longing to hold, caress, hug, and feel intimacy with. We can't fulfill that need because we are women.

79

I do admire the honest men even if it takes time for them to be honest. Who I feel contempt for are the dishonest men who will torture their wives for years by making them think that there is nothing wrong with them—only their wives. These are the cowards who go out and do their thing and continue to lie about it to their wives. These are the men who are denying who they are when they are out there doing their gay thing. These men are not in denial because they are not denying themselves anything. They are in 'DENYING"—DENYING to their wives what the truth is. These are men who want it all—a straight life, gay sex, and a cover for the public at large.

Sadly, too many of these "Denying" men justify their actions by saying that they love their wives too much to tell them. They are willing to keep living their lies figuring what their wives don't know can't hurt them. So often I get letters from men telling me they are so torn because they love their wives so much. Now these are the men who I can convince to do the right thing because they really love their wives enough to stop hurting them. And it ain't easy, believe me. It's a process that we go through where I make them understand how much more they are hurting their wives by lying to and cheating on them. These are the men that I can convince that living a lie is NOT beneficial to their wives. They start to understand the detrimental effect it has on a woman when you are somewhere that you don't want to be because it's not where you should be. You start picking fights just so that sex doesn't have to become an issue. No one wants to make love with a man who is insulting, angry, or detached. Unfortunately, it is rare for a straight wife to ever say, "I'm married to a jerk—he's the loser." Instead she says, "Why doesn't my husband love me anymore? I'm the loser." It's human nature. Women are socialized that way. The failure in the marriage is "their" failure even though they are the best of wives. Sad, isn't it?

Unfortunately, there are lots of selfish, insecure men out there who just will not be honest with themselves or with their wives. These are men who justify their misactions by saying that they are sex addicts, fetish lovers, or bisexuals. A rose by any other name is still a rose I say. The power of "DENIAL" IS VERY POWERFUL.

I also feel anger for the gay husbands who finally come out when they are ready and expect that their wives are just as ready as they are to accept their news. It's taken them 10 or 20 years to come to terms with their homosexuality, but it's only supposed to take us 10 or

20 minutes. Give me a break. When men write to me and say, "It's been a month since I told my wife. Why is it taking her so long to accept it?" I get angry. They lack compassion and understanding. They are in a big hurry to lead their new life without giving their wives the time they need to recover from the news. This is heart aching, marriage breaking news that is very hard for a straight woman to grasp all at once. Those men who wake up one day and decide they can be who they really are and say, "Hi Honey, I'm not home anymore" need to find a better way to make their announcements.

But enough with the bad guys. I'm here to praise the brave men who do what needs to be done, namely, telling the truth and looking for solutions for both partners for the days, weeks, months, and years ahead. I recognize your struggle. I sympathize with your pain. And I admire your integrity for leading your wives out of the darkness so that one day they can see the light again.

OCTOBER 2003

SEXUAL FREQUENCY SURVEY

I am the first to admit that I don't know everything. Or rather, let me say, I don't know or understand a lot of things when it comes to male "out of the norm" sexuality. I wish I did because it would make life so much simpler for all of us. I receive letters daily seeking advice with some of the toughest questions: Here's a sample:

1. Is my husband gay if he says he thinks he is but he has never acted on his homosexuality? How does he know he'll like it?
2. Is my husband gay if he still has sex with me after 20 years?
3. Is my husband gay if he only looks at gay porno?
4. Isn't it true that men who were molested in childhood act out through homosexual acts when they are older?
5. Is my husband gay if he has gay fantasies but swears he will never act on them?
6. Is my husband gay just because he had one meaningless encounter with a man 10 years ago?

7. My husband has oral sex with me. Doesn't that prove he's not gay?
8. My husband says he would like to have a three-some with him, me, and another man. He also wants to have sex with the other man. Does this make him gay or just kinky?
9. My husband wants to have sex with me, but only from behind me. He also wants me to insert a vibrator or dildo into his anal area. Does this make him gay? He says that the thought of sex with men is disgusting.

Now, if I had heard any of these stories, once, twice, or three times, I might think that there are some oddities here. But I hear them often. And boy, are we confused.

So here's my overall answer—BEATS ME. Yep, I'm the first to admit that I just don't understand it all. And guess what? I DON'T WANT TO UNDERSTAND IT ALL. It seems much too complicated for me to analyze and pick apart. It would probably take me years to look for the psychological reasoning of each man's sexual differences.

I can give you the standard gay theory that sexuality is on a continuum. Some people are totally heterosexual, and other people are totally gay. But many are somewhere in between the two ends. So where does that leave us? With a world filled with men who are sorta-kinda gay but not really? I don't think so.

I've been attacked by groups of "Bisexual" men who claim that I see things in terms of black and white when there are many shades of gray. Okay, I'm guilty of that accusation. But let me tell you why.

Even if a man is capable of having sexual encounters with a woman, I have issues with being with a man who is thinking of men, fantasizing about men, viewing gay porno, and finding himself in gay chatrooms for sexual stimulation. It makes me uncomfortable. I would always have to wonder if he is turned on by me or by fantasizing about men when he is with me just so he can sexually perform. I would think about that during every sexual encounter, taking away the possible pleasure even if there could be pleasure.

One of the problems that so many women face is that lack of admission by their husbands about homosexuality. These men claim that they are straight, regardless of the fact that they are into gay porno, videos, chatrooms, etc. When their wives bring up the subject of possible homosexuality, their husbands go into tirades calling their wives crazy, delusional, and paranoid. All this does is further diminish any sense of self-trust a woman has. She starts questioning over and over in her mind if she is imagining something that isn't there. The truth is, women who have straight husbands never have to spend time thinking about this issue.

But then again, what is gay? There is a gay writer, Matt Pearcy, who will soon publish his book of interviews with gay men who were married and their struggle in coming out. To quote his last newsletter, "In my discussions with gay or bisexual married (or formerly married) men I hear them say they don't want to be labeled. They feel that using the terms gay or bi or not-straight is too limiting." He goes on to discuss reasons why men who sleep with men don't want to be labeled. He also states that it is not your behavior that determines what a man is, but rather how he identifies himself. Thus, if a man has sex with another man, but identifies himself as straight, well, then, he is straight. He claims that identity is more than how you behave, it's how you feel about yourself.

Now, Matt's a great guy. He's a great "gay" guy. Matt has no confusion about his identity. He has never had the need to marry a woman to identify himself as straight. He has known what he is for many years and has come to terms with his homosexuality. Matt also tries hard to understand the thinking of men who marry straight women, and sincerely wants to share those experiences with other gay men. Matt himself has never married. And although this doesn't negate his ability to write about this subject, it may cause his opinions to be too one sided to understand the emotional pain that women go through in their lives when trying to unravel this puzzle

I don't believe that Matt is advocating this position, but rather just writing about it based on the responses that he has obtained from interviewing gay married men who like to identify themselves as straight rather than accept or admit to their homosexual behavior. And I've written so to tell him that. I believe that coming to terms with the homosexual identity can be the most difficult step in life which is why I tip my hat to those men who do so and are honest with their wives. Yes, it hurts like hell when you tell her, but it doesn't hurt nearly as much as those men who will never come forth with the truth.

What constitutes homosexuality? Can it only be identified as those men who have decided that they are no longer sexually performing and emotionally involved with a woman? I think not. I know of gay men who still want to bed their wives years after they have homosexual relationships with men. Gay men run the gamut in their sexual desires. My dear friend Becky will tell you how her husband had sex with her on a frequent basis up until the end of their marriage when he left for a man. More amazingly, now five years later, and still with his male friend, he still approaches her for sex whenever he visits the children. Does that make him not gay? I think not again!

We are confused, for sure. What is gay anyway? What happens when you have no proof? And what is proof? Most women think that proof is a full confession smattered with details or finding something so totally concrete like walking in on their husbands having sex with a man. Chances are, in most cases, neither one is going to happen. Then you just have to go on gut instinct because there is nothing else to go on.

Women with straight husbands don't think of gay as the reason for their husbands' alienation or lack of affection. They think that their husbands are having affairs—with women. For a woman to take it to the next step and start thinking that it's a possibility of "homosexuality" means that there has to be some evidence, either conscious or subconscious, that the wife is encountering. This is why I tell women to "Trust Your Instincts." Yep, I tell them that because these instincts come from somewhere—and not from nowhere.

The real bottom line is—CALL IT WHAT YOU WANT. BUT IT IS WHAT IT IS. If your husband is aroused by looking at or having sex with men, is this something you can live with? Is this something you want to live with? And chances are if he wants a man on any level—including fantasy—it's taking its toll on your self-esteem.

NOVEMBER 2003

LIMBO WOMEN

All of you who have read either my newsletters or most recent book, "Doomed Grooms," know that I have written about a phrase I coined, "Limbo Men." Limbo Men are those gay husbands who are caught in between two worlds—neither straight nor gay. They are psychologically straight (at least they think they are) and physically gay. They go through life lying to you, their family, their friends, and most of all, themselves. They don't have the courage to leave the secure straight world and walk into the world that they belong in. They rather just hang out in straight man's land passing through and pretending. Grrrrr.......rrrr. (Sound of a loud growl) It makes me angry.

The reason for my being pissed off is simple. Limbo men create a whole new category of straight wives—namely, LIMBO WOMEN. Limbo Women are the wives of Limbo Men who are stuck wasting years of their lives in unsatisfying marriages because they can never quite get the truth out of their husbands. They know that something is wrong. They know that their marriages are lacking the ingredients for success—namely communication, passion, and intimacy. They have loads of little clues that all add up to homosexuality, and yet, because they can't get a full confession—or even a partial confession—they are trapped.

By the time a wife of a Limbo Man gives a confession, it's usually a partial, such as:

1. I'm not gay, but I like looking at gay pornography as part of a full pornographic fantasy show.
2. I'm not gay, but when I was younger, I had an uncle who molested me on a few occasions.
3. I'm not gay, but sometimes I call gay sex lines because the way they talk stimulates me sexually.
4. I'm not gay, but when I was younger, before I met you, I had a one-time sexual encounter with a man, but I only let him perform oral sex on me.
5. I'm not gay, but there are times I think that I am bisexual because I look at guys and find them sexually appealing. I would never act on it though.
6. I'm not gay, but sometimes the thought of anal penetration turns me on.
7. I'm not gay, but when I was in college, we would all get stoned/drunk and have big orgies where everyone was having sex with everyone.
8. I'm not gay, but I have a fantasy about both of us having sex with another man.

The sad part is that each one of these partial confessions always starts the same way: I'M NOT GAY, BUT.... And now the wife is more trapped than ever. How can they break up a marriage just on their own perceptions based on partial truths?

I have wives that write to me about the extensive research they do on human sexuality. They are looking for my stamp of endorsement for their discoveries that their husbands aren't gay, just sexually "different" or "deviant." It seems if they can get my professional opinion that their situation is not like the thousands of others that I have worked with, they can learn to cope in their marriages and accept that life isn't always a bowl of cherries. On the other hand, it's not always a bowl of pits either. It's actually a bowl of half eaten cherries with the pits still in tact—sometimes, anyway.

These women struggle more than those of us who are given our walking papers or as I like to call it, "freedom." Those of us riding the freedom trail may be hurting for a while, but eventually we can lick our wounds and start life over. We don't have the shackles of homosexuality tying us to a husband who just won't be honest with us or in many cases, himself.

Limbo Women have the lowest self-esteem of all of us because they do personalize that the lack of love that their husbands can show them sexually is because of their failings. After they've exhausted every trick known to womankind without any success or movement, they admit defeat. Nothing they do makes it change. No diet, no breast implant, no sexy clothes, no new hair style, no new approaches to sexual satisfaction is going to move their husbands into the straight zone. Eventually, they admit defeat, but still don't understand why everything they try is not working on anything in their relationship.

Some of these wives cope by developing their own "on-the-sides" personal lives. They meet some straight man on the Internet who can boost their self-esteem by telling them all the things their husbands should be saying but don't say. Sometimes these Internet affairs are lifesavers when women start giving up hope on themselves. Some of these wives cope by finding real-life affairs, going outside the boundaries of their morals, religious beliefs, and vows, making them feel better on one end, but worse on the other. And still other women cope by popping pills that numb their minds and lower their libido just so they can keep living in the state of limbo.

And so life just keeps moving along, day-by-day, week-by-week, month-by-month, and year-by-year. Limbo Women attend family holidays, friend events like birthdays and anniversaries, and office Christmas parties of their Limbo Husbands. They stand like a trophy next to a man who needs a wife to show off to prove to the world that "I AM NOT GAY. HERE IS MY PROOF." The Limbo Wife allays the suspicions that everyone else has about the Limbo Man. It confuses the public at large who thinks it is able to identify people of a different sexual orientation because gay men don't get married? Right? Or even if they do, they don't stay married, right? Wrong.

Limbo Men stay married as long as their wives stay in limbo with them. Limbo Women are willing to fine tune their brains not to think about what they don't have. Rather, they try to focus on what they do have:

1. I have a nice home.
2. I have beautiful children.
3. I have friendly neighbors.
4. I have good in-laws who don't find too much fault with me (namely because you're covering up the family secret for them.)
5. I have a companion when I go on vacations.
6. I have a good friend.
7. I have a good friendship.
8. I have a husband who won't leave.

That's right, Limbo Woman, he won't leave. He's going to be by your side forever and ever because a Limbo Man doesn't leave. If he leaves, that means he might be dealing with whom he really is and what he does on the side might become front and center. This would upset the balance in his life and throw him out of the sphere of being emotionally straight. And that's a scary world that he just doesn't want to have to face. Life as a Limbo Man is too easy for him. It's also safe and secure.

Want to know something funny? Limbo Men think that their Limbo Wives know the truth—at least on some level. They think that all of the little clues that they have been confronted on prove that you know the truth somewhere in their Limbo Minds. And believe it or not, they feel that for this reason, you accept who they are. You can accept their little dalliances and dibs into that foreign world that neither of you really want to talk about. They think that your avoidance of the subject after a while is a form of acceptance. They don't see you running anywhere, and they also see you accepting that marriage can be built on friendship. You've given them the biggest gift of all—the end of sexual pressure. You've learned how to live with them in Sexual Limbo—or abstinence. Your Limbo Libido has gone off into the distance—either with someone else or out the door or body. Whatever. He breathes a big sigh of relief. You are now the perfect wife.

Of course, you're not really the perfect wife. He still finds fault with you because you are a woman. And he is a gay man in disguise. It's never quite the right chemistry. He's never really happy living in between two worlds. He's comfortable, but never really happy. And he'll find ways to blame you for his unhappiness. It will be little things that make you feel stupid. After all, he thinks you're stupid. He thinks you know he's gay and you're willing to live with it. How smart could you be?

The years will pass. Your best years will pass in front of your eyes. Yes, the best years—those years where you could have been living a life without deceit, contempt, and sexual rejection. And before you know it, you'll look around and realize that you can't get back what you have lost. You'll never know how far you could have gone in life because you never had a cheering team cheering you on. You will never be inspired to write poems that have love and hope, but rather your poetry talks of sadness and loneliness. I suppose there is a market out there for poetry of the forlorn. Someone may be smart enough to publish a book on "Poetry for the Limbo Woman." It's sure to sell a million.

And so, my dear Limbo Women, my heart does go out to you. I feel as if you are walking in the valley of No Zone. Not quite here, not quite there. But the good news is that you can move into another time zone. You can join the freedom trail and look at life as a new adventure, just waiting for you. You can make a decision that you've had enough of Limbo Land and want to spend whatever remaining years you have finding yourself and a new sense of enjoyment. You can learn that life can be like a romantic comedy. You can laugh and love again no matter how old you are. Romance is never an age—it's a state of mind. And even though living with your Limbo man has dulled yours, you can still take your life back and live it the way you want to. You may not win the battle, but you can definitely win the war.

DECEMBER 2003

ACT 2: SCENE 3

Quite frequently, women write to me about their lack of viable skills when it comes to securing a job so they can gain financial independence. I always look for transferable skills that would be a good match such as caretaker, nurse, detective, etc. How did I miss the most obvious one, namely—ACTRESS?

Every holiday season, wives of gay men have to play their Oscar award-winning role of "Happy Wife" in front of crowds of hundreds. Of course, there is no golden statue at the end of the season like their movie counterparts, but no doubt, the performances are just as extraordinary. And the holiday season is not the yearly birthday, anniversary, or Easter. The HOLIDAY SEASON is a long stretch that starts at Thanksgiving and continues until Valentine's Day. Between those two points, we begin the family and love ordeal. Thanksgiving is the beginning, followed by Christmas, New Year's, and finally ending on Valentine's Day in February. We are so relieved to have the President's Birthday as a holiday in February because by then, all of our emotional horror of the holiday season is over. Imagine thinking that Washington and Lincoln can actually neutralize and balance out life because after three months of families celebrating family unity and love, we no longer have to cringe when we hear the word, "holiday." The touchy-feely ones are over, and once again, we have not been touched or felt, and in fact, most of us have been living with a Novocain kind of numbness so that we can protect ourselves from crying at any given moment because we are HURTING.

The Holiday Season is such a difficult time for straight wives because it is an upfront in your face reminder of what life was supposed to be like but never became. Or if it was, it's over after years because homosexuality has joined into your previously happy union or what you were hoping would be your happy union. It's almost like having Scrooge find his way into your husband's body and head.

When you want a display of affection and emotion, he's saying, "Bah, Humbug." To this I say, "Ho, ho, no, no more."

You see, even though you may be feeling the pain of this holiday season, it could be your last year to suffer this way. Believe it or not, you can make it your New Year's resolution to be FREE by next year. Free of the pressures and strain of living a lie. Free of the constant questioning of what can you do to make life better with a man who wants a man to make his life better. Free of the mental torture from the mind games your husband plays so well with you, trying to make you start believing that you are losing your mind and it's just your imagination running away with you while he's running around with men. Free of earning your professional detective license while snooping around in a relationship that is supposed to be based on honesty and truth. Free to go to bed at night and feel good about waking up in the morning. Why? Because waking up alone and having peace of mind is always better than waking up next to someone who really doesn't want to be with you and is making you miserable because he feels that you are "trapping" him.

You see, way beyond this being a holiday season of family and love, it is a holiday season of hope. A time to make resolutions that will help you become healthy and happy. Now I know people hate clichés, but this one really catches the essence of the holiday— namely, "HOPE SPRINGS ETERNAL." This little ditty kind of coincides with my own personal philosophy; namely, each new day offers the opportunity of waking up and changing your life. I believe it. I actually did it, and I never look back and regret it. My marriage was doomed. I could have spent 10, 15, or 25 more years of wasting my life with a man who could only make me miserable. But a little bird in my head that became a choir of canaries singing to me, "Don't Do It." Don't give up one more year of precious time to a debilitating situation."

Look, I know that there are women who are now free who are reading my newsletter. You write to me all the time. I'd appreciate it if you could write to share your new life with my other readers who are still trapped to give them hope. Hope for the New Year. Hope for a new life. Hope for happiness. Hope for sanity. I will publish some of your letters in my upcoming newsletters with your permission. Please write to me!

GAY MARRIAGES

In the news as of late, there has been much talk about gay marriages. No, not marriages of gay men to straight wives, but gay marriages to other gay people. Lots of organizations, government agencies, and individuals have taken stands pro and con. Just for the record, I choose PRO.

Yes, I have my own agenda here. It's the agenda that represents over 4 million women in this country when they learn they have gay husbands. And let me be clear—it's not that I believe that if gays can marry gays they will stop marrying straights. I don't think that the two are intertwined issues.

What I do think is that when gay people are treated equally to straight people, they will stop going to desperate extremes of trying to be straight and ultimately marry straight women to prove that they aren't gay when they are. Gay people will stop trying to prove that they can be straight when they can't. They will be allowed to love themselves for who they are rather than run away as fast as they can, shadowed by guilt and public condemnation, which leads to self-hatred and desperation not to be who they are. Upon acceptance, which would mean equality, gay people will start feeling that it's okay to be gay and not feel so compelled to marry straight women.

Laws are a key to change. I'm the first to say that a change in legislation does not immediately change people's hearts. However, without legislation forcing change, there is no chance for change to happen. For instance, during the days of civil rights, Black Americans fought for equality, and as a result, legislation was enacted and put into practice. It didn't change the hearts of many old-school people who were determined to keep living their lives with hatred, but it did set a new stage for future generations who would grow up side by side with people of color and have the opportunity to interact as friends and classmates in school. Now, 40 years later, our younger generation is often seen with friends of all nationalities and cultures, something that was rare when I was growing up. Yes, there are still many people on all sides who have some degree of prejudice, but the younger generation is our hope that this will change in future generations.

The same is true of laws that recognize gay people as equals giving them equal rights and protections. This doesn't mean that in the immediate future people will change, but hopefully in future generations they will become as understanding and accepting of gay people as our children are today of people who look different than they are or who have customs that are different than theirs. Once gay people can feel accepted without fear of retribution, then they won't have to run away and live in a world of denial and deceit.

As wives and ex-wives of gay men, we, of all people, should want this to happen. We see the end result of discrimination of homosexuality all too clearly right in our own homes and marriages. We also know that our chance of having a child who is gay is higher than others because our children have a gay parent. We don't want our children living in a world where they are shunned and rejected because they were born "different."

So, when you hear about "gay marriages," think about the pain that future generations may be able to avoid if they become legal. It's too bad it didn't happen generations ago. Maybe you wouldn't be reading this newsletter.

APRIL 2004

ABOUT THE CHILDREN

This is going to be a painful story. So, if you are weak of heart or not in a good state of mind, please read it at a different time and move on to the next story.

By the time you read this, I will have commemorated my daughter Jennifer's second anniversary of her death from her drug addiction, which is this week in April 2002. I remember the night the call came in so vividly. It was 2:00 a. m. on a Sunday morning. Every time the phone rang at that hour, I cringed knowing it was Jennifer crying to me about how horrible her life was. During her last three months of life, she was so strung out on heroin that this was the only time she called me. She would call me to tell me how someone held a gun to her head while robbing her or raping her. I would cry and beg her to let me take her to a rehab, but she would make promises of calling me the next day after thinking about it. Of course, the calls promised on the next day never came. Somehow, drug addicts lose sense of time along with other sensibilities.

Now, as many mourners tend to do in the early days of a loss, I blamed myself for not being able to save my daughter. It's quite normal to do this when you lose someone who is dear to you, but especially a child. There are thousands of woulda's coulda's, and shoulda's that go through your mind in the days, weeks, and months ahead. It's like playing the "What If" game when you have a gay husband, but 100 times worse. When you lose a child, it's a lot easier to buy into that game than when you have a gay husband. Eventually most women realize they didn't turn their husbands gay, but most mothers always second-guess themselves when losing a child, especially to drugs.

It has taken me two years to come to terms with Jennifer's death. I accept the fact that nothing I would have done beyond what I did could have saved her from the destruction of heroin. I am no longer angry with her or the terrible things she did when she was on heroin. I have come to terms with this by looking at heroin as cancer. Once it is in your system, it is almost impossible to get it out. My daughter tried over and over again, but didn't win the battle. Twelve efforts of recovery in three years and three months were all for naught. She didn't want to be a drug addict. She wasn't weak. Her body was just overtaken by a killer agent like cancer when it takes over a body. That's how I mentally cope after losing my child.

I am not telling you this story because I am looking for sympathy. So many of you, my kind readers and friends, make a point to help me feel better. I am telling you this because a thought came to me two weeks ago that really saddened me.

I think about how so many of you are struggling through life trying to make sense out of something that makes no sense. I think about all of the hours you spend crying because you feel so bad about yourselves and your marriages. I talk to many of you who lead your lives in a dismal abyss or feel like you exist in a deadened state of mind popping anti-depressants to cope with your unhappiness. And then it finally came to me—it's not only we who are suffering from

93

having gay husbands, but our children are losing out as well. Yes, our children.

I remember that I had an epiphany several years ago when I realized that we could have been totally different people if we had supportive, nurturing husbands who encouraged us to maximize our potential rather than stifle it. Now I wonder how different the lives of our children would be if we had straight husbands. If we weren't so busy wondering why we were failures, maybe we would have been better mothers to our children. Ouch. That hurts. It pains me to think about it. But it is a reality that I have to live with—and worse than that—deal with. You see, I can't make up those days with Jennifer because she is gone.

I work with thousands of women each year who are trying to cope when learning about their husbands' homosexuality. Some of them are doing just that—coping. They don't wake up feeling good about life on any particular day because they are living in a haze. They spend numerous hours tracking down the movements of their husbands, only to be thrown off track or sidetracked by their husbands who are doing their best to escape detection. Think about all of the unhealthy hours you have put into your marriages trying to figure out the truth, and even when you do, think of all the wasted time you spend trying to make something work that isn't workable. These are wasted hours that could have been happy, productive ones if you didn't have this deceit to live with.

Do I sound angry? Yes, I am angry. I'm angry because I'm tired of women being told by their gay husbands that they love them, but they don't love them enough to tell them the truth for fear of the consequences of how it will upset their—the gay husbands'—lives. I think of the days when I used to cry and cry because I couldn't figure out what I was doing wrong because my husband didn't love me the way I needed to be loved. Those were days when my daughter didn't see the side of me that made her happy. I took care of her, I didn't neglect her, but she sensed my unhappiness.

Think about it. How many times do we feel frustrated so we take it out on whoever is closest to us—including our children? Worse yet, how many times do we feel trapped in our unhappy marriages because we are afraid to break up a family, and so we subconsciously place that blame on the children we love? Not consciously mind you—but unconsciously, yes.

After two years of mourning my daughter, I can say without hesitation that I don't blame myself for my daughter's loss. But I do regret the lost time with my daughter. I lost many happy days with her because I was sad. These were days when I was confused and frustrated. I didn't know what was wrong, so I had to assume that it was my problem. My husband wasn't unhappy. On the contrary—I was the one with the problem as he kept telling me. He was happy in the marriage. And if he wasn't happy, it wasn't his fault—it was mine. I was too controlling; I was too demanding; I wasn't a good housekeeper; I was too fat; the list kept going on. And not having the knowledge of what was wrong in my marriage, as most of you don't have for years, I believed that I was the problem. Certainly, that took a toll on my ability to be my best as a mother because I second-guessed everything I was doing as many of you do.

Does this mean you are not good mothers? Of course it doesn't. It just means that you can't be the mother you would be if you were happy and living with a supportive, loving husband. Or for that matter, you can live on your own and feel good about life because you aren't living your husband's lie anymore.

This confirms what I already know even more so. Living in a debilitating, limbo, or existing state of mind is not only harmful to you, but to your children as well. The longer you stay, the more time you lose that can't be brought back. As scary as leaving is, it has to be less scary than staying stuck in a relationship where you are constantly feeling that your life is turned upside down and you have lost the sense of who you are.

And so my darling Jennifer, at the end of two years, I'm still hurting for you and for us. I'm sorry that your life was so consumed with the hardship and sadness of addiction. Hopefully you are finally at peace and in a much better place than you were when you were here. Know that I will always have an empty hole in my heart that no one else can ever fill. I love you.

MAY 2004

THE ISSUE OF COMMUNICATION

The most important part of any relationship is communication. This seems to be something that is sorely lacking in straight/gay marriages namely because they are built on lies and deception. Of course, this is not to say that it isn't missing in other kinds of relationships, regardless of sexuality issues, but it is even more so for ours. It's bad enough when we read about straight relationships and the lack of communication because women are from Venus and men are from Mars as the saying goes. But in our marriages, women are from Venus and men are from the Twilight Zone.

I always say that for the most part, straight wives married to gay men are far above the standards of wifedom. You see, women married to straight men have a fighting chance of pleasing their husbands just based on who they are. But we can never please our husbands because of who we aren't—namely men. But that doesn't stop us from trying harder and harder to put that round peg into a square hole, does it? And it never ceases to amaze me how so many of us just can't cry "uncle" and walk away from a no-win situation. We keep trying while we keep crying to figure out where we are going wrong long after we suspect or know the truth. Go figure.

It also saddens me to talk to women who just can't get it. Even when they are faced with the truth, they keep trying even harder to be the perfect wife as if perfection will turn around the gene pool. And I can say that it's not always their fault. Often it is the fault of the "confused" gay husband who just can't let go of the straight world even when he is not confused over what stimulates his sexual organ. Again, go figure.

Excuse me from digressing from my original thought of communication. I have recently revisited a painful part of my past. You see, even when the years have passed, as in my case, and the marriage is long over, the scars still remain. In spite of all of my expertise and counseling skills in relationship issues, I still have to be my own best student. And though it pains me to have to discuss my weaknesses in a forum read by thousands of people, I am a great believer in people learning from each other. So I will proceed to talk about this with you.

One of the areas of self-improvement I work on constantly is self-esteem. This is a definite tie to my ability to communicate in a healthy way in my relationship with my soul mate, which will soon reach the ten-and-a-half year mark. I have found a man who truly loves me more than I could have imagined. And yet, I still have fears that if I ask for some additional emotional support when I need it, I will be rejected. This angers me because it is so typical of behavior by someone who feels she is unworthy, which I do not. So why do I have to keep trying so hard?

My years with my gay husband trained me to be an excellent partner for any man. I am fully seasoned as far as working my hardest to make someone love me like all of you are. And to be honest, I've put everything I have into this present relationship. I work hard to keep it exciting and new after all of these years. We're middle-aged, but we feel like we're young and in-love. Our relationship is solid. I trust this man with my life. It took years of working at it to get it this way. We have both learned to compromise. He works hard to meet my emotional needs because to me, that's an important part of a relationship.

Well, to get to the point, several months ago, my soul mate didn't meet my expectations concerning something that was very important to me. I was hurt and angry. It was something simple that required very little effort, and yet it was very significant to me. He blew it and he knew it. He knew it instinctively and also because I did tell him. I honestly think he felt worse than I did because the last thing he ever wants to do is hurt me. In the following two days, he tried his best to make up for it by buying me flowers and cards that said emotional things. And I acted like I forgave him even though in my heart, I was still hurting.

So life went on and all was well—or so I thought. But over the days and weeks that followed, something was amuck—with me, not him. I didn't worry about it because I am pre-menopausal and expect to feel highs and lows. But the feelings I had were neither high nor low. There was a slow but gentle decline in my feelings for my soul mate. I went through the motions, but I wasn't feeling them. My soul mate knew something was off, but I kept saying it was everything but what it was.

Although I made excuses for why this was happening, I was unable to discover the real reason until weeks later. As I started to see that nothing was improving and it started impacting on our intimacy, I realized that there really was a problem that I needed to work on. I did some mental backtracking to the time when my feelings started to shift, and voila—I finally figured it out. It all led back to the time when he screwed up weeks before. And although he tried his best to patch it up with words of regret and flowers, I hadn't inwardly resolved the hurt.

I analyzed why I buried the hurt and it all comes back to the same thing--lack of self-esteem. Lack of feeling worthy enough to express my true feelings for fear he will back away or think that I am "nagging" or "suffocating" him. My gay ex-husband had me very conditioned not to ask for what he didn't want to give me. It always started a fight and I always lost because he had better verbal damaging skills than I had. In fact, all these years later, he still knows how to trigger those buried feelings of inadequacy whenever we have an argument. He can shout me down and shut me up because I don't like fighting on such a low level. I find it degrading.

My soul mate is not my ex-husband. He is kind and gentle, caring and giving. If I am upset about something, he takes it to heart. He has worked hard to change so he can meet my emotional needs. And 98 percent of the time, he does. It's the two percent of the time that always gets to me. And most times, I let it slide because no one is perfect and I know he has tried so hard to make me feel good about myself and about us. But this one time was something of great importance to me, and the usual "I'm sorry" just didn't cut it.

Once I recognized where the problem stemmed from, I sat down with him and said we need to talk because I finally understood what the problem was. And guess what? He didn't laugh at me or blow me off. He wasn't annoyed or angry. He listened and accepted my feelings, acknowledging that the hurt was deeper than we both realized. All was well again after that conversation. It was like a dark cloud being chased away and replaced by a lovely day.

It taught me a lesson, which is why I am sharing this with you. Through the years that our feelings are ignored or scowled at, we become conditioned not to ask because we would not receive. This behavior is easy to carry into our new relationships because we are still trying hard to please our new partners, subconsciously feeling that we failed with our gay ones. Every time we can't express our feelings fearing rejection, we are giving in to the horrors of our past marriages. Not being able to assert yourself in a relationship only continues to build on your feelings of inadequacy even when you are sure that they are dead and buried. It doesn't take much to revive them no matter how much you think you've left them behind.

Unless you internally believe that you are deserving of more, you will always settle for less. This is why I tell women who are leaving marriages with their gay husbands to wait before they jump into a new relationship with a man. You need time to relearn who you are and to work on the issues that can haunt you forever if you don't face them. Coming out of relationships with there is a lack of trust, intimacy, self and sexual esteem, and communication takes time. If you don't give yourself time to repair, chances are you will jump into the wrong relationship, or take a potentially good relationship and destroy it all on your own.

I have seen women who have met good men but destroyed the relationship because they haven't resolved their own issues with their gay husbands. They transfer them into their new relationships and disaster occurs. We allow our feelings of inadequacy and mistrust to surface anytime there is a problem, rather than allowing ourselves to rationally work it out. That's why we all need time and breathing space after our marriages to regroup and regenerate.

Now, this is not to say that you have to stay home and become a hermit like I did for many years. You can go out and have fun—and practice for your soul mate. But before you get in the relationship mode, make sure you work out kinks from your marriage. If you don't, you are setting yourself up for a big fall. You may choose the wrong partner because you still haven't restored your own sense of self-esteem. And one thing I've learned—no one can make you feel better about yourself except you. Only then can you find long-term happiness and fulfillment.

The most important thing to work on is overcoming your fear of asking for something that is important to you for fear of being rejected. We've tiptoed around our gay husbands, not feeling worthy because they could never love us the way we needed to be loved. In a new relationship, stand up for yourself and don't be afraid to ask for what you want. That's how communication in healthy relationships works. Don't allow your insecurities of the past overtake your happiness in the future.

SEPTEMBER 2004

RECONFIRMING MY POSITION AND MY NEW EPIPHANY

Since the "coming out" of Governor McGreevey in August, I have received an onslaught of media requests for information and hundreds of new letters from women in pain. I suppose I should be thankful that the Governor got "caught" in this situation, because it has focused some pretty powerful attention on the subject of straight/gay marriages.

For those of us who feel the pain of isolation and shame for being the wife of a gay man, there has been a sense of real jubilation as so many of you have stated to me in your letters this month. Sometimes after revealing the truth to others we get reactions from even our closest family members or friends like, "You must be imagining it—after all, you have children together" or "But he seems like such a great guy, how could that be?" to "He doesn't look gay to me, are you sure?" and "He obviously wasn't gay when he married you. What happened?" That last one, by the way, is not necessarily verbalized, but you see the person looking at you with that look of, "WHAT DID YOU DO TO MAKE HIM GAY?"

Ah, we straight wives have suffered the indignity of the ignorance of society for the same amount of years that gay people have been ostracized and condemned. This accounts to why we are "stuffed in the closet" next to our husbands. Shame. Blame. Insane. We know every emotional feeling that all comes down to the bottom line—INEPT.

But thanks to Governor McGreevey, people see us in a new light. We are now the sympathetic figure, much like the stoic Mrs. McGreevey who stood by her husband's side while her husband made the announcement that their life together was a lie. Yes, when you are married to a gay man, your marriage is a lie. You can slice and dice it any way you like, but in the end, it's still like scrambled eggs—beaten up and shattered.

A number of you wrote to me feeling assured that I've been in touch with Mrs. McGreevey to help her through this trauma. Others wrote to me asking me to send her a copy of my books. Still others told me to call her to offer her counseling. One writer: "Maybe you should invite her into our chatroom. She could really benefit from the support." To all of you—the answer is NO. I have no clue how to reach Mrs. McGreevey. She hasn't called me, and chances are, she's not looking for me! However, by now, if she's been reading the New Jersey newspapers about her husband, she will have found my name in the various interviews where I was quoted in case the day comes around that she needs support.

People ask me what I would say to Mrs. McGreevey if I have the opportunity. My answer is this: GET OUT. Run as fast as you can. No trappings or trimmings can compensate the agony you will feel in time from being married to a man that wants to make love to a man instead of you. No outside physical beauty will matter because you will start to feel ugly as rejection takes over your psyche. No amount of self-esteem will save you from the peel down facing you each day when you start second guessing what you were so sure was right but now makes no sense at all. Every time your gay husband tells you that you're "Imagining things" or "thinking crazy," you'll really start wondering why these suspicious feelings keep gnawing at you in spite of his denials, beginning the process of self-confidence erosion.

I have expertise in straight/gay marriage issues. I'm not the only one out there who has experience in working with straight/gay couples, but among others in this arena, I think that I'm the one who makes the most sense. I cannot condone these relationships. I can't put sophisticated labels on them like "Mixed Orientation Marriages" to try to make it sound better like gay men who label themselves as "bisexuals" in order to make their infidelity with men sound more palatable while they are married to a woman. I can't dress it up and make it look more attractive to the public eye. AND I WON'T. I will call it what it is—A MISTAKE - a big mistake-or, to term my own phrase, a Mismarriage.

Here's the interesting thing. We all make mistakes. It's part of being human. When gay men marry their wives, I believe there is no ill intent in almost all of the cases. Our gay husbands don't marry us because they want to be gay and lead secret lives. They marry us hoping that they will be straight. And yes, some of them have no clue because some men's gay feelings don't surface until they are in their 20's, 30's or even 40's. And no, not all gay men knew something was different or wrong when they married us. Some knew—some didn't. And for those who knew, well, they hoped against hope that those

feelings would vanish if they loved us enough. Most of them tried—
and tried very hard. But it doesn't work. It can't work. As the old
saying goes, you can't shove a square peg into a round hole. In the
case of gay husbands and straight wives, one or the other will try to
shove those pegs and holes into each other as if by forcing or by
pushing hard enough, it will make them fit. All you end up with is two
bashed pieces, broken, splintered and whittled away.

To err is human. To keep the mistake going is inhumane. You
need to stand up to the error and correct it as quickly as possible. The
longer you stay, the harder it becomes to leave. Now some of you
would think that the longer you stay, the more disgusted you'll
become and the easier it will be to leave. That is not the way it works.
The longer you stay, the less confidence you have in yourself and this
makes it more difficult to leave. The longer you stay the more
comfortable you become with physical surroundings versus a healthy
mental state so you are willing to sacrifice happiness for material
security. The older you get, the more difficult it gets to start over. The
longer you stay, the more of your life you throw away.

Sometimes women feel trapped in their marriages. I understand. I
am not without sympathy and understanding. But even when you're
trapped physically, it doesn't mean you have to be trapped
emotionally or mentally. You can't lose sight of getting out of your
marriage at some point of your life. Otherwise, you've given up hope
and surrendered. This is sad. It's also bad. It means that you've
settled for living in the land of the zombies. You've accepted the fact
that you're going to exist to please everyone but yourself. You're like a
Stepford Wife. Mechanical. Yuck. This is why I refuse to give support
to women who write to me for ways to stay in their marriage. I refer
them elsewhere—to the groups that work with "Mixed Orientation
Marriages"---after I explain to them that they are wasting valuable
years of their life.

I have many women say to me that they can't wait until they have
the proof they need to confirm their husbands' homosexuality. They
hang in there day after day, watching, waiting, checking pockets,
wallets, cell phone bills, computers, websites, and anything else you
can imagine. Still—no proof. To those of you who are spending years
in a loveless, sexless marriage, you need not wait any longer. You
have your proof. Straight men want sex. It's their nature. And when
they go through personal stuff that lowers the libido, the good news is

that it returns when the problem subsides. Gay men just reject you. Period. They don't want to make love to you. They do it because they think they "have to" to keep up their illusion of straight. And in time, they just stop doing it and turn it around to make you feel like you're the "abnormal nymphomaniac."

I had this new epiphany while I was in my Sunday chatroom a few weeks ago. I don't remember what made this new point so very clear to me. I have an epiphany every few years. The last one I had was in 2001 when my friend Jay inspired me with his words to realize that we could have all been very different women if we were married to straight men who nurtured, encouraged, and inspired us with love that gay men are not able to give us. We have no idea what we could have achieved if we hadn't spent years becoming prisoners of our own insecurities.

Now, I realized why I can't encourage women to stay with their gay husbands under any circumstances. Here is my new epiphany: If a woman was living with a straight man who was physically or emotionally abusing her, I would never tell her to stay in that relationship and try to work it out when I knew there was no way it was going to change because her husband could not change. Living with a gay husband is living in an abusive situation. No matter how nice your gay husband is, knowing that he wants to be with a man and not you is emotionally abusive. And I refuse to condone this situation because it would make me irresponsible. This is not to say that your gay husband is intentionally abusive—but the whole situation is abusive.

I have advocated and strongly encourage couples to co-parent their children from separate homes. I have also said that people can make all kinds of financial readjustments in their lives even if they have to live without so many materialistic objects. But peace of mind and sense of worth is something you cannot achieve when living with a gay man. Period.

As I embark on my 53rd year of my life (September 26), I felt the need to relay that message to you, my readers. Some of us have been together for a long time forming a deep friendship over the years. Others of you keep in touch with me through occasional emails letting me know how your life is progressing. Some of you have moved on to new wonderful lives; others of you are still struggling to find the way through the Alice in Wonderland mirror of twisted, upside-down life. But for those of you who are physically stuck, you're not giving up. You write to me letting me know that these newsletters give you the courage to hang in and think ahead.

I also needed to restate these thoughts because this summer, I've had some real scary times with health issues. Thankfully, I'm on the mend, but it made me realize how valuable every day of life really is. It made me think about how lucky I am to be free of the mistake that I made 26 years ago. I am also so blessed to have found a soul mate who makes me feel good about myself throughout my own years of weight struggle. See, a gay man would find fault with the looks of Mrs. McGreevey. But my straight lover finds me beautiful even though I've gained 80 pounds in 10 years. More of me to love, he says! Well, now I'm working on less of me to love so I'll be around for him to love!

And so my dear women, please do what you need to do and salvage the years you have ahead. We are given one chance at life, and every precious day you stay in a debilitating situation is another day that can't be taken back. Every day that you live in your unhappy marriage is another day lost that can't be returned to you. Start preparing to take back your life!

OCTOBER 2004

LIVING IN FEAR OF BEING DISCOVERED

I bet you're thinking that I am going to write about your gay husband and his fear of being discovered, right? Wrong. I'm going to talk about you—the straight wife. And I'm going to talk about a situation that may hurt some of you to think about, but we need to discuss it so that you will stop feeling worse about yourself and this situation than you already do. And this does NOT apply to many of our sisters in pain, but it does apply to enough of you to compel me to write about it. So for those of you whom it doesn't apply to, just read along for the ride.

The complexity of straight/gay marriages has enough twists and turns just by the nature of what they are—distortions of life. We spend years trying to unravel all of the threads of this situation, thinking to ourselves, "Where did we go wrong?" Sometimes thinking about where we went wrong stops us from thinking about something else that we have conveniently tucked away in our subconscious—namely, WE ALWAYS KNEW. Ouch. That one really hurts.

Truth be known—some women suspected or knew something ahead of time. There is no shame in this—NONE WHATSOEVER. Why? Even if we knew it, we DID NOT UNDERSTAND IT. I would stake my reputation on the fact that less than ONE PERCENT of women who know or suspect their husbands are gay want to marry a gay man. Yes, there is always an exception to a rule, but the rule holds pretty steady. For that rare woman who has issues with sexuality and prefers to remain mostly celibate because it is meeting an emotional need rather than a physical one, you are the odd woman out here. The rest of us are women who want straight husbands. And if we had any clue that our husbands were "bisexual" or "gay" before we married them, we didn't think they really were, but rather they had one or two same sex experiences. According to sex experts across America, a little dabbling in same relationships is not that uncommon and DOES NOT define sexuality or rather homosexuality. WHATEVER.

We were so sure. We were so sure that even if we knew there were inklings or attractions they would go away because we would love our husbands enough to help them overcome those fleeting feelings. We thought those feelings were similar to indigestion, which can be resolved with a bubbling pill every time it attacks your stomach. In time, we found out this was not the case. The harder we loved our gay husbands, the more "trapped" they felt. Our love started to strangle them and they started to strike back at us. And even though it's difficult to be nasty to someone who is so good to you, it didn't stop our husbands from the barrage of mental haranguing. These men don't want to be there, and every day that they look at you becomes a painful reminder of their unhappiness, no matter how hard you work to make them happy.

Most of us are raised with the concept that homosexual means "same sex." We see gay people everywhere in the media—television, movies, magazines, and radio. We think that this is what gay people are: funny caricatures of men with either extreme distortions in their walk and talk, or little effeminate tones. Those are the gay men that are easy to spot. Those, for the most part, are not the "marrying kind." It's the variety of men that we marry that no one ever suspects. Well, for the most part, we don't suspect. But sometimes we do suspect. Sometimes it's a subtle clue or hint. It could be a lingering look, a slip of the tongue, or an insinuation to something sinister in the past.

But when we fall in love with someone, a person's past seems to be just that—his past. We believe that if we are the present, we will be the future. And our husbands, with their trails of "I love yous" following every step they take, are most convincing. Marriage is the ultimate commitment. Surely if a man wants to make a LIFETIME commitment and cement it in front of God and everyone in a long line of family and friends, why would we think that he is gay? After all, the vows state forever and ever, not just for a number years until the gay thing takes over.

I know that I've addressed this in the past, but I felt the need to bring it up again. This stumbling block seems to stop women from moving on to new relationships. It seems that some of you fear that if you made the mistake once, you'll make it again. I'm not saying people haven't made this mistake twice, but it is so, so rare. Most women learn from this experience what to look for in a new relationship—namely passionate sex—and won't settle for someone who wants to be "respectful." We all know what that sense of "respect" really means!

NOVEMBER 2004

WORDS MY MOTHER TOLD ME

This was a card from my mother who sent it to me nearly 17 years ago following my divorce decree. I thought for sure the card was gone with the wind so to speak, but there it was, carefully hidden away inside a file box that I wouldn't have ever looked in if Jay hadn't inspired me to do so.

My mother passed away in April of 2000 from lung cancer at the age of 67. She was the most beautiful of women both inside and outside. My mother was my best advocate throughout my life. She encouraged me no matter how much she may have disagreed with my decisions. I was the oldest of five children, so I had the benefit of spending the most years with my mother, developing a close a loving adult relationship with her after a rocky relationship throughout adolescence. I always walked to the beat of a different drum, which can be quite taxing to those who are walking on a straight line. But over time, my mother came to appreciate our differences and never failed to supply whatever material help or emotional support I needed in the difficult years of being a single parent after the breakup with my gay husband.

My mother's life was not an easy one. As I always tell my readers, gay husbands do not have a monopoly on irresponsibility. There are multitudes of straight men who are equally if not more irresponsible—my father standing high in the ranks. My father left my mother walking away from five children, bankrupting his business, moving 3,000 miles away, and leaving us virtually homeless while he lived next to Beverly Hills with all the luxuries life has to offer. Back in the 1960's, the courts were not very responsive to child support and my mother lacked the resources to fight my father in the other end of the country. And so my mother began a struggle to survive and feed us. They were very bad years, but she had a great sense of inner strength. With nothing more than a high school diploma, no viable work experience, and five children, my mother went to work as a typist for $75.00 a week, and struggled to jump over every possible obstacle life presented. I was 16, but my sisters were babies—2, 4, and 6 years old. I was rebellious and clashing and always on my own page. And yet, my mother was able to overcome whatever adversity was thrown her way. She battled back, educated herself in the world of business, and in time, became a highly respected marketing manager for a major insurance company, spending her last working years in the World Trade Center in New York. When people ask me where I get my strength, I tell them from MY MOTHER. She was my role model to look up to and emulate.

My father tortured my mother long after he walked out on her. He purposely delayed getting a divorce for years playing all kinds of psychological warfare games with her. One day, many years later when he decided to get remarried, he gave her the divorce. I mention this so you'll understand the context of the words she wrote to me. Here are those words:

Dearest Bonnie

This is not the funny card I was going to send, but instead one the color of sunshine, the sun bringing to mind that whatever happens to people, joys, tears, health, sickness, weddings, or divorce, the sun always rises bringing new life, spirit, and vitality to the world. Remembering the words, "On This Joyous Occasion" from the first time, those occasions change, and we do the best we can to look ahead to brighter days and happier times. Divorce is a finality and a conclusion to a mistake. You should be proud that you brought this to an end from a legal standpoint and a morale standpoint. Your children will someday admire your decision, as to not divorce but know of his life would lower their feelings of strength they see in you and count on for their future. Someday, they may have to accept his failings but never your weakness. My life, in limbo all these years to suit your father's fancy, has been unproductive, restrictive, and foolish on my part. Now it is too late to recapture my years, but I'm comforted in the fact that you face a free new road. Enjoy your freedom and strength. I am proud of you always.

Love Mommie.

My mother was a woman of few written words. That was why I was so overwhelmed when I received this card with pictures of rainbows and sunshine. Re-reading it all these years later reinforces for me how lucky I was to have such a wonderful mother. That's why I feel so saddened when I get letters from some of you who tell me how your mothers don't support you or your decision to leave your gay husbands. It's not bad enough that we have to travel through a maze of confusion and hurt, but to not have family support with this makes it so much more difficult.

So, that's why I wanted you to read the words my mother told me. In case your families don't give you the support you need, hang on to the words of my mother, because they were written to me, but I'm sending them to you for support.

DECEMBER 2004

ONE MORE GAY HUSBAND CLASSIFICATION

Several years ago when I coined the phrase **"Limbo Man,"** women from all over the world congratulated me on finding a way to describe those men who were caught in between two worlds. These are men who are emotionally straight and physically gay who hover in between the two worlds never really feeling comfortable in either one. You see, these men pass as "Bisexuals" to the outside world. They have them convinced themselves and sometimes their wives that they could actually be husbands to their wives and lovers to other men. Sad to say, there are some women who buy into this concept—but NOT MY WOMEN! There are women who belong to other groups that get give and get support to keep these mismarriages (my term for marriages of mistake) in tact, and, in fact, expect the woman to be happy living this way. But—NOT MY WOMEN! My women know that there is no way in hell that they are going to be happy in these marriages. They may be temporarily stuck due to circumstances—but they are not doomed forever.

Then after that, I realized there is another category of gay husband and I gave him a new terminology –"**The Straight Gay Man.**" This is a gay man who parades in the skin of a straight one, never admitting to himself that he can possibility be gay because he's so straight. In fact, he's so straight that he'll make fun of gay people, imitating their stereotypical effeminate walk and talk. He'll refer to gay people as "faggots" and other derogatory terms to really throw you off-track because in his heart, he knows it isn't him, when it fact, it is his sense of self-hatred that pushes him to talk that way. This is the kind of man who doesn't have gay relationships, but rather sexual encounters only. Anonymous sexual encounters for the most part that won't follow him back to his comfortable house for fear of being "misunderstood." After all, he's in denial anyway. He blames you for all of your unhappiness in your marriage—"You're the one who isn't happy—I'm perfectly happy in this marriage." And this is the man that will definitely remarry if you leave him. He'll be happy to make the life of some other "unsuspecting" woman just as miserable as he is making you. Besides, he's trying to make you think you're crazy, so even if you think of revealing any of this to his next wife, DON'T BOTHER. She already thinks you were the cause of all of the problems in his marriage with you. He's convinced her. Trust me on this.

And recently it dawned on me that there is a third kind of gay husband. I have named him the **"Have Your Cake and Eat It Too"** gay husband. This is the man who knows he is gay, knows that you know he is gay even though he won't admit it exactly, and he'll deny it after he lets it slip out because he doesn't really care what you think. You're stuck with him, and if you decide to ditch him, well, you're the bitch. How dare you?

These guys don't dare reveal their sexuality to the public or to their families. They are not like the Limbo Men who are really stuck in between both worlds and never happy totally in either one thinking that they are "bisexual when in fact they are gay. They are not like the Straight Gay Men because they don't live in a sense of denial. They are a class unto themselves.

These are the men I dislike the most because they feel they have you where they want you—stranded in "Never Never Land." You may as well join the Lost Boys because you will be feeling lost. Well, actually, you may as well take over the role as Wendy because you will be the mother to this man who won't grow up. Wife? Let's not be ridiculous. You will be his "caretaker." He won't be a husband to you because a real husband would be there for you emotionally, physically, and sexually. He'll be there physically taking up space in your life, but forget emotional and sexual. Knock, knock—nobody's there.

The Have Your Cake and Eat It Too gay husband will leave just enough information and clues around to let you know he is gay. He'll get caught in some way or another at least once. Then he'll tell you it was a mistake. He really loves you. And you're not going to break up a perfectly good marriage for one little indiscretion, are you? Of course not. And he's remorseful for a few days or weeks. He shapes up temporarily sometimes to be a model husband—acting like he cares about your emotional feelings and even approaches you physically for probably the best sex to date. But it's a temporary stop-gap or as I call it, the false illusion of a second honeymoon. It fades as fast as the first honeymoon. And then you are left with a pocketful of doubts that he keeps reinforcing in odd little ways. These are they

110

guys who need to remind you over and over and over again how inadequate you are as a wife, mother, woman, human being, worker, etc. By knocking you down a notch on a regular basis, in time you start believing it. These guys perfect their style of beating the hell out of your sense of self-esteem and self-worth. It's not necessarily by yelling and screaming, it's by their utter looks of disapproval or needling comments and remarks that make you feel stupid. Mission accomplished. On some level they think you really are stupid. After all, you know they are gay and yet you stay married to them. How smart is that? Well, since you're not that smart anyway, why not knock you around some more. That's what these guys think. Urgh. That's my sound of throat gurgling while growling at the same time.

These are the men who are so controlling that they make you fearful of finding any support or telling anyone about their homosexuality. And these are the guys who will blame you when you bring it up. You are the cause of their gay indiscretions because you have failed as a wife. And some of you are convinced that there's a strand of truth in those accusations because you have been stripped of who you were before the marriage. You have become a dishrag, much like I was during my marriage. I was slumped over looking like one emotionally. These are the wives that have to fight so hard to regain any sense of self in hopes of someday being free. But it can happen and it does happen so you can't give up hope. If you are married to a Have Your Cake and Eat It Too gay man, please grab support wherever you can get it. You're going to need it. That's why people have generously volunteered to be pain pals and why we have online support chat twice a week. Help is always there. Just ask!

FEBRUARY 2005

HAPPY VALENTINE'S DAY TO MY READERS

I'd like to wish all of my readers a Happy Valentine's Day, even though this message is a few days late. Valentine's Day is traditionally a day of love for people, and of course, without clouding the issue, a day of love for lovers. While so many of you are living in the mist of confusion and depression, it's hard to feel happy about a day that makes you feel cheated in a big way. It is difficult to find kind and loving words to say to a man who is living his lie with you on a daily basis. For those of you who have recently moved on, you are feeling a sense of hopelessness that all of us feel when we first leave our marriages. Then there are those of us who have lived past the black hole days and life has resumed—better than ever. We can once again appreciate the meaning of this day and give hope to others who need inspiration.

During my eleven-year exile away from men following my marriage, I looked at Valentine's Day differently. I tried to take the "romance" aspect out of it and just put the love into it. I looked to my loved ones like my children and family, as well as my friends. I started enjoying it much more than when I was living with my gay husband and wondering who his real valentine was going to be on that day—because it never was me. That's not to say that he didn't give me flowers or jewelry, but the love and romance was not there. And usually, he wasn't there either, so I knew he was with someone else. This made the gifts seem very trivial in comparison to the pain.

One of life's great lessons to me is that the most important person to receive love from is YOU. This means that you need to find yourself again or the person you were before you married your gay husband. Most of us lose ourselves in our marriages to our gay husbands because we are trying so hard to be who we are not, just like they are trying to be who they are not. I know that may hurt to hear, but it's the truth. When you feel like a failure in a marriage on an ongoing basis, you make every adjustment that you can to make to try to keep making your husband want you, because you personalize the fact that he is not responding to you as a man should. And for most of us, we look for reasons to blame ourselves rather than find fault with our husbands, especially when they throw us some loving crumbs. The crumbs are the words with no back up with the action. And the longer you stay in these marriages, the more you realize the true meaning of the words, "Actions speak louder than words." That's because we have no action—only a lot of lip service filled with excuses or a finger pointing in our direction placing the blame.

So my friends, wish yourselves a happy Valentine's Day with a pledge to work on loving yourself better and harder so that some day, you'll be free of the unhappiness you feel when this day comes around. From a woman who knows, there is life after gay husband, the best is yet to come!

LIVING IN THE DISCOMFORT ZONE

I have approximately 7,000 people who read my newsletters each month. It is always rewarding to me when I have people write to me telling me that for the first time, things that were incomprehensible finally make sense. I have women who are in all stages of life with a gay husband—those who just find out, those who have known for a while, those who are planning their futures to be free, those who are "stuck" due to numerous circumstances due to health, those who can't walk away because of finances, and those who are "just there" because they are "just there." No real reason so they say—just afraid to find out where somewhere else will be.

Now, I don't like to alienate people who are taking time to read my words. I always hope that when they are ready, they'll know that there is someone out there who is trying to be their advocate. So I try not to push or probe too hard when I see women who are sitting on the edge of the fence hoping to fall over to the other side with gentle nodding. But every now and then a woman in pain makes a comment to me that I feel so shaken by that it forces me to comment.

Recently, I was chatting with a woman who was telling me about the painful existence she was living with her gay husband. When I asked her why she is staying in an abusive situation, this was the answer she gave me:

I am comfortable living in the discomfort because this is the way it has always been.

Ouch. That hurt. That's probably the saddest statement I've ever heard. It's like that saying, "Is it better to have love and lost than to never have loved at all?" So let me see if I can rephrase this. "Is it better to have never been happy in your marriage than to have been happy and then made miserable when the news about your gay husband happens?" Or, "Is it better not to be happy through your whole marriage so you won't be disappointed when you remain unhappy throughout the years?" I'm not sure of the right way to phrase it, but it all ends up the same. Some women stay because they are so used to just staying and accept that this is what life has to offer.

Why does this sadden me so much? Women who don't remember what life was like without this stress or unhappiness lose sight of what life can be like again when they walk away from it. Unlike those who are temporarily or even permanently stuck due to circumstances beyond their control, these are women who are stuck because they don't know what it's like to be "unstuck." They don't feel the sense of "urgency" to get up and go for something better because they have forgotten, or in some cases, never knew any life that was better. They know something is wrong, but they don't have a need to fix it. They accept it because life without any substantial meaning has become acceptable to them. And this is what really what saddens me.

We all have one life to live. If we give up and think there is nothing better than our current status quo, then we are doomed to a life of existence rather than living.

APRIL 2005

SOME PERSONAL THOUGHTS FROM BONNIE KAYE

First, let me congratulate myself on the start of my fifth year of newsletters. It's hard to believe that I've been churning them out month after month, but it's true!

Some months I have to really discipline myself to sit here to write because you think to yourself, "How many things can I keep writing about without sounding repetitious?" And sometimes I am repetitious. But guess what? None of you seem to mind or complain. That's because some of these words need to be repeated again and again and again.

Nearly two hundred people have remained on my mailing list from the very early issues of my newsletter. Since that time, my newsletter has now grown to a readership of just over 7,000 people each month. Some of you live locally in the United States; others live internationally including Europe, Australia, the Middle East, and Asia.

As difficult as it is to keep writing each month, nothing is more rewarding or inspiring to me than the number of letters of appreciation from my readers that come to me after each newsletter. How can I not feel wonderful to know that I have brought sanity to the marriages of insanity? How great is it to hear from women that I have saved them or rescued them from a world of isolation and confusion? I am proud to have letters from women who have thanked me for saving their lives because they were seriously on the verge of suicide. What could be greater than helping save a life?

Some of you have written to me that this newsletter is your "life line." That's why as I embark on this fifth year of newsletters, I am going to speak some serious business. My words will have to hold you over for the next month because I am about to embark on a new chapter of my life—one of better health. On April 25, I am scheduled to have a gastric bypass to help resolve some of my health problems that have resulted from my lifetime of obesity. As I have progressed into my 50's, my health issues have become more plentiful. And now at 53, I feel relieved and excited that something other than my lifetime of frustrating dieting will truly make the difference in my weight and health.

Of course, anytime you go to surgery, there is always a risk. And although I plan on being one of those successful statistics, you never really know. And so, I am going to write all my words of wisdom as if this could be my last newsletter because too many of you need to hear them. I've said them before, but I need to say them again.

Here are words you need to take to heart. These are 10 most important lessons I have learned about being in or out of a straight/gay marriage. And by the way, I never dignify them by calling them something chic like "Mixed Orientation" marriages. To me, "Mixed Orientation" means Jewish/Catholic or White/Black, where people know way up front before marriage what the obstacles are. Straight/Gay marriages are more like Alice in Wonderland marriages—distorted at best. Never feel the need to have to "apologize" for these marriages by cleaning up the way they sound because it's hard on the ear. If anything, call them what I call them— MISMARRIAGES, meaning a mistake in marriage.

Here are my lessons learned:

LESSON 1

Some of you have been languishing in a destructive marriage for years. You are throwing away valuable years of your life that can never be returned. Once they are gone, they are gone. Some of you feel compelled to stay in these marriages because you have no proof that your husband is gay. You know you're unhappy. That's enough of a reason to the leave the marriage. You don't have to prove that a husband is gay to get a divorce. Just suffering in a marriage with someone who lacks passion, compassion, intimacy, and respect is grounds for a divorce. When women who are married to straight men decide they want a divorce, they don't have to spend years figuring out how to justify it. Why do you?

LESSON 2

This expression has come up several times in recent newsletters. I wish I could take credit for it, but I can't. However, I will repeat it: Stop spending your life being a detective. There is nothing more debilitating than to spend your valuable time investigating your husband. I did it for several years—checking his pockets, his notes, his papers, listening to his phone calls from the other side of the wall with a glass—you name it, I tried it. Why did I keep obsessing over this? I needed to know that my suspicions were more than my imagination. So when I thought I had concrete proof and I confronted him, he went into a rage telling me that I was crazy. And guess what? I was relieved because **I WANTED TO BELIEVE**. And please don't tell me that I was stupid because I know the majority of you out there want to believe as much as I do that this nightmare is anything but what it is. You don't have to confront your husband—you just have to know the truth for yourself. That should be enough. And when you do know the truth, then you need to set yourself free, because living with a gay man can never fulfill your expectations of what you want out of life. No way. Ever.

LESSON 3

Although it takes two to make a marriage, when you're married to a gay man, it only takes one to make it fall apart—namely him. Any other natural failures of straight marriages are not applicable here because your life is a distortion when your husband is gay. Whatever he objects to is through the eyes of a gay man. When he is angry with you, it is because he is frustrated being in a marriage with a straight woman and will look to find fault with YOU rather than face up to his responsibility of being honest. This is not to say you are perfect, but it wouldn't matter if you were. He would still find fault with you because you are a woman. And a lot of you are almost perfect. That's because the unhappier he is, the more you try to make him happy, internalizing and personalizing that his unhappiness is your fault. Untrue. He can't be totally happy or fulfilled living with a woman no matter who the woman is. Accept it. It's his failure, not yours. And this is not to say that he is a failure as a person. He is just a failure as a husband to a straight woman. He can be a great guy, but he belongs being your friend, not your mate.

Lesson 4

Love hurts. Loving a gay man really hurts. Even losing a gay husband in many cases hurts. This is why it is so difficult for us to recover from these marriages. Sometimes we have wonderful men who are our best friends. Then one day out of nowhere, a new man appears who is a stranger to us. The man we thought we were tied to for life now tells us that he can't go on being "untrue" to himself. He tells us that as much as it pains him, he has to tell you that he is gay. By the way, the ones who tell you are really the wonderful ones although it's hard to believe when you're hearing the truth. It's the ones that refuse to tell you and accuse you of being crazy that are contemptible. It is going to take time to get past the pain of this. You need to give yourself the time you need to go through all the stages of mourning just like you need to mourn for someone who died. This is the death of a marriage, and in many cases, it is a very ugly death.

Lesson 5

You are not stupid. You start beating yourself up over your stupidity in not recognizing that your husband was gay. You start looking back and examining all of your moments in the marriage wondering how this could have happened. How is it that the person who was supposed to love you and cherish you forever was leading a life or thinking about leading a life that was totally foreign to you? You trace and retrack your years together. You look for the clues or the signs that something was wrong, but you keep missing the clues. This is because you were fooled by someone who was most likely fooling himself. And when he stopped fooling himself, he kept fooling you because he was scared. He was scared that if you knew the truth you wouldn't want him anymore. These guys can be great deceivers. And we of good hearts want to believe in the love we have for our men.

<u>LESSON 6</u>

Some women find it so hard to say that they knew something about their husbands prior to marriage lest they be accused of knowing they were marrying a gay man. UNTRUE. I say we don't understand homosexuality. We don't understand how someone who is supposed to be going with someone of the same sex is now marrying someone of the opposite sex. We believe that even if they did try it, they didn't like it because they are not gay. Even if your husband hinted that he was attracted to men, he has now "outgrown" those feelings because he loves you. And after all, sexuality can be confusing, so maybe he was just confused. But now he knows what he wants and there's nothing to worry about. Stop kicking yourself for being blindsided by this. There is no way that we can understand such a complex situation when our husband's can't understand it.

When I was 25 years old, I reunited with a high school boyfriend after seven years. He had become a doctor and had nurses galore dating him. When we found each other again in a different place and space, he revealed to me that he had tried a relationship with two men on two different occasions. He actually lived with these guys for a period of months. He then told me that he also lived with two women for a period of time. He realized that he was not gay from those two experiences with men. Women were his thing and I believed him. He dated me, made love to me, and wanted to move in with me. Although I knew that something was missing, I didn't think it was an issue of sexuality. I thought it was because he was a Cancer. Hey, astrology was big back then. People believed in the zodiac signs. I thought that his July birthday accounted for his sometimes-aloof reactions to me and to us. It wasn't for another 8 years that this man came to terms with his sexuality and found his man mate. Ironically, I left this guy for my future gay husband. Like how stupid was I, you want to know? I don't think I was stupid. I think I was uninformed. Look, I had sex with both of these men. Maybe they weren't the best, but they were adequate. And in your 20's, adequate is good enough. It takes us time to realize that making love is so much more than sex.

You find these good-looking, sensitive, conversational men who want to spend their lives with you. Gay? We may think there are issues, but gay isn't one of them. Even before I married my gay husband, someone came to me with his suspicions that my soon to be hubby was bisexual. I felt a sick knot in my stomach much like the same knot that occurred years later when my suspicions started to kick in for real. When I told him about my friend's accusation, he took the table where we were dining and nearly threw it over, yelling, "How dare someone accuse me of that?" I was so relieved. Hallelujah! My heart told me to proceed without caution because I had the confirmation I needed. Was I stupid? I think not. I was just UN-INFORMED. Some people may think that it's not normal to find yourself involved in two relationships with gay men. Well, I had been involved with dozens of relationships over the years with straight men. It was not something I was seeking out. It was just by chance that it happened--chance and ignorance.

LESSON 7

Some of us in our desperation to hang on to something that we should let go of will look to make a million excuses of why we need to stay. One of the common reasons I hear is "THE CHILDERN." People want to believe that children need two parents living under the same roof no matter how miserable they are or how that roof is always caving in. WRONG. One important lesson I have learned from my own life experience is that children will not be happy unless you are happy. My mother stayed with my father for far too many years. They would both fight and inevitably, fight about the children. This made me feel as if I were to blame for their misery. CHILDREN KNOW WHEN THEIR PARENTS ARE UNHAPPY AND THEY DO PERSONALIZE IT. Trust me on this one. If you or your gay husband is unhappy, your children know it and most likely internalize the blame.

The other problem of staying in this type of marriage is role modeling. Children copy their parents. If they see you staying in a loveless marriage, chances are they will think this is the norm for marriage, which is very sad. Certainly you don't want your children to be condemned to a life of unhappiness when they get married, but we often repeat the mistakes of our parents. I marvel at how many women who had abusive fathers marry the same type of man. So, if you are staying in your marriage and think you need to do this for the security of your children, STOP.

LESSON 8

WAITING FOR YOUR HUSBANDS TO CONFESS CAN TAKE A LIFETIME. Too many of you are hanging in there waiting for a confession to something that will be the DECISIVE factor in your decision to leave. All you have to do is CATCH HIM, right? Then you'll get him to confess. Well, let's forget this one. Some of them will never get caught, and many of them will never confess—EVER. Some gay husbands are in deep denial. If they can't even admit it to themselves, why do you think they'll confess it to you? When you do catch them they come up with the world's best stories on how the porn got on the computer, how the condoms got into their briefcases, how they contracted a sexually transmitted disease (which they usually claim to be your fault), or how your imagination is running away with you. It's just not happening, so stop looking for it. If you are questioning your husband's sexuality, YOU HAVE A REASON. Whether it's a hint, an instinct, or proof positive, go with it. Women don't suspect their straight husbands of being gay. Trust me on that one. This goes back to a few of the previously mentioned lessons. If you are unhappy in your marriage, no matter what the reason is, get out.

LESSON 9

Breaking up is hard to do, even under the worst of circumstances. There is no easy way to leave a marriage. Most women need a readjustment period to filter the information through their heads totally. There's lots of second-guessing during this time, as well as questioning your sanity or stupidity. "How couldn't I have seen this coming?" "How come everyone suspected this before me?" And other people start questioning it too. "What did you do to make him gay? He wasn't gay when he married you, was he?" "Men don't just TURN gay. You must have screwed up somewhere." On top of all of the hurt we are going through, we have to deal with other people's ignorance and stupidity, which compounds our own feelings of inadequacy. And you know what? Not every straight wife finds me in her early days of confusion or even ever for that matter. They sit and suffer because they are unable to find help or a voice of sanity to tell them they are not at fault. That's the saddest part of all. Lack of support keeps women in a long state of depression and confusion.

Wives of gay men have to contend with so many issues that wives of straight men don't face. This makes things much more complicated and uncomfortable. You see, I contend that women who have straight husbands don't have the set of problems that we have. Most women who are wonderful wives LIKE WE ARE with wonderful marriages to straight men don't have husbands who are sneaking and cheating on them because their husbands are happy. We, on the other hand, are the best of wives but are made to feel like we are worthless. How do great wives feel when their husbands start abandoning them emotionally, physically, and sexually for no apparent reason at all? What does it feel like to think you have to "beg" for sex from the man who is supposed to be you soul mate in life? How do you think it feels when you uncover his little secret only to find that all of those times he was saying no to you he was saying yes to a host of men that he met for casual sex that was so casual that he never even necessarily saw their faces or knew their names while he was making you feel as if you were sexually abnormal for wanting to share intimacy with him? You feel dirty because he makes you feel that way. You are not good enough for him to make love to—that is his message to you.

As women who have been emotionally abused in this way, we have to start rebuilding the long stripping of our sense of worth, self, and sexual esteem. We now have to worry about what to tell our children, and if they will hate us for breaking up their family. We end up protecting our ex-husbands in so many cases, keeping their secret while they are out there living it. You see, it's okay for them to do it, but they'll tell you it's none of your business to discuss it. After all, you're only the wife, right?

You can be in what you think is the beginning or the middle of your marriage and suddenly, your husband announces that, "I am what I am," and his own special creation is your worst nightmare. You have two or three children and limited resources as a single parent. This gay husband who comes to terms with his sexuality, unlike the straight/gay kind of husband that stay forever to torture you, is now walking out on you to begin his life as a gay man. All your dreams are up in smoke so to speak, and you're left to pick up the pieces. It's not unusual in those early years of gaydom for husbands to be scarce when needed. They are off in their new life and very, very busy. It seems like he's forgotten you, the children, the house, and the money it takes to run a family. He does seem to have money for his new life and lovers, and there seems to be no balance. You pay, he plays. And you're also exhausted. Yuck.

It can be any one of those situations mentioned above, but the end result is all the same—misery. That's why some women who are so pealed down mentally to start with, never can reach the finish line to proclaim themselves the "winner." It's hard to run a race if you're wearing yourself out doggie paddling just trying to keep yourself from drowning. That's why I never judge how long it takes someone to leave—as long as she knows that she is going to leave someday. Mental freedom is three-fourths of the battle.

LESSON 10

Beauty. Hmm, let's see—it's in the eyes of the beholder—namely YOU. Self-esteem has to be rebuilt before you can truly love yourself and realize how beautiful you are. I have seen the most physically beautiful of women learn to believe they are ugly and undesirable. When they look in the mirror, it's like an anorexic reflection showing fat when the person is skinny. When you don't feel good about yourself, you don't see yourself objectively anymore. You feel ugly inside, so you see your reflection as ugly outside. It's such a shame and makes me so angry. The self-damage that is done has to be worked on before you pursue any kind of new relationship because you leave yourself open for other unsavory men to find and grab you. They aren't gay, but they are losers. They are controlling, angry, abusive, and in other cases, useless. These guys see a "sucker" coming and they lunge after you. They know you are ripe for the picking. Give you a few "I love yous" or "you're beautiful" and you belong to them, few questions asked. If they have sex with you, you feel redeemed from the marriage to your gay husband so you settle for the wrong relationship because it seems less wrong than the last one. UGH. More bad years wasted again. ☹

The song The Greatest Love of All has the right line in it—learning to love yourself, it is the greatest love of all. If you can't love yourself in a generous healthy way, you'll never be happy in any future relationship.

And so my dear reader, keep this message close to your heart. It sums up the writing of the past four years and starts the fifth year off with the lessons you need to be reminded of when you find yourself with a gay husband. Hopefully my recovery will go well and I'll drop you all a note next month. And hopefully you'll realize that I'm recovering and you'll be generous enough to send me letters to share with others to make it easy for me. Never stop believing in yourself, because if you are reading this newsletter, it means that you are fighting back in one way or another. I send my love and hope to all of you in big doses to keep you safe in my absence in the weeks ahead.

JUNE 2005

A CONTROL ISSUE

Several weeks ago while I was in my support chat room, one of the women mentioned that her husband told her that, "You will never meet anyone who loves you as much as I do." When she uttered those words, a flash from my past hit me in the heart. Those were the same exact words that my gay ex-husband used to tell me on a daily basis. Well, they started out as the words he used to tell me. Then he used to cut the sentence in half from time to time just stating, "You'll never meet anyone who loves you." Period. But by that time, I was so beaten down, that I bought the message loud and clear—and sadly, I believed it.

Remember, when you are living with a gay man—even if you have no clue your husband is gay—your sense of self-esteem and sexual esteem is being stripped away layer by layer, day by day. After a while, you are so confused you don't know how to make any decision without questioning it, because you have lost faith in your judgment.

Your husband makes sure of that—ESPECIALLY IN THE BEDROOM.

I say this because there are some women who write to me to tell me that their gay husbands are their best friends. They have wonderful friendships with them and love being with them to go shopping, vacations, dinners, outings with friends, and family holidays. I'm not sure if these women are luckier or not. I really have to think about it for a few more years. You might think this is odd, but it's like the women who write to me sometimes wishing that the emotional abuse was physical abuse because that way the bruises would show and people would believe how they are suffering. Women with the wonderful gay husbands are sometimes in worse pain when their husbands leave them for their new found lives and lovers. "We were the perfect couple. I thought we were the perfect couple. Well, I thought other than sex, we were the perfect couple." I think some women just don't get it. Without sex, there is no perfect couple. Sex is part of the foundation of having a relationship. It's not the icing on the cake, it is the cake. It's not extra sprinkles, it's the cake. In other words, if the marriage is missing the sex part, there is SOMETHING WRONG. Also, the women with the best husbands except for the gay part have a much more difficult time moving on after the marriage is over. They still keep hoping that their husbands will be disillusioned in the gay world and come back to live their wonderful marriage—or friendship—or relationship—or arrangement—or whatever you want to call a sexless marriage.

I'll tell you the sad part about these women who "lucked out" with the nice guys. I've heard this story hundreds of times through my 21 years of listening to sad stories from straight wives. These men loved their wives to the best of their ability. They just knew in time that they couldn't keep living a lie after so many years. In most cases, these guys have met someone and it is often the first real interest in pursing a man to man relationship on both an emotional and sexual level that they've had. Sometimes it is 10 years into the marriage—sometimes it is 30 years into the marriage. What happens so often is that the man leaves his loving wife and goes into the arms of his new male love. The woman goes through her heartbreak questioning everyday why this man that she loves is throwing away everything they have—their children, home, business, family—all over sex. She doesn't really understand gay at all yet. She thinks it's just a "sex" thing. The man who is so excited with his new found happiness usually finds himself devastated when the gay relationship doesn't work out. In almost all cases, the first gay relationship doesn't work out. That's just how it is. And when things come tumbling down, and the gay husband is devastated, where does he find himself running? He runs right back into the comfort and safety of his wife and their previously happy marriage.

Guess what? Straight wife is glad that gay husband has come to his senses and she takes him back. He promises that he's learned his lesson. He's not meant to be part of the gay world. He tried it. It wasn't for him. He's so hurt that he knows that the only thing that will take away his pain is the loving support of his wife, children, and family. She forgives him because she loves him and she wants their marriage to go back to where it was before this nightmare took place.

Guess what again? He is so grateful that his wife has taken him back to the security he longs for, that in most cases, he throws in some sex to show his gratitude. It may happen for a few weeks or even a couple of months. He does anything he has to do to reassure his wife that they are going to live happily ever after. It's one of those "honeymoon" periods that I've written about before. For the wife, that's the icing on the cake. It's still not the cake because it's only for a short period of time before it's over again. But oh, how delicious it tastes while it's being savored.

See, this is why I'm not sure if this kind of husband is better than the cruel, nasty, controlling ones. To skip to fast forward, these good guys leave again once the new love of their life comes along—which is almost always. It may take a few months or even a year or two, but once the taste of gay grabs a gay man, the need for it will continue to progress until it overtakes him again. This is human nature—and gay nature. It's also nature. Gay men should be with gay men—not with straight women.

Once again, the woman's heart is broken, only this time it's even worse. She was so sure that things were returning to "normal" when in fact, there was never any real "normal" in an "abnormal" marriage. Worse, I know women who allow their gay husbands to come back a third and even fourth time, unable to accept the reality that a gay man will always be a gay man.

Last weekend, I watched the movie "De-lovely," the story of composer Cole Porter. I watched it because I have always been a big

Cole Porter fan, and I heard that the movie had wonderful music in it. I was no stranger to the reality of Porter's life. I knew he was gay and married. This movie was quite upfront about Porter's homosexual relationships and how it affected his marriage. Did his wife, Linda, know before she married him? Yes. Like some of us, she had heard that her husband-to-be had done some messing around with men. Did he tell her that's all over now that they are getting married? No. And she said that she could live with it as long as it didn't interfere with their marriage. It was 1919, and who knew what anyone expected from marriage. Back then, people didn't talk sex—they just did it whenever the man wanted to. Linda was coming out of an abusive marriage, so marrying a wealthy famous socialite seemed like a good bet. According to reports, there was never sex initiated in the marriage. Cole loved his wife like a best friend and she loved him like a gay husband. Eventually, they split up when they relocated to Hollywood and he was having too many indiscretions that were being noticed by the general public. But after he had a terrible accident horseback riding, she returned to him and lived her life out with him while he went through operation after operation to help him walk again. She died from lung cancer while he took devoted care of her.

I was thinking of this movie while I was writing this to show how some women sacrifice their lives to gay men without ever having more than a friend or companion. Linda Porter had the strength to walk away, but came back out of love, pity, and compassion. This is the same reason why some of our straight wives take their husbands back when they are devastated after their gay relationships don't work out. No matter how nice the nice guys are, taking them back is a mistake. It leaves you open to continuing heartache and heartbreak.

Getting back to my original statement, never believe that no man will love you again. When my ex used to say to me, "No man will ever love me as much as I love you," over time my thinking changed. I started thinking that I don't want any man to love me the way he loved me. His love was cruel and hurting. That's not the way that love is supposed to be. In fact, it taught me that the word "Love" was just another four letter word. My ex was so unhappy in our marriage that he looked at me as the cause of his unhappiness instead of himself. As he grew older and matured, he was able to be honest about it not only to me, but also to himself. Up until then he wasn't honest about it at all. I was the cause of his unhappiness. I was the one who wasn't supportive enough….caring enough….thin enough….etc. etc. and so on and so on.

Whether your husband is abusive or he's your best friend, marriage to a gay man is an unnatural state to live in. If your gay husband makes comments to you such as, "You'll never find anyone who loves you as much as I do," you can answer him very simply. Just tell him that you are happy to hear that. Tell him that when you find a straight man, he will know how to love you the way a man should love you—in the bedroom and out of the bedroom. Explain to him that a straight man will love you for all that you do, unlike a gay man who will never be happy with what you do because you are a WOMAN.

Whenever your husband makes his negative comments to you, learn to BLOCK the sound of his voice out of your mind. Pretend that you are going to a horror movie, and he is the star of the show—like Freddy Kruger. Pretend you are at a movie that can be classified as horror FICTION. When you have a gay husband, that's what life is—FICTION.

Always remember that the best solution when you are stuck in this muck is to start rebuilding your own life and stop focusing on your gay husband. This will give you the strength you need to move on for your future.

AUGUST 2005

REPEATING YOUR LIFE IN FUTURE GENERATIONS

One of my support group members, Pat, asked me to address this question:

How does staying in a straight/gay marriage affect children, especially daughters? I mean, they see almost no affection or touching over the years.

It's sad, but true. Children are usually doomed to repeat the patterns and mistakes of their parents. This is because children develop "learned" behavior from their parents. If they see no affection or touching in your relationship, then chances are they will think this is the "norm." It comes down to the old saying of, "Monkey see, monkey do, monkey act just like you."

When children see their parents setting the tone of no affection, they often fall prey to mates who are the same way. And yes, unaffectionate people, for whatever the reason, know how to seek out partners who are accepting of this behavior. Just like I contend that a gay man seeks out a certain prototype of woman, men with other sexual or emotional issues which cause dysfunction know how to seek out women who won't be expecting much from them in or out of the bedroom. If your children lived with parents who couldn't express love, most likely, they are the prime candidates for partners who lack the emotional depth or the ambition to work on the problem. It's just the way it goes.

Women who write telling me that they are staying in the marriage because it's the best thing for the children really need to rethink this thinking. I've written about this before and I can't say it enough times—STOP DELUDING YOURSELF. Children who grow up in an environment where there is no visible love and affection are well aware that "there is something rotten in the State of Denmark" as the saying goes. Children sense when there are problems in the marriage. The real tragedy is that they attribute the problems to themselves—not you. Often the children become the target of frustration in the parents' arguments even if they are not the underlying problem. I know because my parents did this constantly. They waited until my brother and I were sleeping, then the fights began waking us up. Our names were often mentioned during these fights making us believe that we were the cause of the fights. Ultimately, we felt bad about ourselves because we thought we were causing our parents pain. Pity, isn't it?

So, the answer to the original question is YES. Living in a marriage void of affection and love will definitely affect the futures of your children.

FEBRUARY 2006

Happy Valentine's Day to All of My Straight Wives

February is a bitter/sweet month to many of our straight wives. That's because the world is celebrating Valentine's Day, the holiday that commemorates love, the foundation of what a relationship is based on. This year, I have printed numerous letters from women who have taken back their lives and taken "a chance on love again" as the words to one of my favorite songs goes. But many of my readers are still stuck in the muck or recently out of it and not feeling too keen about this day that feels like a jagged edge, blades and all cutting into their hearts.

For those of you who are still living confused, unhappy lives, let me reassure you that reading this newsletter means you are fighting back. It's a small step in a long line of steps, but at least you are moving forward, not content to be complacent or oblivious to your unhappiness.

I am not the judgmental type—really I'm not. When a woman tells me that she is unhappy but can't leave, I never say, "Of course you can," Life is never that simple. I like to remind women that I was able to do it because my ex-husband walked out and gave me a week to breathe. If not, who knows how long I would have stayed and languished with him. My ex gave me the gift of life—literally—and saved mine by leaving. At that moment, he thought he would teach me a lesson. He was so convinced that I could never make it on my own and that I would jump to take him back under his terms. When he returned a week later, suitcase in hand, I had the strength to say, "No more. It's over." That one week was all I needed to know that no matter how hard I would have to struggle with two little babies and no money or career, it would be better than living in an upside down world always dodging distorted mirrors. I was tired of being Bonnie in Wonderland. I never regret making that decision 23 years ago.

Some of my women have been living in an emotionally abandoned situation for 10, 15, 25, and even 40 plus years. Those years of being stripped down layer by layer by a man who is uncaring to your emotional well-being and who is often controlling leaves you in a battered state. Some women are given the message on a daily basis that they can't make it without their gay man, and they start to believe it because they have lost who they are.

Girlfriends, I understand how difficult it is to end a marriage, no matter how unhappy you are. I never sit here and say, "If I can do it, you can do it." That would be cold and insensitive on my part. What I do say is that if you want to do it, someday it will hopefully happen, but it may take some time. The important thing is to keep sight of what the goal is. The goal is to take back whatever good years you keep losing and to find happiness within yourself again. You don't have to find the love of your life; you just have to start to love your life and be free of the pain. Many women write to say that they wish they could meet a wonderful man who will be their partner in life. But you can only meet someone who is your true love after you relearn to re-love and trust yourself again. Then it will fall into place.

No woman is an island. We all need help and support. Living with a gay man is isolating enough because we live our lives as detectives, waiting to trap him. And then when we catch him, we think we need more evidence and want to catch him again. That's because every time he's caught, he denies your evidence, waters it down to being some kind of "curiosity" moment, or promises it will never, ever, happen again. Right.

Well, actually, I meant to say "wrong." Your gay husband will not change. You can wish for it, pray for it, or go for counseling for it, but it is not happening. He might try in earnest and be sincere when he says it won't happen again, but he's fooling himself—and you. Gay is not a choice—it is a state of being. People can control their behavior, but they have no control over their sexuality. What does this mean? It means that your husbands have no choice in being gay—but they have a choice on acting on it and on being honest with you.

Some women believe that their husbands love them and their marriages enough to deeply bury their homosexuality. And, some men really do make the effort. But guess what? They are not happy campers. They love you, but you can't fulfill the need they have within them either emotionally or physically. I believe that they have a mental need to be in their marriage, but their thoughts and hearts are always somewhere else. They are gay. You are a woman. You can't give them what they want aside from being a security blanket.

Some gay men can have sex with their wives. They still want a man. A few gay men can even satisfy a woman. They still want a man. A few RARE women have told me that their husbands were great in bed. I believe their husbands were great actors. One gay husband recently wrote to me that he has spent years studying how to satisfy a woman because he loves his wife to make sure she is satisfied. But—he still wants a man. She is satisfied—he isn't.

When a man isn't happy with his life, he's not happy with his life with you. He may love you, but either consciously or unconsciously, he starts to believe that you are the obstacle standing in the way between him and happiness. And so he looks to find fault with you because it's easier than accepting responsibility for it himself. Once again, this isn't about love—it's about sexuality. And sexuality isn't always just about sex—it's about the things that go with sex like intimacy—something that he wants from the same person he wants to have sex with—which isn't you.

Some women tell me they have intimacy with their gay husbands. To them, intimacy means laying side by side—with or without holding each other—and talking about "stuff." It is intimacy without sex most of the time. And some women have confessed to me that this is better than the sex. They don't mind not having sex. This makes me very sad because what they are really saying is that they never knew how wonderful making love with a straight man can be as far as fulfilling, gratifying, and satisfying. Many of these women have had only one man in their sexual lives—their gay husbands. They have nothing to compare it to or judge it by. They just know that they don't mind not having it. After all, sex is not all it's cracked up to be, right? Wrong. Rather, having sex with someone who doesn't want to have sex with you is not all it's cracked up to be.

There are lots of complex issues revolving around one common problem. But, in spite of it, Happy Valentines Day to all of you. I'm sending lots of love your way. Don't be afraid to reach out for support. I'm here for you, and so are some very incredible women who come to our support chat.

MARCH 2006

PAYING FOR DIVORCE

In my support chat, I have some of the most extraordinary women that you can ever imagine. They are bright, funny, and insightful, willing to give of themselves in their quest for giving and getting support.

The issue of divorce and legalities often comes up as women have to struggle in the aftermath of their divorces to receive child and/or spousal support. A few women seem to do fine depending on the state where they live. But the vast majority of women I work with usually end up on the short end of the stick.

One of the issues why women tell me that they stay with their gay husbands is because they can't afford to get a divorce. I have heard some staggering figures of monies paid out as legal fees. Most women don't have that kind of money to use in finding a reputable divorce lawyer.

The more I think about this, the angrier I become. If a woman wants to end a marriage because her husband is gay, why should she have to pay the legal fees? She entered into the marriage in good faith with a man she believed was straight. And please don't misunderstand me—I believe her husband entered into the marriage hoping that he would be straight just by trying hard enough or wishing it enough. Most of these guys try hard—at least in the beginning. They love their wives to the best of their abilities, but the bottom line is they are gay. In time they can't be who they are not, and that's when things start breaking down.

I'm not faulting gay husbands for marrying their wives knowing they truly hope that their nagging attractions for men will dissipate in time of they have a loving family of their own. I understand how confusing the issue of homosexuality is for most men. But once they feel this sense of frustration, they start acting on their needs and forget or neglect to mention it to their wives until they are either caught or meet someone they want to leave the marriage for. At either point, the news is out.

My bottom line is this. If the man you married in good faith turns out to be someone who is a stranger to you, and if your dreams of the marriage are now nightmares, why should you have to chip in to end it? I am not trying to place blame. There is no blame for homosexuality. But I am trying to push the issue of accountability. You've already lost so much—why should you, the straight wife, have to pay towards a divorce? I think it's only fair that all legal fees for both parties be paid for by the husband. What do you think?

APRIL 2006

NEW GAY MAN CLASSIFICATION

For the past 22 years, I have been working with thousands of women who learn that their husbands are gay. Some women are able to accept this and say the word GAY. Others can spend years not accepting it and call it something else—like BISEXUAL. And yet other women can't accept either one of those names and call it something else—like "Bi-curious."

Look, if you know me, you know I have a big heart that goes with this still big body! I feel for any woman who has to live with this disaster. But one of the great stumbling blocks that I continue to run smack into is the woman who hasn't caught her husband in bed with a man yet. And it's amazing how some women feel that's what it will take confirm their suspicions. In other words, the gay websites, lack of marital sex, phone calls to gay talk lines, and numerous other signs just don't do it. You can suspect—but you can't convict. Yadda, yadda, yadda.

I would say about 50% of the two to three thousand women who write to me yearly start out by telling me they are unsure. Sometimes women want to so not believe this news that nothing short of watching their husband in the act would convince them. Also, I get plenty of flack from gay men who claim that I can only see things in black and white—gay or straight. No in-between.

You see, the problem is I don't know where those shades of gray belong. I'm confused. I admit it. I'm called narrow minded because I believe for the overwhelming number of men who call themselves bi-sexual that this is a cop-out because they are emotionally straight but sexually gay. They need the credibility of the straight world to make

133

them feel complete. They marry women because they want to be straight. And yet, they have sex with a man, which to me makes them gay. But these guys are bothered by my lack of sensitivity to the bi-sexual issue. And to add more injury to the situation, their confused wives believe what they are told—at least in the beginning.

So, to eliminate all of the confusion and hard feelings, I've decided to throw away all my previous labels. I'm going to give my ladies and their men a better way to look at things. No woman wants to say that she has a gay husband. So now I've come up with my new terminology—STRAIGHT MEN WHO WANT OR HAVE GAY SEX.

I think this will let everyone off the hook and make the situation easier to deal with. This way, when a woman writes to me and says, "I don't think my husband is gay, do you?" I can respond with, "No, he's a straight man who wants gay sex."

This way, people who can't accept labels will be happy and maybe I'll be more popular in some of those scary corners that call me narrow minded!

As for me personally, I don't really need to label anyone. I just don't want to be with a man who wants a man. I don't care what anyone calls it. In the end, it's all the same!

JUNE 2006

As a tribute to Father's Day, I am dedicating this newsletter to issues that concern our gay husbands/ex-husbands.

SOME THOUGHTS ABOUT GAY HUSBANDS

Although my area of expertise is working with straight wives of gay men, I think I know a lot about the gay husbands of these women. They come in all different varieties from men who are truly struggling with their sexuality to those who aren't struggling at all but refuse to be honest about it. In the past, I've talked about the Limbo Man caught between two worlds, the Straight-Gay Man, stuck in the straight world due to his own cowardice and torturing his wife out of resentment, and the alleged "Bisexual" man who justifies to himself that he is not gay but just enjoys sex with men.

Let me be very clear—the process of coming out to your wife is the most difficult moment in time for any gay married man. There is never a good time or an easy time. There is never a right day or a wrong day. And although some women may not agree with me, it is the most courageous act that a gay husband can do for the woman that he loves.

I say love because I still contend that gay men love their wives to the best of their ability. When they marry us, they truly are hoping against hope that any nagging attractions to men will magically disappear because we, their wives, will love them enough to become Houdini's and perform feats of the impossible.

Even in this day and age people are still misinformed about homosexuality, it is easy to understand why some gay men would think that. It is still a common misconception that "GAY IS A CHOICE" like choosing between vanilla and chocolate ice cream. "Come and get it—straight or gay." Well, I refuse to believe that gay is a choice any more than skin color is a choice or eye and hair color is a choice.

Keeping that thought in mind, people can buy blue contact lenses for their brown eyes or use blonde bleach in their black hair, but as you know, they are cosmetic fix-ups. That's what it is for a gay man who marries a straight woman—a cosmetic fix up. It looks real good to the public including family, friends, and employers, but once the contacts are taken out, or once the hair roots grow in, you still have brown eyes and black hair. A gay man can "cosmetically" fix his life, but inwardly it is what it is—and it ain't changing.

Too many men languish in "unnatural" relationships with women for years because they don't know how to do the right thing for a number of reasons.

One reason is they don't want to be gay. They may be thinking about it, looking at it, fantasizing about it, and in many cases acting on it, but they still don't want to be gay. Gay is nothing something people want to be—gay is something people are. We still live in a very homophobic society where it takes a lot of courage—a lot—to do be honest about your sexuality, and in many cases, even with yourself.

Some gay men have been thoroughly indoctrinated by family and religion that gay is a choice that leads to eternal damnation on earth and in hell. They believe that by staying with their wives, they are "choosing" the right way to live. They fear the repercussions from their families and friends if they are honest. And so they crouch and hide, hoping they can just get through life this way without "rocking the boat" and tipping it over.

Other gay men fear that they will lose the only sense of security that they have in their lives—their wives and children. I believe that gay men who stay in their marriages love their families, at least on some level. Maybe it's not the kind of love they are seeking or you are seeking, but love comes in different forms—including complacency. You may not feel the pitter patter of your heart, but love is more than that…or so some people say, even if I'm not one of them.

I admire men who find the courage to tell their wives the truth because I work with too many women who have husbands who are cowards and will never tell the truth. Or maybe they tell some of the truth 30 years down the line after denying any possible hints by their wives that homosexuality may be the cause of problems in their marriage. The greatest act of love a gay man can do for his wife is to **TELL THE TRUTH**.

Those men who are content to keep the truth from their wives don't really love them because they are too selfish to understand what love is. Love is not watching a woman who loves you suffer day in and day out wondering what she is doing wrong when she is doing nothing wrong other than being a woman. And yet, I contend that probably half of the gay married male population will continue to live like that until physical death do they part, going down with their secret. The emotional death is a daily occurrence.

If you have a husband who has been honest with you, consider that a gift. It doesn't change the years of emotional neglect or abuse you have been through, but it does explain it. Think of all of the women who never find out the truth and internalize that the problems are their fault. At least you have a chance to see the light of day again and understand that the problems are not YOUR problems.

I always say that being gay is NOT a choice—how you live your life with it IS a choice. You have the choice to be honest about it although it may be the most difficult choice at the moment. And to any men who may be reading this who are still having trouble "doing the right thing," I have an excellent support network for you with some wonderful men who have done the right thing and will help you get through it. All you need to do is ask. I'm there for you—and so are they.

THE ABUSE EXCUSE

Over the last five years of working with so many thousands of women, I've noticed an emerging trend of women who tell me that their husbands are gay because they were sexually abused during youth or adolescence. What I find so interesting is that of the several dozen or so of gay men I am in contact with through friendship or business, I've asked them if they were abused as children, and so far, only one has said yes.

So, I went to my good friend Michael who runs the site at www.marriedgay.org and asked him for his thoughts on this. He has added this page to his website. He's such a gem! Thanks, Michael, for giving such a great perspective.

EXCUSES, EXCUSES

We are full of excuses......

A colleague wrote to me and asked whether I thought being sexually abused as a child was a valid reason for their homosexuality - she calls it the "Abuse Excuse", something that she has discovered is used by something like 80% of all Married Gay Men.

There are lots of other statements:

- "I was not strong enough to deal with the baggage of coming out......"
- "I lived in a male dominated society......"
- "I was raised in a family with a strong moral code......"
- "I was brought up to believe that acting on my homosexual feelings was totally unacceptable......"
- "I suspected that I had other feelings and did not date for a long time......"

Many of these statements are perfectly valid and explain what has happened to the individuals concerned, but with any excuse that is not valid, we should try to be more honest with ourselves, and to understand what really happened.

For instance, with the "abuse excuse", the abuse may have happened and that is perfectly valid, but not as an excuse for explaining a person's sexuality. Sexual abuse does not cause a person to be gay, but it does trigger emotions and feelings that a person may not have realized were there. The person who is abused, is traumatized, and never wants to go through the experience again, is probably not gay. The person who is abused, is traumatized, but realizes that they do want to go through the experience again, is most likely to have gay tendencies which were already there.

To make it easier for ourselves, why not try to come to terms with those tendencies, and understand ourselves better?

It has been said many times, I make no excuse for repeating it, but honesty is almost certainly the best policy in the long term.

If any of you have not visited Michael's website, please do so and fill out his informational survey so we can have more clarity about the straight/gay marriage situation. It only takes a few minutes, and we are learning so, so much from his research.

JULY 2006

AND THE PASSWORD IS.....

Each week, I receive over two dozen letters from straight wives asking me if I can help them figure out what the password is for their husbands' computer activity. I guess I've been getting these letters for so long that I missed the obvious issue. Sorry about that girlfriends! Sometimes you're just so close to the situation that it blinds you.

Well, now I've finally come up with my computer password epiphany. Hold on to your hats gals: WHY DOES YOUR HUSBAND HAVE HIS OWN PASSWORD?

That wasn't too obvious, was it? But think about it. What reason could a husband possibly have for keeping his email private? What is it he doesn't want you to see? Based on this circumstantial evidence alone, I would vote, "GUILTY!"

So, here's my scenario for those of you in this situation. If you see that your husband has a different password, first ask him why. I'm sure he'll come up with some reasonable explanation. And after he does, reassure him that you understand, and then ASK HIM FOR IT.

If he says that he's not giving it to you, ask him why not. After all, you are his partner in life. Be reasonable. Tell him that you have no intentions of using it, but you would like to have it. Explain if he refuses to share the password, you will feel that he is looking to "keep" a secret from you. See what kind of explanation he gives you at that point. And do me a favor—send me his answer. I would like to share them in a future newsletter to let women know what they will encounter when they build up the courage to ask.

By the way, there is only one way I know to find out the password if he gives you a resounding "No." That way is to buy spy ware that can be purchased online for under $100.00. It's a simple download, and it will record every key stroke he types in. Then you'll see everything going on. There are certainly other things you can to do to check things on the computer such a view computer history or check for temporary Internet sites. For directions on any of this, just email me at Bonkaye@aol.com and I'll be happy to send you the instructions.

If you are reading this and have any other suggestions to help other women who are struggling with this, please send me the tips so I can reprint them.

MARCH 2007

LIFE AFTER THE DEATH OF A MARRIAGE

Several weeks ago, I received this letter. I will comment on it at the end because I think this is an issue that we don't discuss enough:

Dear Bonnie,

I first contacted you over a year ago when my husband of 19 years told me he was bi. I went online and read all the other women's comments but felt too overwhelmed to get into a conversation. Even though I didn't participate I found comfort in reading these women's feelings and hearing your gentle but firm advice/empathy. Looking back I now realize I was unable to join in as I wasn't able to accept that I was one of the group. Denial kept me on the sidelines.

Since then I bought you book "Straight Wives, Shattered Lives" and it truly changed my life. The testimonials followed by your thoughtful and insightful observations and affirmations expressed all my feelings. Even my most personal and private emotions and fears were addressed - where I felt alienated I now felt a part of a group. Misery does indeed love company!

I must admit that I get frustrated or maybe just plain jealous when I read about women that meet a straight man and fall in love and therefore move on. I wish that could be my story but raising two young children alone is all consuming and leaves no room for taking on searching for a man. I also have to admit that I made terrible choices when my husband left me and flung myself into the arms of creepy straight men, as we women who only know gay men don't know how to navigate with straight men.

I learned the hard way that attention and flirtation from a straight man may fill the void that rejection from a gay husband created. But you can get used up and spit out very easily while lacking the confidence and experience to see that they only want sex and manipulate women to get it. Therefore once again, I found myself feeling rejected and lonely. Although I am relieved to hear that there are women who had gay husbands that find new healthy love with a straight man I want to share my message to the rest that haven't that they must be careful not to sell themselves short.

If any woman who has just found out that her husband is gay reads this I want to encourage them to avoid sexual experiences until they are not fragile. I believe women like us are desperate to prove that we can be attractive and sexual. We lack confidence as we have been so broken by the terrible realization that we were lied to and have wasted time on fake love/sex.

But being used doesn't help a woman to heal - it only creates more pain. And most importantly - integrity is the one thing woman like us share in that WE while were believing in the marriage, our gay husbands were cheating and lying to us. Therefore we should never lower ourselves to their level where we trade integrity for cheap useless sexual encounters.

Thanks for your support,
Trish

Trish's letter definitely saddened me because it brought back so many of those painful memories about the horrible feelings that I suffered with for so many years following the end of my marriage. So let me give you my take on this.

After a marriage breaks up and the woman knows or suspects that her husband is gay, there are two roads that are the most traveled. The first road is celibacy; the second road is promiscuity. There doesn't seem to be much in between for most women. We either find ourselves unable and unwilling to trust our own instincts again and hibernate, or have the need to make ourselves feel "desirable" which drives us over the borderline. I've seen it go both ways and there's no way to predict this ahead of time. Trust me—I make no judgments at all either way.

I went the way of the first road—celibacy. I was walking down that road for 11-- yes eleven--years following the breakup of my marriage. And guess what? I was perfectly fine with it. Well let me backtrack—I did have one sexual encounter after six of those years, and it was a disaster. That sent me back into my world of safety for another five years.

After the breakup of my marriage, my sexual esteem was at an all time low. Ironically, I had been very sexually active prior to that marriage. I was married to a straight man at least once or twice before! And I had a string of men over the years because I was always a romantic in love with love. How could one man have affected me so badly to send me into sexual hibernation? Believing that I was a sexual failure did just that. I knew that I didn't make my husband gay, but just living with him and feeling the sexual rejection and humiliation were enough to make me feel that no other man would want me ever again. And he kept telling me that throughout our years together. "No other man will ever love you as much as I do."

It's funny how that word "love" just became another four letter word to me. In time, I found it just as offensive as other four letter curse words. Over the period of our marriage, it had the same impact—it would make me ill just to hear it. How could someone "love" me and constantly berate me and talk to me with contempt? How could someone make me feel so inadequate as a wife, mother, and lover? How could someone who "loves" me weaken me into a heap of jelly with no spine left to barely stand up for fear of being knocked down verbally? There's was never physical violence, but we all know only too well how those "invisible bruises" last much longer than the black and blue ones. And they are inflicted more often and push—or shall I say penetrate--your most vulnerable emotional buttons.

When my marriage ended, I was nowhere ready to be with a man. My ex kept reminding me how my weight would turn off any man like it had done for him. After all, hadn't our sex life been reduced to nothingness because I had gained weight and was no longer worthy of being a sex partner? So now that my gay husband was out of the picture, why would a straight man want me?

The FEAR OF SEXUAL FAILURE was an overwhelming emotion that stayed in my head in those early days, months, and years. And so I learned how to suppress my hormones. I focused on rebuilding me, my life with the children, and getting an education. I became a super achiever and started to rebuild my badly beaten down self-esteem. Back then, I believed that this was enough to make me feel good about life. I had family and friends and I was a single mother. I was happy. I kept very busy going to school so I could have a future for my kids. Ob-la-di Ob-la-da, life goes on, brah.

I am not going to lie to you—for many years I felt no sense of loneliness, but rather a sense of freedom and independence. I had never really been manless, because I always equated manless = unworthiness. And believe me, I wasn't justifying my life—I was truly happy. I learned to LOVE MYSELF again and TRUST myself again. Those emotions take a long time to rediscover.

Let me not leave out learning to trust my judgment again was a key factor in allow myself to trust a man again. Some of you have been married 10, 20, 30, and even 40 years to a man who has hidden his true identity. Knowing this destroys our own sense of being able to make decisions, especially about men. We keep asking ourselves how we could have been so blind…stupid…misled. We start to wonder what else happened in our lives that was illusion, delusion, and smoked mirrors.

I think that almost all women who are in recovery start to suffer from what I call "gaynoia," or the fear that every man we meet is gay. I hear it constantly. When you discover that you have a gay man, every man after that is suspect for a long time. Sometimes years. After all, our husbands didn't "appear" gay and they were. So what do we know about gay? As we say in our support group, "All men are gay until proven straight!" When we start to recover our sense of judgment again, we realize that there are many men out there who are straight and possible soul mates. But that takes time too.

For me, it took eleven years before I was ready to find love again. My body and mind started to want it. And once I was ready, I fell in love again. On that road of getting my soul mate to fall in love with me (which took a year-and-a-half of relentless pursuing), I dated and dated and dated and dated. I had lost a lot of weight, started looking good, and built up the confidence in myself that I lacked throughout most of my adult life due to my weight problem. In that year-and-a-half, I made up for 11 years of void. I met guys, went out with them, made out with some of them, made love with a few of them, fell for some of them, rejected some of them who cared about me and was rejected by a few whom I wanted. Yep, the rejection hurt, but I just kept moving along to the next guy. It was a learning experience. Some of those experiences were a little scary, but they served as excellent material for my book "ManReaders: A Woman's Guide to Dysfunctional Men" which was published in 2005.

On the other hand, there are women who are jumping into the beds of men the week that their marriages split up. I see this happen often. "My husband rejected me—but some 'normal' man out there is going to want me." There is no doubt that some normal man is going to want you because you are a woman. Straight men want women, ESPECIALLY FOR SEX. Men are sexual beings. It's not that easy to find women who are willing, ready, and able to have encounters. So when your radar goes up, they come running.

At first, this is a morale booster. After feeling deflated for so long, it feels wonderful to be "inflated," even if it's for a quick sex fix. I am woman, hear my roar! And it does feel good to feel wanted, desired, and sexy. After being pushed away for so long, it's nice to have someone pull you in. The big bonus here is that you get to have sex with a STRAIGHT MAN—and for many wives of gay men, you can finally understand for the first time how wonderful making love can be.

The problem is, as Trish so beautifully put it, when the night becomes day, we are often left with the feeling of being "used," and that feeling negates the feeling of the moment when we felt desirable. That's why I always tell women to give themselves a chance to heal before seeking out worldly pleasures. If you jump into a relationship before you have healed, you are likely to make the same mistake with a different player. This does not mean you will necessarily meet another gay man, but it does mean you will likely meet an unworthy man who will rob you of your self-worth in a different way than your gay husband.

Here is why. After the breakup of the marriage with our gay husbands, most of us suffer in one way or another from LOW SELF-ESTEEM (LSE). Straight men who are predators have are drawn to women with LSE like sharks are to blood. They sniff and smell. They are pros. They recognize us before we recognize ourselves. And they know how to charm us which doesn't take much because we're so desperate for approval and love. The problem is that you haven't spent enough time learning to love yourself, and until you do, you can never find a happy, healthy, and emotionally nurturing relationship. That's just the way it is.

I am not here to discourage any woman who wants to take the plunge into bed with a man—rather, I here to warn you about some of the problems in the aftermath. There is no right thing or wrong thing to do during your recovery. You have to take back your life and take whatever steps are necessary to do this. You can make mistakes along the way, and that is human. There is never shame in making a mistake—the shame is not fixing it. Hopefully in time, you will meet your soul mate IF YOU WANT TO MEET HIM. You always read happily after stories in these newsletters, so never give up hope. And if you make the decision to live your life without a man because you are truly happy, that's fine too. You never have to apologize or explain to anyone.

If you are willing to share an "aftermath" story like Trish that will give women insight as to what to expect, please let me know so I can share it with our other sisters in pain. After being isolated for so many years, we need to now share our lessons so no woman feels alone again.

Trish, I thank you so much for sharing your emotionally moving story. I know that your words will touch our readers.

JUNE 2007

WHY THE ABUSE?

I consider myself to be one of the most understanding, open-minded women when it comes to gay husbands. I consistently state that I understand why gay men marry. I contend that the overwhelming majority of them love their wives when they marry them and hope against hope that their love will negate or erase those sexual feelings for men. I even believe that there are some gay husbands who don't realize they are gay when they marry because their sexuality has not been clearly defined at a young age. And I even understand those gay men who do know they're gay but marry anyway really intending to be good husbands, vowing that they will never cheat on their wives even though they can't keep that promise later on.

I get lots of flack from some women in pain who are sure that their husbands married them to "cover" their identity while having no intentions of being faithful. I truly don't believe that is the case in almost all of these marriages starting out. I have worked with nearly 1,000 men through the years in helping them in their pursuit of honesty. I am committed to doing this because I know how deep the fear of loss is to a gay man who wants to do the right thing. I know how some of them linger far too long—long after they know and understand that they are not straight—in marriages for fear of losing the known rather than facing the unknown. So many of them are afraid of a world that they have been taught is decadent, unstable, and morally wrong.

Now you know, once again, where I stand on this issue, even if you don't agree with me. You know I am not in the least homophobic, even if I am sometimes gay husband-phobic. And I admit that I sometimes am. Here's why.

I don't understand how a man can marry a woman proclaiming love, and then after he leaves, becomes your enemy. I see this happening time after time after time. It's not bad enough that your marriage is ending and that you have lost years of your life, but now you have a new enemy—your ex-husband. I hear horror stories—and

145

I mean horror with a capital H. So let's push the fast backwards button and revisit this.

A gay man marries a woman whom he promises to love and cherish til' death do they part. A woman puts all her hopes, dreams, and aspirations into the marriage, working her butt off to please the man she loves. In time, she realizes that there can never be enough done to please him, but she still doesn't understand why. She feels like the failure because the husband can't be honest or truthful with her. But that doesn't stop her from trying harder and harder. Nothing works. No amount of tears, therapy, plastic surgery, or weight loss/gain seems to make a difference. Her husband doesn't desire her and finds 100 reasons why she is at fault for the problems in their marriage—especially the sexual ones.

One day, he decides that he can now accept his homosexuality and tells her the truth. Or sometimes, he is caught by his wife who has now become a better detective than Columbo. The marriage ends because it needs to end, and they both move on separately in life.

Now, personally, this is how I FEEL. If you are a gay man, and your marriage ends because you are gay, you should do everything humanly possible to make sure that your wife has the emotional and financial support that she needs while making this transition into singledom. And I have met a few wonderful men who do exactly this which always revives my faith in men. But the MAJORITY of men that my women are dealing with are NOT these men. They become strangers in our midst, as if an alien ship grabbed them up and reprogrammed them to destroy their wives who are their new enemy territory. I just don't get it. As if the wife doesn't feel depleted enough from dealing with the collapse of her life as she knew it, she now has to become a mental kung-fu fighter to block the constant attacks by her husband.

Many of these men become very mean spirited. They are angry. They plot revenge—usually financial revenge. And when they "lose" that battle, as some feel they do when the courts divide the assets equally—they are really, really mad. Then they take out their frustrations on the children by badmouthing their ex-wives, the mothers of the children. By the way, plenty of men win the financial battle leaving their wives with a pittance of what they need to survive.

What are they so mad about? I don't understand it personally. I say if you're a gay husband, you don't have the right to be mad. You

146

have taken from your wife of some of the most valuable givens in life—self esteem, sexual esteem, and the sense of trust. I'm not saying you hurt her intentionally, but you hurt her. You can't give her back the time and territory she has lost, but you can try to make it better by being a better ex-husband.

Gay men need to understand that their marriages didn't end because of their wives—it ended because they are homosexual and don't belong in a straight marriage. So what if your wife is angry? She should be angry. This is the natural emotion for someone to feel when they've been "robbed" of what they think was theirs to keep. But if you act responsible in a meaningful way, she will get past that anger and hopefully build a road to understanding with you. Gay husbands have no choice in being gay, but they do have a choice in being honest, understanding, emotionally supportive and financially responsible.

I do feel very blessed to have a wonderful support system of wonderful gay ex-husbands who are always willing to help men who request help to move forward, giving them the advice I would give them myself. To those men, I say a great big THANK-YOU. My women need to hear more from you to restore their faith in men in general.

With this thought in mind, below is a letter from my friend, Joe, who would like to send you a message:

Dear Bonnie:

Thanks for asking me to write to your readers. First of all let me say that coming out to my wife was a real struggle. I had decided to tell her about myself after I came to grips with my own self. I was on my cell phone one day and she overheard my conversation with my friend. After I returned inside the house she confronted me as to what she had heard and at that point I had no choice than to tell her all. Since then she has been struggling with it all. She has been blaming herself for what is happening to our marriage.

Ladies, don't blame yourself, it's not your fault. Many of us gay husbands got married in the hopes that all would okay. Well when your born gay, you are gay. I have done extensive reading on the subject and it seems that it is a proven fact that there is an area of the brain that is different from most men that causes our homosexual tendencies. Unfortunately it is you, our wives, which after many years of dedication to us gay husbands learn of what our preferences are. It is devastating, its earth shattering, it shatters your self esteem, it shatters your emotions, it shatters your self confidence and trust in men for life.

I too have been struggling at what I have done. I really didn't want it come out the way it did, but it did and now I have to start picking up the pieces in the hopes that my wife will understand. Understand is a very difficult term in this situation because I really don't think that she or any other women in the same circumstance will ever "understand" the whys. I have spent many sleepless nights, many days just sitting and crying at what has transpired and at what I have done to ruin, devastate and shatter the hopes and dreams of a very wonderful woman. I have crushed what use to be a very energetic and loving woman. Her depression began worrying me and I finally spoke with our family doctor about the situation and he too was very shocked at what I told him.

We are now both seeing a psychiatrist in the hopes that the doctor can help both of us, me in overcoming the guilt, my wife in hopes of repairing her very low self esteem that she is now feeling and the blame that she is inflicting on herself. To this day I still cannot come to grips with my guilt. To compound the injury our son has started to catch on that something is different about mom and dad, the constant disagreements and our own anger being inflicted on him. What we have to realize is that even if there was no child in the mix, the sexual part of the marriage was over and would have ended eventually.

I guess the next question is why did I get married, why did I go through it when I knew 24 years ago that I was gay? I fell in love with a very wonderful woman, I fell in love with the hopes that she would change the way I was. For many years after we got married it was great, there was desire, there was pleasure and happiness. We all know that no marriage is perfect and that there are always times when disagreements will take place but they are forgiven after a calming down period. But a situation like this is not forgivable.

Many women become so dependent on their husbands for everything. This is the case with my marriage. At the start it felt great that she was depending on me for everything, from taking her grocery shopping to helping her make decisions on what color dress to buy for the occasion. She has become so dependent on me that even making the simplest of decisions like defrosting the fridge is sometimes a major ordeal. Regardless she has been a devoted wife and a wonderful mother to our son. There are so many emotions to deal with when the time comes that both parties have a great amount of struggling to contend with.

Just remember one thing ladies don't blame yourself for what has happened; you had on way of knowing the truth, you had no way of knowing how your husbands felt or who they were. I know it's not fair to you because you have given up so many years of your life to be with a man that you love, but a man that has been dishonest and unfaithful to you. If there are any women out there that suspect their husbands are gay or fooling around on the side, be open and confront them with the issue. You will begin to notice the patterns from loss of sexual desire to making up excuses why they are late or not at the office when they should be. Take it from the voice of experience, its difficult to come out and tell your wife that you are gay.

Again thanks to Bonnie for letting me put forth my little story about my "screwed up" life. I really hope that this has shed some insight into the male side of things and what some of your husbands may be going through.

Joe

JULY 2007

THE NEW "A" WORD

Have you noticed how the lingo keeps changing throughout life? First it was the "B" word – "Bisexual." This was a word invented by married gay men to throw their wives off track. You see if a man says he is "Bisexual," that gives you adequate false hope that he could choose YOU instead of a man. But over time, these men realize that the "B" word puts a lot of sexual pressure on them while their wives are living in this state of false hope. They see that their wives don't get discouraged—in fact, they will keep loving them harder than ever in hopes of sharing a piece of the pie or in their minds, a "piece of the meat." They've also discovered that the "B" word creates suspicion in their wives' minds whenever they use the computer or go out past the expected time creating that "nagging" suspicion that bothers them so much. What's a gay husband to do?

Not to worry—now there's a new excuse. It's what I refer to as the "A" word. Now men are using the excuse that they are "A-sexual," meaning they don't want any sex with anyone. They have no sexual drive—not for a woman or for a man. What I find surprising is that even though they have no sexual desire, it does not stop them from viewing gay porn or masturbating.

I've had a half-dozen letters from women in the past two months who are trying to convince me that their husbands are "A" sexual. I keep explaining to them that the "A" really means GAY. They even rhyme—**A and Gay**. Actually, I like the "A" word better than the "B" word. The "A" word is telling you, the wife right up front that you should **FORGET IT—IT'S NEVER GOING TO BE HAPPENING**. The **"B"** word keeps you dangling, telling you that maybe one day, if you're a very, very, very good wife, you're husband will pick YOU instead of a man. And once in a while, you actually do get "lucky" when he's feeling guilty or obligated to put in his straight performance to keep throwing you off track.

Ladies, please trust me when I tell you that it doesn't matter what letter the word starts with. Any word that comes before "sexual" other than "hetero" means you are in for a big disappointment. Don't be lulled into a false security of thinking that you're safe because your husband won't be cheating on you with anyone. He will be—trust me. And if he's looking at gay porno, it means he's thinking of a man sexually, not you. And one last thought—if he doesn't want any sex with you because by chance he is A-sexual, then you don't need to be his wife.

DISPELLING THE MYTH ABOUT GAY MEN AND THEIR FATHERS

As of late, I am hearing more and more about the theory that gay men are gay because they have a poor relationship with their fathers when they are growing up. Recently, there has been a lot of publicity focusing on my old best friend from high school days, Richard Cohen. Some of you may have seen his antics on The Daily Show, and if you missed it, I'd be happy to send you the link if you care to watch it. Email me and let me know.

Cohen's book "Coming Out Straight" was released one month before my first book "The Gay Husband Checklist for Women Who Wonder" in 2000. The irony was that I had written about Cohen in that book, never having a clue that he had a book coming out at the same minute.

In my book, I tell about our relationships through our high school days and post high school days. I also explain how he was a leader in a prominent cult-movement during the 1970's which brainwashed him into becoming "straight." It's an old story, so I won't re-bore you with it. But it brings to light the growing adoption of his theory by other anti-gay thinkers that men are gay because they didn't have fathers who were warm and emotionally bonding. As a result, they are seeking that love in a man-to-man relationship. And guess what? For a lot of money, Cohen can "convert" these emotionally abandoned gay men back to a healthy life of being straight—just like he claims to be.

For the record, I want you to know that this is the most ridiculous theory I have ever heard. If every man who had a lack of emotional bonding with his father was gay, then at least half of the population in this world would be gay. If there is any validity to this theory, how come all sons who come from the same father aren't gay? Does this mean that no father of a gay man ever had a close relationship with his son? And is this a condemnation of all fathers who have gay children? Are they all emotionally distant?

And if a man was truly seeking out emotional bonding from his father, how does this translate into sexual activity? Wouldn't this imply that gay men have incestuous desires? How does wanting a father's love end up in a sexual act?

And what about women who didn't have close relationships with their mothers growing up? Are they lesbians? According to Cohen, they are. Now that I'm thinking about this, I'll go one step further. My daughter, Jennifer, who died in 2002, was a lesbian. Did I make her a lesbian because of my lack of emotional bonding with her? I think not. We had a warm, caring, and loving relationship for 22 years. But then again, I guess some of us women have extra special powers. After all, if we are able to turn our husbands gay like some people think, why not our children? Hmmm....that will give us all something to think about!

The bottom line is this—gay is NOT a choice. I don't know any gay person who would consciously choose to be gay if he could choose to be straight. We all know how these men so desperately WANT to be straight—after all, we are/were married to them. They try very hard to make the STRAIGHT choice because they are told it's the only right choice to make. As a result, we lose years of our valuable lives trying to fix something that can't be fixed.

Gay isn't curable—it's NOT a disease--and the sooner people can accept that, the easier all of our lives will be. It saddens me when my women and gay men write to me about the horrors of counseling that they go through from people taking their hard earned money to help them stay miserable living a life that is unnatural for both of them. This thinking is a sham.

We need to stop looking for reasons about WHY, and we certainly need to stop thinking about ways to CHANGE WHAT CAN'T BE CHANGED. And we also have to stop looking to place the blame for something where there is no blame. It just is. We need to accept what IS, and the sooner we can do that, the sooner life can move ahead into a place where it belongs for our straight wives and gay married men. Thinking such as Cohen's gives you false hope that will someday come tumbling down in front of your eyes.

By the way, if you do watch the Daily segment, you'll notice how Cohen has men lay in his arms as he holds them tightly. If you think for one minute that he's not getting aroused by this behavior, then you are more naïve than you realize! Trust me, no straight male therapist would be holding men so closely and so tight. You can bet on that one!

Sadly, there are too many disqualified counselors in the field giving destructive advice for people in our situation. If you have had experience with bad counseling from therapists who don't understand the straight/gay marriages, please write to me and share your story.

SEPTEMBER 2007

THANK YOU SENATOR CRAIG...I GUESS

It's sad that we have to wait for a public figure to be exposed in order to get some publicity on the topic of straight/gay marriages. It's really a shame that it takes a controversy such as this for people to realize that we have a plight. But in a lot of these cases, these issues really backfire in our face, especially when these gay men "doth protest much too much" that they are NOT gay. The latest line of men caught in a compromising position is Senator Larry Craig. You know how I always say that if it "looks like a duck, walks like a duck, quacks like a duck," then it's a duck. In this case, Craig was not only quacking—he was tapping. So I guess I'll add that to my thoughts, "If it taps like a duck...."

I say that these issues can backfire because people actually want to believe these men are straight and not guilty of the gay gossip. They can't conceive that "straight looking and acting" men are those stereotyped images that we conjure up in our minds of the flamboyant gay character that people see in the media. Oh, that's right—we were married to them. Some of our women tell me that people doubt their discoveries because they hear from family and friends, "There's no way your husband could be gay. He doesn't 'look' gay or 'act' gay." Yep. We know. If we could have "seen" they were gay, we wouldn't have married them. They still don't get it.

The Larry Craigs and Ted Haggards of the world just have to add in a pinch of denial to put everyone's mind at ease. And their wives stand at the front of the DENIAL line to seal the deal. They are so relieved to hear their husbands say, "What? Me Gay? Don't be ridiculous!" And regardless of how overwhelming the presenting evidence may be, these wives aren't looking. And they're not looking because they just don't want to find what they should be looking for.

In the end, it only hurts our women more because it fans the fires of self-doubt. And this is a process that gay husbands are so excellent at perpetuating—making you doubt yourself. This is why so many women who come to me feel the need to have concrete proof that their husbands are gay. I have women who can't accept their husbands are gay no matter how overwhelming the proof appears to be. They have found gay porno on their computers, but their husbands refuse to admit that this is an indication of being gay. It's just CURIOSITY—and this convinces our women that "curious" doesn't mean that it will ever actually happen. Trust me, if they are curious, it's happening. I have other women who find sex toys in their husbands' briefcases, but when confronted, their husbands claim that these are not for them—it's for their wives in case they want to "try something different." Why would the wives want to try something "different" when they don't even have something "regular"? I have women who find condoms in their husbands' glove compartments, but that's just because they forgot to bring them into the house to use with their wives. Of course, they're not having sex with their wives. None of this is concrete proof enough for some women because their husbands' constant denials and lies leave them thinking that they are hopefully wrong. For some women, anything less than walking in and finding their husband in the sexual act with another man will never be proof enough. But I suppose that some women, even if they walked in to the room with their husband in a compromising position with another man, would find a reason to believe their husbands' excuse of, "I was just giving him a massage."

Denial is a powerful emotion. And it's even more powerful for the women living with it than the men who are dishing it out. That's why even though prominent news figures bring the issues to light, they don't necessarily bring the light to our women in doubt.

OCTOBER 2007

REVISITING AND REVISING THE KINSEY SCALE

Most of you have heard of the Kinsey Scale. Gay men use this as an argument to prove that they are not gay, but rather on some road or continuum that never seems to get to where you know they are going or have landed.

The Kinsey Scale was first devised in 1948 by Dr. Alfred Kinsey. His research broke sexuality into seven steps starting at "Totally heterosexual" to "Totally Homosexual." There were a number of other steps in between. According to Kinsey, these are the steps:

0. Exclusively heterosexual with no homosexual
1. Predominantly heterosexual, only incidentally homosexual
2. Predominantly heterosexual, but more than incidentally homosexual
3. Equally heterosexual and homosexual
4. Predominantly homosexual, but more than incidentally heterosexual
5. Predominantly homosexual, only incidentally heterosexual
6. Exclusively homosexual

According to Kinsey, "Males do not represent two discrete populations, heterosexual and homosexual. The world is not to be divided into sheep and goats. It is a fundamental of taxonomy that nature rarely deals with discrete categories... The living world is a continuum in each and every one of its aspects."

This scale has widely been accepted and utilized by many professionals in the field. I look at this scale as being an excuse for gay men as a way to prove that they are not gay, and I regularly see it being used to that end.

Quite frankly, I don't understand this whole concept. For instance, what is the difference between the Number 1 and the Number 2 position on the Kinsey scale? Number 1 is: Predominantly heterosexual, only incidentally homosexual. Number 2 is: Predominantly heterosexual, but more than incidentally homosexual. What determines if someone is "incidentally" or "more than" "incidentally" homosexual? For that matter, what does "incidentally" mean? An "incident" happened one day or night? And how is a man predominantly heterosexual but more than "incidentally" homosexual? Hmmm, beats me. And quite frankly, let's skip up to Number 5 on the scale: 5- Predominantly homosexual, only incidentally heterosexual. What does that mean? Very confusing, isn't it?

I believe that there are men who are "emotionally" straight. They are unable to come to terms with the gay world. They dread the thought of being "labeled" as gay due to societal or religious pressures. They enjoy the security of living with a woman in a "heterosexual lifestyle" where they don't have to fear the rejection of their families, religions, and communities. However, this does not deserve a space on the ladder climbing up to homosexuality on the Kinsey Scale.

I think the Kinsey Scale is an excuse for people who can't accept their sexuality. I believe that some gay men can perform sex with heterosexual women when the emotional need is so great that they can talk themselves into it. And I believe that these men feel much better talking themselves into being a 2 or 3 on that scale rather than a 4, 5, or 6. That scale convinces many a man that he's okay staying in a marriage because he's not a "6."

The Kinsey Scale is a product from 50 years ago. I believe it needs to be updated and simplified. So now, I've come up with a "Bonnie Kaye Scale of Sexuality." The scale has two levels – Number

1 and Number 2. Number 1 is Heterosexual. This is a man who craves sex only with a woman because these are the only sexual feelings that arouse him. Number 2 is for all the other men who desire a penis on any level—"incidentally," "occasionally," "every blue moon," "just out of curiosity," or "in a fantasy." Think of all of the anguish this new scale will take away from people who are intellectualizing about where they stand on the Kinsey Scale. Think of all the worry they could avoid as they inch up the ladder and move from a 2 to a 3 or a 4 to a 6. I can't even imagine the fear a man would have who is on Number 4 and creeping up to Number 5. Does he sit and worry how long it is going to take him to get to number 6? Will he try to convince himself to have sex with a woman so he can downslide to number 3?

I like the idea of my scale so much better. Men don't have to sit and worry about "how gay" they are or will be. They have nothing to prove if they desire sex more with men. It won't change their number—they will still be a Number 2. Wow—wouldn't that take the pressure off of men who are trying so hard to fight their own gay desires and behavior?

And wouldn't it make things so much easier for our women also? Women wouldn't have to wonder if their husbands/boyfriends are moving up or down a scale. It would be much more black or white. If you want a heterosexual man, that's fine. If he's anything else, well, it's not fine—at least not fine for a marriage. We could eliminate the fallacy of "Bisexuality," or Number 3 on the Kinsey Scale which always gives false hope to women. "Bi" implies to women that they have an equal chance to winning their man as a man has-- which we know is not the case. It reinforces false hope that if they "love their men enough or try harder to be better wives/girlfriends," their men will pick them. It just ain't happening, is it? The need for a penis is always there. All "bi" men would automatically fall under the Number 2 category. Even men who are "just fantasizing" about other men would be in the Number 2 group. After all, if a man gets "aroused" by a penis, it's definitely the Number 2 category.

I think the "Bonnie Kaye Scale" will help women make easier decisions. You don't have to sit and debate anything at all. It all comes down to one question—do you want a man who wants a woman or a man who has a penis on his mind? Why does something this simple have to become so complicated?

DECEMBER 2007

HAPPY HOLIDAYS—TO US

Dear Friends,

This time of the year is so painful to all of you who feel the loss of your marriages. It seems as though we are outsiders looking in—observers rather than participants. We go through the motions of smiling, filling out cards, buying gifts, but there is still something NOT RIGHT. We try to hide it, mask it, numb it, or dull it, but we are still in that dark tunnel that pulls us in closer than ever during this time.

Please know that this is normal. You are suffering from the opposite of Holiday Cheer—namely Holiday Fear. It's the normal time of the year to be reminded of what you don't have and what you thought you did have—and would always have—namely a loving marriage with a man you thought was your soul mate. Bah humbug. Instead of enjoying Christmas parties, you are finding yourself immersed in a big old-fashioned pity party.

Guess what? That's fine. You're entitled to pity yourself. Don't feel guilty—indulge. Allow yourself to cry—allow yourself to vent and be angry. You deserve it. One of our problems—universally among straight wives of gay men—is that we have been so emotionally suppressed for so long because of losing ourselves to who we are that we don't let ourselves go through the emotional steps it takes to recover. We still believe that we have to put up a brave front even when we feel like breaking down—or breaking things around us.

My dear friend Dina in California once wrote something that is so true—anger is an important emotion because it means that you are fighting for yourself. We spent so many years trying to fight for our broken marriages that we forgot that we have entitlements as well. We gave so much of ourselves that we forgot that we have the right to expect something in return. We were always looking to fix what was wrong, hoping if we could try just a little harder, our detached husbands would love us just a little more.

We internalized what should have been external. We believed we were to blame for something that we had no control over. It broke down our self-esteem, our sexual esteem, and our sense of self-worth. We started questioning ourselves wondering what we were doing wrong because our husbands sexually rejected us. Instead of their being honest, they were quick to place the blame on us. "You're too pushy... demanding... unsupportive.... sexual.... unappealing.... fat.... thin.... you name it, we were accused of it. Anything to place the blame where it didn't belong.

This week, I did an interesting interview segment with WE (Women's Entertainment) that will be aired during their new season in the spring. Part of the interview included a counseling phone session with my support system member Shawne in California. I met Shawne last summer when I was making my West Coast visit. Shawne is a beautiful woman inside and out. She had found out about her husband the year before and was devastated. She was still trying to be the "good wife" and do the right thing. By July of last summer, she realized the right thing was to leave him for the sake of her two daughters and herself. She wanted to be a role model to her children and not give them mixed messages for their future.

During our conversation, she mentioned how her husband told her that she should "get over it." Sound familiar? Many of us hear this not only from our husbands, but also from our families and friends. After all, half of all straight marriages end in divorce, and life does go on. While that is true, most of those marriages don't come with the baggage that ours do. Our marriages are unique. We all share the same problems that straight divorces have, but we also have added issues that other divorces don't have.

Other marriages may have ended due to a number of problems including incompatibility, financial problems, growing apart, being married too young and not understanding it, mental health issues, abuse issues, or drugs and alcohol. But at least the women in these marriages knew what the problems were. They weren't living someone else's lie and not understanding why they were facing the emotional turmoil and distancing. Our marriages included a number of these common issues, but the worst issue was not the one we could see—but rather the one we couldn't see, didn't know, didn't suspect, or understand. Our marriages were ruined without any ability to get better because they weren't able to be fixed. Homosexuality is not a problem that can be resolved in a marriage—it's a problem. PERIOD. It doesn't belong there lurking, hiding, or rearing its ugly head.

Nothing strips away a woman's sense of self-worth like being sexually rejected. Sexuality is a major part of who we are. Kill that, and you kill part of what makes us a woman. We weren't meant to be celibate. We didn't join the convent to live a life without sex. That takes an extreme kind of commitment. We got married to be part of a couple. Part of a couple means every aspect of being a couple— especially intimacy and love making. No woman should ever have to feel as if she is begging for what should be hers. There is nothing that degrading like being rejected sexually, and most of us are. Some sooner than later, but in time, almost all of us have that rejection and internalize that it is our fault. That hinders many of us for years to come when we want to start new relationships. We feel like damaged goods. All of this could have been avoided if our gay husbands had been honest with us. Sexual recovery is another step we have to make that women in straight marriages don't usually have on their plate.

The issue of trust becomes a major issue—not just trusting other men, but more importantly learning to trust ourselves. We lose the ability to trust ourselves because we were not able to trust our ability to know what was wrong in the marriage. The person who was closest to us was not the person we knew at all. And often, rather than accept responsibility for who they are, our gay husbands made us doubt everything we were doing including our parenting skills. It was so much easier to throw us off track than take the responsibility and tell us the truth.

The list of issues goes on, but since we all know them, I won't keep harping on them. I bring them up to you because I never want you to feel for one moment that just because you can't "get over it," that there is something wrong with you. It's a lack of understanding and sensitivity of those pointing that accusing finger—not you.

One way to get past the holidays is to try to make an major mind adjustment—at least to get you through the worst of holiday times. Those of you who have read my newsletters and have known me for a while are aware that I lost my greatest treasures in life—my son, Jason, in 2005, and my daughter Jennifer in 2002. Holidays have become so difficult because like everyone else, I seem to focus on what I am missing, rather than what I have. I try to remove myself from that space and place and surround myself with caring, loving people—like so many of you who have become my own personal support network and friends. I keep busy which doesn't allow me time to think too hard about anything too horrible. I close my eyes when those images appear and place a happy thought in there—like my soul mate of 14 years in January or my family and friends. I reach out. I make a call. I send an email. I break my never-ending diet and eat something I want but shouldn't eat. It always soothes the soul. I move forward—pushing, pushing, pushing, knowing that in a few days, the holidays will be over. My sorrow won't be over, but the constant reminder of what I've lost will be if you keep busy and distracted enough.

That reminds me to thank all of you who are there for me all year round who give me friendship and support. I never take your caring for granted for even one minute. Whether you are in my support chat, part of our support network, or one of my gay men friends who is always there to give me insight and guidance, I thank you. I wish all of you the happiest of all years. So many of you have moved ahead this year to places you never believed you would be a year ago, and hopefully, many more of you will be there by next year at this time. The New Year is a new chance for hope for all of us!

Remember—you are never alone. There are many of us out here who want to give you the support you need. Just ask! Isolation is the surest way of desperation. Don't allow yourself to stay in that dark place.

I would like to share the following letter with you that will hopefully start you on that path to hope. I felt it was a wonderful way to confirm this holiday message:

Dearest Bonnie,

As the year of 2007 is ending, and the New Year is about to begin, I feel compelled to write to you to let you know why this year is so much different than the last 20 or so that have passed me by. This is a year that I can celebrate—not the New Year as much as my New Life. Since you were the main instrumental part of that, I wanted to share my story and thank you, as well as ask you to print this story to give our other women the hope that they need during this time of year.

When I came to you over two years ago, I was scared and feeling mentally depressed. I had known for years that something was "rotten in the state of my marriage." It was there, but there was no passion or compassion. I was walking through the days, one after another, knowing that each day would be the same—VOID. I spent 20 years trying to "fix" something that I didn't know how to fix. I told you embarrassingly at that time that I had tried EVERYTHING to make my husband happy, but nothing worked. My husband was detached. For all intents and purposes, I was in a marriage all by myself. It was almost like I was living with a shadow that I could never grasp or hold on to.

In the early years of our marriage, when the sex seemed to vanish like smoke, I kept asking him what was wrong. First it was the pressures of the job. Then it was the pressures of having a new child. Then it was one ailment after another. And then it was the emotional battering down of how inadequate I was at EVERYTHING. I was never a good enough housekeeper; I was not as attractive as I was when we married (I gained 10 pounds over 20 years). I spent too much time taking care of our two children. I wasn't supportive enough. What did that mean? I LOVED MY HUSBAND. I spent year after year trying to figure out what would make him happy, but nothing did.

I believed that I was the cause of his unhappiness—not that he was the cause of mine. I spent long hours crying and asking him to help me become the kind of woman he wanted. He would snarl some nasty words at me and tell me to stop complaining and expecting so much from him and from our marriage. He would tell me that I was watching too much television and that we were not "Ozzie and Harriet." Those marriages were not real, so stop expecting him to be that way.

When I told him I wanted to go for marriage counseling six years into our marriage, he started yelling at me and telling me that our marriage didn't need counseling because there was nothing wrong with it except I wanted too much. And in time, I learned to stop asking and start accepting that I must be the problem.

Everyone who met my husband thought that I was the luckiest woman alive. He was a chameleon. His outside face to the public was charming, loving, and personable. How many women told me, "I wish I had a husband like yours!" That was funny because I wished they had him too. I wished they knew how all of that energy shown in pleasing the crowds magically disappeared when we were alone. All the communication that seemed so easy to him to have with others was "un-haveable" with me.

And then two and a half years ago, the day of suspicion came for me when I overheard a phone conversation that was not meant for my ears. It was late at night, and I was lying in bed pretending to be asleep as I often did because it often would take me hours to fall asleep. His cell phone in the den was ringing and he jolted out of bed to answer it. I heard him laughing quietly, telling the person on the other end how he couldn't wait to see the person the next day and how excited he was about the fun they would have. I felt as if I had been hit by a bowling ball right in my heart. I didn't say a word but waited to see how he would handle the next day ahead where we had "family plans" with my family.

At breakfast, the cell phone rang and my husband answered and made a big fuss about a problem at his job. He put on an act like there was a crisis that suddenly arose and he was being summoned to his office. This certainly wasn't the first time—but it was the first time that I realized there was no office crisis. Just to confirm my suspicions, I went to his office and his car was not there. I checked five times that day, circling a five block radius around his office, just to believe it myself. Now I knew. He was having an affair.

There was a woman out there who was able to make him laugh, unlike me. There was a woman out there he was willing to see at all costs including lying to me—unlike being with me. I cried my eyes out wondering why he could be so happy to run to another woman but so unhappy to stay with me.

I was determined to be what you call "my own private detective." I started looking through every scrap of paper around the house searching for clues. I don't know what made me think to check his computer, but I was hoping to find something there that would tell me who my demon was. I wasn't very computer savvy at that point, but I knew that my husband was spending a lot of time on it. I saw a history button and decided to look there. In between a bunch of websites for insignificant information came was the name "BroadMan.com." I hit into it just on impulse, and to my shock, a site of naked men appeared with inviting other men to "come and have fun." I found myself wanting to vomit. This couldn't be—it had to be a mistake.

Thankfully, when my husband came home and I told him how I "accidentally" discovered the site, he told me it was a mistake. A friend sent it to him in an email as a joke. He thought it was a site for large men's clothing. He was tall and muscular and needed specialized clothes. When BroadMan.com appeared, he assumed it was a specialized catalogue for large men. He told me how he had gotten "ill" when it popped up seeing a gay sex site, and I felt relieved.

I then confronted him with my suspicions that he was having an affair, and he got very belligerent telling me that I'm "paranoid." Again, I felt so relieved. When we went to bed that night, I lovingly approached him hoping to find something that would encourage me not to believe he was looking elsewhere. He pecked my forehead and told me how exhausted he was from working all day. I didn't have the nerve to tell him I went by his office looking for his car.

Once those pictures of naked men were in my head, I became obsessed with the thought that my big strapping handsome husband might be gay. I found you on the Internet when I typed in "gay husbands," and I wrote to you with the signs, and you assured me that he was gay. I remember sending you a nasty note back stating that considering you didn't know me or my situation how could you just so quickly "jump" to that conclusion? I wanted you to tell me that the website was a fluke. I wanted you to reassure me that one gay website does not a gay man make. I wanted you to get rid of the horrifying fear that I was facing. You were of no help to me at all that day.

Even though I wasn't very nice to you, you were very nice to me. You sent me a long set of your past newsletters, and I forced myself to read them. All of the emotions that I was reading about were MY emotions. All of the circumstances you talked about were MY circumstances. All of the denial you spoke about was MY denial. I kept sending you short notes hoping you would tell me that I could be wrong, but you refused to allow me to stay in my own state of denial. You told me to install spyware so that I could find out the truth. I did—and I did.

In those following weeks, I became glued to the computer every time my husband left the house. I became obsessed with reading about his life, as if I were reading a novel about someone else. Who was this man that I lived with for nearly 20 years and thought I knew? He was a stranger to me. I had no clue who he was as I read email after email with notes about "hook ups" and "casual sex encounters." I didn't say a word to him. It was as if I was watching a soap opera of someone else's life and I was glued to the television.

I started to write to you almost daily, sending you the information I found. I didn't know how to confront him with the truth. You advised me, consoled me, and listened to me when I was almost banging my head against the wall. You encouraged me to take one step at a time rather than jumping into quick sand that I couldn't pull myself out of. You advised me to get legal advice before I did anything because I feared the financial repercussions of leaving the marriage. You had me make a plan—a week by week diagram for the next few months of how to take each step when I seemed overwhelmed with just waking up in the morning.

I carefully stepped one step at a time. Sometimes I went three steps forward and two steps back, but you told me to get up and keep moving "straight" ahead. Each day I woke up and read my goals as you had me put down on paper to keep me focused. The funny thing was my husband never suspected a thing. He was so unemotionally involved in our relationship it never occurred to him that I was now just as unemotionally involved with him anymore. This made it easier for me to do what had to be done.

It took me over a year to put all the pieces together, but you were there with me every step of the way, never pushing—just encouraging. And then the day of confrontation came. I was totally prepared. With evidence in hand, I told him to sit down because it's time for a discussion.

Of course, he was annoyed. He was on his way out to meet with one of his sex mates and I was taking up his valuable time. I didn't beat around the bush. I had my folder of evidence in my hand. I told him, "This is your day of reckoning. I am letting you know now that I know you are gay. I know you have been lying to me and cheating on me for years. Don't bother denying it—all the proof is in this folder. Don't try justifying it—there is no justification for it. Don't try running from it—the truth is out, even if you're not. Most importantly, our marriage is now ending—and it's not just because you're gay—it's because you were dishonest and unfaithful. If it were just gay, we could have ended it being friends. But because you ruined every ounce of self-worth I had by blaming me for your unhappiness, I don't want to be your friend. I will do my best to be civil about this as long as you do the right thing. That means leaving immediately and being responsible to your family."

I had this all written down as you told me to do in case I got nervous. I practiced it 100's of times in my own mind, waiting for the day when I could say it. I didn't leave it open to discussion or argument. And for the first time in 20 years, he didn't try to argue. He said okay and raced out of the house. Of course he was late for his date, but I didn't care what his reason was.

The next day, he packed whatever I hadn't had a chance to pack and moved in with a "friend." I didn't cry, but I was still feeling stunned. Women have to understand that even ending a bad marriage is difficult. You told me that so many times, but I didn't believe it until he took out his suitcases. Our two children, in their late teens, were told the truth. I told them. I felt they had the right to know. They were at peace with my decision. They loved me and were tired of seeing me beaten down. I told them both that this was not the right way to live, and I apologized to them both for having them endure the years of mistreatment with a man who was frustrated with himself and taking it out on all of us.

December 28 will commemorate the one year anniversary of being out on my own. It's been a year of rebuilding and rediscovering who I am. I like this new me much better than the old me because I didn't even know who the old me was anymore. I was living in my husband's closet, living in his shadow, living to please him without thought of pleasing me. That has now changed.

I spent this past year of what you call "gay husband recovery" getting to know myself again—the real me. This was the me that somehow was lost for all of those years trying to be someone he wanted, not someone who I wanted. I isolated myself from my family and friends over the years—or shall I say my ex-husband made sure I was isolated. I have spent this year reconnecting with people who can give me the support I need.

I have just recently gotten up the courage to start seeing a wonderful man that I met at a company in-service day. I have only been on five dates with him, but wow—I feel like a woman for the first time since I can remember. This is a man who thinks I am beautiful, interesting, and intelligent—all of the things I never heard from my husband after the first year of our marriage. I'm not ready for sex yet, but I love how he holds me, cuddles with me, and kisses me. In time, I will be ready to move to the next step. Even if he's not my "soul mate" as you call it, I will do as you say—"practice, practice, practice" for when my soul mate does show up.

Bonnie, I know this is a long story, but my life has been so enriched through your help that I wanted to tell it the way it is. I am forever grateful that you brought light into my darkness, and hope to me when I was hopeless. I wanted to let your other readers know that the holidays are a painful reminder to all of us about what a family should be, but isn't. I ended my marriage last year right after Christmas and right before the New Year. The thought of being alone of New Year's Eve was very frightening—but not nearly as frightening as not being alone and being with a man who held me in such contempt. As you said, "You are alone even if he is there—if not more alone!" You were so right.

Waking up every morning without knots in my stomach and colitis and spasms during the day is just one of the many benefits of being on my own. I may work harder because of the financial situation and now being a single parent of two teenagers, but it's worth every ounce of effort to work hard so I can be independent. And it doesn't take me hours to fall asleep anymore! I can do it in minutes and have peaceful dreams about my future—not nightmares about my past.

Good luck to all of our women who have to make that tough decision to save themselves. Please know that your life will be enriched and feel fulfilled once you "take it back" as Bonnie says.

Happy holidays to all of you,
Catherine C., North Dakota

Thank you, Catherine, for sharing your story of hope. Let's hang on to that hope and know that it is within your reach! Happy holidays to all of you, and a happier New Year filled with the dreams that you want that you can make happen if you start to believe in yourself again.

JANUARY 2008

SEEING AND BELIEVING

Happy New Year to the thousands of my world-wide support network members who faithfully read this monthly newsletter. Many of you write to me monthly to tell me how my words are your "lifeline" to get you through the dark days of your marriage and after-marriage mourning phases. I hope this is a year of peace, happiness, and love for you. When I say love, I mean love for you because that always seems to be the hardest obstacle to climb over. Women who marry gay men in general love too much, but their love is misplaced. Too many of our women don't understand the concept that love should first be about yourself—and then you can function as a healthier human being making the right decisions instead of dwelling in the muck of smoke and mirrors. This is because too many of us focus all of our strength in trying to get our gay husbands to love us enough to be the kind of husbands we were hoping they would be, while our own feelings of value and self-worth evaporate until they disappear. We focus so much of our own time and energies on being "detectives" and trying to "prove" or "validate" what we already know, fearing people will accuse us of making up this information. Add to that a splash of strong denial by our gay husbands every time we ask, and it's a recipe for even stronger self-doubt in our ability to see what is sitting right in front of us.

There are still numbers of women who write to me each month stating that they are afraid of ending a marriage because they don't have enough proof of homosexuality against their husbands. What is enough proof? For some women, it will be nothing short of walking in and seeing their husbands engaged in hardcore male sex. Obviously, finding websites, emails, cell phone bills, and credit card bills still doesn't give them the proof they need. All their husbands have to do is say, "I was curious," or "I love you too much to ever act on it," and their wives feel redemption from the whole sordid mess. Then they write to me to tell me that they have to give it another chance because their husbands are "trying" to change things around.

Please! Give me a break. If you've read the huge mounds of newsletters I send to each and every woman who wants the past editions as well as every new one, you have to know that this problem doesn't go away—it just hides for a while in a bigger and better way. Once your gay husband knows you are on to him, he finds new ways to keep you from learning the truth. He gets smarter and wiser. He learns how to hide his evidence better. And you, the loving, trusting wife want to believe that some miracle has occurred—at least at first. Then he reaches his comfort zone of your lull back into denial and he says a big "Whew!" He's safe again. Eventually when he lets his guard down, that's when I hear from you again. This time, you're SMARTER AND WISER. You know that old saying—"hit me once, shame on you—hit me twice, shame on me." Sometimes that second blow is what does it.

Women need to learn that gay isn't a choice—it's not a lifestyle. Just because your husband doesn't hang out in gay bars or participate in gay pride parades doesn't mean he isn't gay. Gay men can be straight looking, straight acting, and some even homophobic just to throw you off kilter. They think that if they protest enough, this will allay your fears. And "Whew!" again. It generally works!

MARCH 2008

LEARNING TO LOVE YOURSELF—GREATEST LOVE OF ALL

Last month, I wrote about finding new love after a disastrous marriage. My dear friend, Melody, shared her love story with you about finding true love after the horrific end of her marriage of 25 years when her husband was discovered soliciting a policeman in the park. When Melody first came to me, she was shattered. But she was determined to salvage the good years left in her life and start a new chapter. I just heard from Melody following her new marriage and honeymoon. This made my own heart feel so, so good. Nothing makes me happier then when a woman can take back her life and salvage it.

That being said, I did hear from a few of you who nicely reminded me that you don't have to find a man to have happiness in your life. Sour grapes? No not at all. It's the truth. Many of our women have found happiness on their own and don't feel the need the need to have a man in their lives to make them happy. Is this possible? Of course it is.

I remember how I felt in those early years following the break-up of my own marriage. Yes, I was wounded emotionally. The thought of meeting a man was my very last thought. I had to put my own life together before thinking about a man. I had two little children to raise, college to attend, a career to put in place, and somehow find a way to rediscover who I was before my marriage. A man in the mix at that point didn't make any sense to me.

I spent the next 11 years of my life without a man. Guess what? I was quite happy and fulfilled. I didn't feel as if I was missing anything by not being in a relationship. I wasn't angry or bitter against relationships or men. I was just happy to be on my own. I had spent most of my life up until that point under the false illusion that I needed a man to validate my existence. I was a child of the 50's who grew up on the Cinderella story. I was expecting Prince Charming to enter my life and bring me my happiness on a silver platter. As each of my princes seemed to revert into toads, I realized it was not going to be easy. This, however, didn't stop me from trying, because in my immature mind, I truly believed that BEING LOVED BY SOMEONE WAS BETTER THAN NOT BEING LOVED BY ANYONE. And guess what? A lot of you when you're honest with yourself will admit the same thing.

I did love my ex-husbands. Yes, husbands with an "s" meaning more than one. I didn't enter into marriage just to be married. I was in love, or as my loving departed mother used to tell me, "I was in love with love." Maybe, if I'm honest about it. I have always been a romanticist. I do love being in love, but it took me many years and hard knocks to learn that love is a two way street. I don't have to love someone who can't love me back or who can't meet my emotional, intimate, and sexual needs. In my earlier relationships, that's what I did. I did most of the loving, and the men did most of the taking. That's when I realized that I wasn't ready to find love again UNTIL I learned to love ME first.

This was a process. It didn't happen overnight—it took years. First, I had to learn who I really was, not who I had become in the shadow of the men who overpowered me. I had lost myself in my constant need to make them love me by becoming the woman I thought THEY wanted me to be—not whom I wanted to be. And after I found myself, I had to learn to LOVE myself. I had to take those words from the song "The Greatest Love of All" which states: Learning to love yourself, it is the greatest love of all." Those are powerful words when you really think about them.

Is loving yourself a selfish act? No. Quite the opposite. It's the most unselfish act. You can't truly love someone else in a meaningful way if you don't love yourself enough to have the expectations of what love should be. If you love someone more than yourself, your needs are not taken care of. That's when you become needy and co-dependent and willing to stay in a relationship that is never going to give you the satisfaction you deserve.

Don't confuse loving yourself with being self-absorbed. It took me nearly half a decade to love myself and believe that I was worthy of love in a positive way rather than a negative way. And if you do enter into a relationship, loving yourself gives you the ability to communicate your needs rather than to feel crushed when your partner isn't meeting them because you are afraid to tell him what is bothering you. Most of us are coming out of marriages where we were shut down or degraded when we expressed our feelings of loneliness in the relationship. How many times have you told me that you were more lonely living with your husbands than without them?

If you learn to love yourself, you can find the peace of mind of living on your own. Not every woman has the same needs. Not every woman wants the same thing. And guess what? That's fine! The most important thing is for you to be happy with YOU—whether it's on your own or in a new relationship.

MAY 2008

BUT YOU MUST HAVE KNOWN....

A few weeks ago, my support network member Shawne was on Dr. Phil with her ex-husband on a show talking about marital problems. The couple was telling the story of their marriage and how homosexuality was the cause for the problems they were having. Since the show aired, the couple has split, but they were together when they taped it last year on their way out of it.

I'm not a Dr. Phil watcher, but I made sure to watch Shawne on that day. Although Dr. Phil gave the couple the correct advice in dissolving the marriage, he said something else that really angered me. He was admonishing Shawne for not admitting she knew about her husband's homosexuality before the marriage. After all, he had so many "obvious" characteristics that should have convinced her. So on some level, she needed to accept responsibility.

Okay, let me get ill. How sick am I of hearing that "on some level, we must have known"? It feeds into all of our already shattered self-esteem when people confront us on this. So let me ask you this. Are there really signs we should have seen but didn't? Does it mean that a man who listens to you and cares about what you have to say is gay? How about a man who likes to shop? Or a man who likes the same movies you do? Is every man who has an eye for decorating a queer guy with a queer eye? Does that mean that straight men don't ever like decorating? And how about the men who cook? Is every male chef gay?

I can guarantee you that almost all gay men who marry us had not come to terms with who they are when they marry us. They didn't believe they were gay, so who were we to challenge that? They loved us, made plans to spend their lives with us, have children with us, and do all the same things that straight men do. Some of these husbands are our best friends which is why it's so difficult to end many of these marriages. It's not like you've been living with the "enemy" from the beginning. You were often living with a man who was your best friend. And marriage is supposed to be about living with your best friend— just not your gay best friend which is why the marriage fails.

The point is that there is no way for us to anticipate that we are marrying a gay husband. Trust me, if we did, we wouldn't do it in almost all cases. I say almost because there will always be women who are trying to change men because they are young and confused. Or older and confused. Or even old enough to know better and confused. But I say that 95% of us go into this marriage with the hopes and dreams of living the rest of our lives with a straight man, not a gay man. For people to assume that on some level "we should have known" is truly insulting and upsetting. But, come to think of it, that's why our latest book is titled "How I Made My Husband Gay." People think we can do magic tricks as well!

JUNE 2008

THE "P" WORD

As my long time readers know, "DENIAL" is a very powerful thing. That's why so many of our women linger in relationships long after they should—seeking the "TRUTH" while wasting years of their lives that can never be returned. I'm not quite sure why so many of the women who come from me have to have "POSITIVE" proof before taking action to end their marriages to gay men. I always give them my standard line of, "Look for the symptoms, and you'll eventually find the disease bringing toxicity to your marriage," or "Look for the clues, and you'll evidentially find the evidence." I try to relate it to medical and legal terminology to make it simple.

And yet, women want so badly to believe that the worst is not the worst, but rather some mistaken moment of stupidity.... weakness.... boredom.... mid-life crisis.... past sexual abuse issues resurfacing... and so on and so on. Here's the funny thing. These women come to me looking for the truth, but when I give it to them "straight," they don't want to hear it. It's like I need to be challenged at least once a week by some woman who will insist that her situation won't be like the other ones I write about. After all, her husband has always been so good...so honest...such a good friend...you know the story. These women are way beyond swimming down the river of De'Nile; they are building a Mountain of DENIAL. I send them directly to those other groups on the Internet who sit and complain while they figure out why life is so much better living with a "Bi" man than "No" man.

One woman sent me an interesting thought. After gathering information about her husband's homosexuality and confronting him, he replied, "I'm not gay—I'm straight with problems." Wow—a new category. Now I could add that to the "A" sexual," "Bi-Sexual," "Metro-sexual," "Limbo," and "Straight-Gay Man" categories that are taking up a lot of my mental time explaining to women, but I've come up with my new terminology that will stop men from having to pick and choose which column of the menu they are on at any given year or what rung they are standing on of the Kinsey scale while they are scaling up and down between 1 and 6.

From now on, we can call these men "Penis Men." It's so simple—it's not a choice of where a man is, but rather of what he wants. We don't have to use that ghastly "G" word anymore—we can use the trendier and more upscale "P" word. If a man is thinking about it, viewing male porno sites, fantasizing about it, or actually acting on it, he's a "P Man." It sounds more honest than "Bisexual" and gives no false hope that he's going to want you, a woman, more one day than he does a man.

"P Men" sort of sound like that Elton John song "Rocket Man." We can even change the words to our cause:

And I think it's gonna be a long long time
Till touching down there brings me round again to find
I'm not the man they think I am at home
Oh no no no I'm a Penis Man
Penis man burning out his fuse out there alone....

Since Elton John is an open "P Man," maybe he won't mind too much if I adapted those lyrics for the future.

Bottom line for our women—if he's a "P Man," you know that means he's a "G" man. But we'll let him think he's just a "P"!

JULY 2008

ABOUT GAY HUSBANDS

Each year, I receive approximately 200 letters or calls from gay men who are seeking answers to their confusing situation. Some of them are open to listening and HEARING what I have to say. They feel scared, sorry, remorseful, and a bunch of other appropriate adjectives that express how sad they really are about the situation. I love hearing from these men because I feel their wives will have an easier time in making the adjustment out of the marriage.

But then I hear from too many gay men who JUST DON'T GET IT. Either they feel like they are the victims or they feel their wives are not. They look to make excuses as to why their marriages have moved downhill and give me a long laundry list—literally. "My wife is lazy—she won't even do the laundry." Okay. That must be the reason why your marriage is broken. When I mention the "G" factor, I'm assured that's the least of the problems. After all, they are good, loving, supportive husbands. Some of them even pay the rent. Doesn't that prove it?

Somehow, they are trying to justify what can't be justified—their homosexuality in the marriage. I always say that people have no choice in their sexuality. I will always believe that to my last breath.

173

However, what they do with it is another story—that is a choice. And you know that I am sympathetic—much more so than many others in this situation. I know the pain gay people go through living in a world where they are constantly reminded that they are making their own choices and will spend a life in damnation for it. It's easy to see why those who can, choose the "escape route" of marriage. And you know I'm also a strong believer that these men do love us when they get married in almost all cases. They really want to be good husbands and fathers and make the marriages work. They believe that love will cure all—including their homosexuality. We all know that doesn't happen.

But where I have a hard time feeling sympathetic is when there's no sense of responsibility for the years of deceit that so many of these husbands put us through. Case in point: I recently had been in touch with a gay husband who is getting ready to split. He knows that his marriage is a sham and he can't keep living cooped up in a lie. He had no problem being honest with me, but he said he does have an issue with being honest with his wife. He asked me, "Why is it necessary to be honest with my wife? Plenty of marriages split up. Why do I have to make it because it's a gay issue? Why can't I just say that it's because we're not compatible?"

Yikes!!! Actually, double Yikes!!! He doesn't get it. I've tried to explain to him that your wife has suffered for years wondering why your marriage isn't working and blaming herself. She hasn't tried hard enough…looked good enough…been supportive enough….we all know the drill.

I explained to this man that he OWES the TRUTH to his wife. Yes, she'll be angry. Yes, it will be the worst day of his life and the hardest decision he ever has to make. But if you love someone, you owe it to her to tell her that she is not the problem in the marriage, but rather homosexuality is. At first, he said no thank you. He didn't like my advice, but he was a reasonable, receptive man. After a few correspondences, he was at least thinking about telling her down the line. I told him NO. Down the line is too long and too far away. These guys don't understand that every day we live with this ball of confusion is another day that we lose of ourselves.

Too many of our women spend years and years of their lives living in a world of deception. Ten, twenty, and thirty plus years is too long of a life term to spend wondering why we can't make the man we love

174

happy. We try to comfort him in every way known to humanity to try to make him happy, and yet we fail. We don't believe that this failure is self-induced—we internalize it and blame ourselves.

Whether it's emotional rejection or sexual rejection—IT HURTS. How many nights do our women go to bed crying themselves to sleep wondering why their marriages aren't gelling? How many times do we sit and wonder what there is about our bodies, our shapes, our odors that repel our husbands to spiral away from us sexually? Do they realize how hurtful a simple comment like, "You smell bad" when they touch our womanly parts makes us feel? Is it any wonder that we just give up for fear of feeling "dirty" or "inadequate"? Do they have a clue as to how we eventually let that part of us die rather than be called names like "sex crazy" or "nymphomaniac"? And when your sexual esteem is destroyed, part of your identity as a woman is destroyed as well.

I try to explain to gay husbands that it's not just about ending a marriage. It's about ending a dream for many women who went into their marriages filled with love, ideas, life-time plans and expectations. And yes, plenty of marriages between straight people end as well. But they "feel" different. I know. I've had both. The issues are different. The deterioration of the relationship is different. And that is because in additional to the standard problems that all couples face, the emotional distancing and sexual rejection is an added feature that most straight marriages don't go through. I haven't run across too many straight men who don't want to have sex or belittle you because you want to have it. In fact, I find that straight men WANT to have sex—and beyond that, they enjoy "making love." They cherish it and enjoy it—and they want YOU to enjoy it. I'm blessed to have a wonderful partner who after 14 and a half years still excites me with passion and sexual fulfillment. And we're middle aged!

I think what these husbands just don't get is that it is not just them who are living a lie. They are dragging us through their lies as well. They think they are "hiding" their secret lives from us, but we know that things are off kilter—we just don't know why because they are not honest. Even though telling us the truth will not be pleasant or easy, they owe it to us. For every day we have suffered with self-doubt about ourselves as women and wives, they owe us at least that. Too many of our women will never know the truth because their husbands

175

are cowards. They would rather have us sit and suffer than step up to the plate and tell the truth. This is the tragedy.

PART TWO

LETTERS FROM MY WOMEN

THE MAILBAG LETTERS

Every month, the members of my support network send me letters in response to the newsletters. I am sharing some of the most emotionally hitting ones that everyone can relate to. Hopefully they will confirm everything I am saying—and everything you are feeling.

Dear Bonnie,

I anxiously await your newsletter each month and it has been so helpful and true. I would just like to comment on two points that you brought up in this January letter: Abuse.

This may sound so sad and pathetic but I thought I needed to share it with others: I used to pray that my husband would hit me or physically do something so I could go to the police or a family member for help. How can you go to someone and say "he calls me names or he makes me feel worthless?" The local police would have laughed me out of the station. How low could one woman go as to wish she could get beat up in order to be relieved of the pain?

The second point that I would like to bring up is the eternal denying of being gay and even the possibility of him marrying another woman to prove to the world that I am a liar, (bitch, pick a name) etc. At the urging of my husband's therapist he finally told me and our 14 year old daughter that he was gay. A few months later he was able to tell his parents and sister. Now he is begging us all not to tell anyone. He now claims his therapist says that it was a scheme he thought up because it was the only way I could understand that he wanted a divorce and didn't want to hurt me. In other words he is really not gay. Yea right. I am begging women not to fall into this sick elaborate trap. What kind of a mind could think of this? Apparently a very scared and sickly complex one. Five years ago I would have believed it. I would have wanted to believe it in the worst way. But all I can say is you have to be ready to hear and feel it. Nothing I say or you say can convince a broken heart but reading about it takes you down the path you may not initially want to be on but you know it is the right road.

Very sincerely yours,
Susanne

*　*　*　*　*

Dear Bonnie Kaye,

I could just HUG you!!!!!!!!!!!!!!!!! Your newsletter is RIGHT ON TARGET this month!!! I could never put into words how bad I felt about myself for the snooping and suspecting any man he ever talked to, the wild thoughts and visions that filled my every waking and sleeping moments ..... and the mental torment I put myself through, beating myself up for that!

It is SO NICE to be OUT of the TWILIGHT ZONE, as you so perfectly put it! Admittedly, those thoughts or visions still creep in occasionally and I still have those "DUHHHHHH CLUE # 4,653 moments" when I remember something he said or something he did .... but, I know it was NOT MY FAULT and we truly WERE in different ballparks, although he had hung Yankee signs in the Boston park and I thought I was in NY.

Thank you - thank you - thank you!!!!!!!! I REALLY needed this today!!!

Keep up your good work ... you are helping more people than you will ever know!

Joanie

*　*　*　*　*

Bonnie,

Not taking the whole thing personally, like "If I had been a better wife, mother, and lover, I wouldn't be divorced!" is very hard. I need to remember that from time to time. On the subject of how they try to make it our fault, my ex told me that I spent too much time reading, doing craft projects and going to church. He accused me of wanting to make him into "Pot Roast Harry" whoever that is.........

I love you!

Judy

*　*　*　*　*

Dear Bonnie,

Wow. You really hit the nail on the head with this one. I feel like you totally understand what I went through in the years of my failing marriage and the self-blame in addition to my ex-husband's blame of me for its demise. I wish he could read your words and understand what a hellacious existence that was for me but alas, he still has his blinders on and will never really "get it", especially as intent as he is on hiding the truth and deflecting responsibility. He still insists we were both responsible for the break-up of our marriage and that my faults were grossly understated in relation to his big revelation about his attraction to men. He says all the things you mentioned: I was a nag, paranoid, had trust issues, couldn't love, couldn't give, was selfish, demanding, couldn't be pleased, had an attitude against men etc. etc. Damn, was I awful or what??

And despite all this, he is still (2 years post-separation and divorce) trying to get me back and incredibly, sometimes the words even sound good to me! We have gone on some dates and been intimate a few times (I should shoot myself) but I don't know why I keep doing this!! I hate being a single parent and now being away from him its sometimes easy to get lulled into that false sense of security that maybe he's changed. (I am the one who wrote to you several months ago about his abuse and our ugly court battle) I have to see him all the time because of our 6 yr old daughter and it royally sucks because I can't seem to get on with my life. He is heavily involved with the church and still won't admit to anyone his gay feelings etc. He insists he's never acted on it and yet he said that during the marriage and I was there when he made an open pass at another married guy!

It was devastatingly painful and thanks for this last newsletter reminding me of the craziness of that time. I swear to you, I had almost blocked it out. I am vulnerable and lonely and he still knows the buttons to push. Not to mention that I never wanted this--- to be single and a single mom and have no money, family life, support etc. I left HIM which he still insists is my fault but that he'd forgive me if I just came back to him etc. I only left him b/c of what you described! I couldn't win! Thank you so much for saying in words what happened because I've been getting as delusional as he is again.

Why on earth do you think he still wants me back? After the court battle, the ugliness and everything? He insists he has attractions to men but they're only a result of his insecurity and lack of feeling masculine and that he'd be faithful to me. I don't even know why I'm entertaining these things except that my self-esteem is very shot after all that stuff and now I don't feel good enough for anybody. Plus, I'm scared to death of losing custody of my little girl b/';c he presents so well and can make me look emotional and crazy. He is quite the actor, which I tend to forget at times. He swears he loves me and that he wants us to be a family again and sometimes I am just so WEAK, b/c that's what I always wanted and may never have. But I know it would never be real with him and I'll never trust him. I guess, I'm just pretty messed up huh?

Anyway, thanks for listening. I get a lot out of your newsletters. I even showed him a few when we'd gotten together and he thinks it's evil that anyone would be so much for the woman without understanding the men's point of view. He thinks you paint us as angels and the gay ones as devils, but I know that isn't true. You simply understand that we've had enough blame. We have been devastated by husbands who refuse to look at the wreckage THEY created. And as usual, and probably for always-- he just doesn't get it!

Thanks again,

Callie

✳ ✳ ✳ ✳ ✳

Dear Bonnie,

I just read the newsletter. Seems we have something else in common that really hit home. I tried to commit suicide 4 times in my life. Twice it was official because Dan found me and took me to the hospital (gee, thanks Dan). The last time wasn't all that long ago, and I ended up losing my 2nd leg because of it. I got up and probably rammed into a wall in my wheelchair, and ripped open my foot. Shortly thereafter I lost the leg. Was it all because of my marriage to a gay man? I'm not sure. My first suicide was when I was turning 21, and was so lonely and depressed, I took a bunch of my father's pills. Just made me sleep, but honestly was an attempt to take my life. I truly wanted to die. My life was so unhappy. This was exactly the time I met Dan, he pulled me out from that depression, but it was right after finding out that the love of my life (another man) was gay!!! Thinking about this, yes, it is because of gay men and my trust in them, that I've been so suicidal.

Anyway, thanks for sharing such intimate thoughts with all the people who read your newsletter. That was a brave thing to do. I'd really love to talk to you about those times. To actually have someone

who understands what suicide is all about! Well, I could use that.
 Love, Holly

*   *   *   *   *

Dear Bonnie,
 Thank you, Bonnie for your newsletters. Keep 'em coming! I'm especially looking forward to reading your next newsletter, as my husband keeps telling me his online gay porno visits are more of an addiction than a sexuality issue. He feels he is in touch with being bisexual, but is committed to me and our marriage, etc.....
 By the way, I'm in the throes of a really rough time dealing with this, and your newsletters are like a lifeline for me. My husband has been very desperate to keep the marriage going and has made suicidal statements. He is finally in therapy (after me begging him to talk to someone for three weeks) and has let his gay brother know what is going on (only after I went to his brothers office and told him, though). He actually went to three therapists before he settled on the husband/wife team he's currently seeing. The first two confronted his denial, and the third was actually a child psych we were consulting about how to tell our son we are separating (he hoped the psych would talk me out of it). But his brother and I don't anticipate he will be able to fully come to terms with this for quite awhile. His brother gives him two years, but I can't wait that long. His brother has begged me to stay with my husband for a couple months just to help him "catch up" to where I am.
 Meanwhile, my husband has tried EVERYTHING, including making reservations on a cruise (I immediately told him to cancel them) to try and get me to stay in the marriage. Just like you warned in one of your earlier newsletters -- he has become an Olympic champion trying to prove his true love (and sexual attraction) for me.
 I feel even more betrayed, because I really trusted that my husband would have been honest with me about his sexuality. However, I'm seeing that he is so closeted EVEN TO HIMSELF that he is only beginning to fathom how his dishonesty has affected me.
 I am basically hanging in here (but not allowing any physical contact) for my son's sake until the end of the school year. I feel like we're setting up tag-team parenting. It's hard having to stay in the same house because I've never lost my own sexual attraction for my husband -- do you understand? And we had a pretty good sexual

thing going on occasion. We had just come back from a two-week beach resort vacation and had a pretty good time -- but of course, it was just a week later I found all this porno stuff going on. And my reaction was not one of hurt or surprise, but rather, resignation, I think. It was like an "ah-hah; so THAT's what's been going on" moment.

I want us to be able to maintain a friendship so that someday we can sit next to each other at one of our son's basketball games, and cheer for him together, even though we may by then have different partners. I know that's somewhat of a fantasy, but perhaps it can be a goal...So, all of this to say how important your newsletter is for me.

Danette

* * * * *

Dear Bonnie,

I just wanted to tell you what a light in the darkness you have been. I think your strength through all your trials--your gay marriage, and losing your beloved daughter--is a true testament to the human spirit and an inspiration to all of us who have been or are currently married to gay men.

I always shouldered the burden for my husband's unhappiness before reading your letters. I also never allowed myself to be angry at my husband's treatment of me. Do you remember that quote by Gordon Liddy, the one he made while holding his hand over an open flame? He said "the trick is not to mind it." That quote went through my head constantly during my hellish marriage, and reading your and other women's stories made me realize that I did mind it, and that I should mind it.

Even now, my husband is coming back wanting some way to "work out" our marriage. I was able to show him your letter "what if we were married to straight men". I read him the sentence where you state that at best, it is a friendship and how it will never be the stuff that love songs and poetry were made of. How glad I was to have that the time when he was using 25 years of conditioning to convince me to return to the old life. So, thank you, I only hope now that I am stronger, I can pass the strength you have given me along to others.

Beth

* * * * *

Bonnie,

I read with interest your newsletter on anti-depressants. Let me give you my story about myself and tgo (the gay one)... we were not married, had, however, lived together for several years - we both have children, but not with each other - my child is grown, his are with his ex wife):

It was during the time that I knew "something" was wrong ...there WAS an elephant in our living room... of course, *he* knew it wasn't an elephant, he knew it was his secret lover. "I" was the one with the problem, all was well with him... he couldn't "understand" why I felt something was wrong...it *must* have been in my head.

That's when I started to feel like I was losing it. Looking back, it was a *"Gaslight"* situation, but I didn't know that, then. I just knew I was losing it and I had the hole in the gut feeling that something was wrong, yet I couldn't put my finger on it.

That's when I started to snoop. That's when I found "the love letter". That's when I hightailed it to my doctor and fell apart in the office. That's when I started on anti depressants.

I didn't tell him I knew.... and I didn't/wouldn't let him touch me. I left, making an excuse that I needed to live with my dad for awhile, because he needed help (it was less than 2 miles away) and I would still see him every night... I just wouldn't sleep there.

That was a hellish time... it only lasted about 6 weeks... 6 weeks of me knowing the truth, hinting at the truth, driving by on nights that I told him I 'couldn't make it over' to see the that strange white car in the driveway... wanting for him to tell me, but not wanting to hear it.

Hoping I was so wrong. Hoping that it was not at all what it seemed. I remember borrowing a friend's car, putting on a man's coat and hat and a pair of big glasses and following the 2 of them ... they just went to Lowe's, but dammit, "THEY" picked out the kitchen wallpaper border and put it up that night ... I could watch them as I drove by ....the car was there until the next morning, and the guest bed hadn't been slept in... I booby trapped it so I would know if someone slept there. The next day, he "surprised" me with the wallpaper, saying he did it all by himself just for me.

Every time I looked at those stupid little apples, all I could see was gay sex.

By then, I guess the anti depressants had kicked in, it had been over a month and I did not drive my car over a cliff or into his gay face, so they must have worked. (Joanie without the anti depressants would not have been so kind.)

I finally broke him down into admitting the truth to me 6 weeks after I found the love letter. Then, I wanted him to suffer. I wanted him to await my test results... I wanted him to see me cry. I wanted him to know that I thought he was a liar and a snake and that he had lost any ounce of respect I ever had for him.

I wanted him to feel the pain. I would go there every night and make him admit all the times he lied and told him in EXPLICIT words what I thought of him. He had to sit there, shut up and take it, or I would out him to the world and he knew it. I wanted him to feel my pain, which of course, he never could. After about 2 weeks of this, I had said all that needed to be said, and told him never to contact me again or I would 'out' him to his family and the world.

Things were fine .I stayed on my meds and started moving on...even dated someone wonderful.... even had real straight sex... got back my group of friends, and started living again. Life was good.

A few months later, he called... he said he "knew he was risking everything "but it was worth it to him because he loved me and it was a "mistake" and it would never happen again, blah blah blah. Well, I think that at this time, the meds had made me so complacent, that I fell for it. Without the meds, I would have taken the telephone to his house and put it where he probably would have enjoyed it.

Anyway, for several months, okay, over a year, I started seeing him again... I did NOT move back in with him, but we did resume a sexual relationship (I know --- duhhh) and I guess we had what you would call the honeymoon stage. Slowly, the nasty side of him started reappearing - not the gay sex thing - I would have killed him - meds or not. But, his frustration started coming out in many ways and he started treating me like dirt. I was taking it and didn't know why ... I knew better.

So, I went *off* the meds (under doctor's care) and a couple of months later, I had the strength to finally tell him "ENOUGH" of his abuse, lying and gayness.

I finally found my strength again.. the complacency was gone ...and so was I. It has now been almost 6 months. I have changed my home phone number, blocked his email and threatened him with a restraining order and his face on a billboard advertising butt plugs if he ever even THINKS of contacting me again.

We live less than 2 miles apart, and I have changed the grocery store I shop in, and have avoided being anywhere near his house - have not driven by once (YAY!) because I do not CARE what he does now. He is not my problem, anymore. But, I had to respond to your letter, because the anti-depressants helped me to *SURVIVE* in the beginning ... but, they also allowed me to foolishly *GO BACK* and "try to work it out" - because, at the time, the meds made me unable to realize the sheer futility of this. (I always wonder how much farther ahead I would be had I not dumped the great straight guy I was seeing and gone back to the gay one). Stopping the meds finally helped me *LEAVE* at the end.

So, in the beginning they saved my life, (and his) but later on, they prolonged my letting go and moving on. Hope this makes sense. Keep up your amazing work!!!! I wait for your newsletter every month!
Joanie

* * * * *

Dear Bonnie,
Your most recent newsletter rang true to my situation. You may use my letter and first name if you wish.

Looking back, my 30-year relationship seemed to be lacking. I knew something was wrong but was afraid of the truth and my partner was a master at deceit. In the last 6 months, I've learned he's been having sex with men. He says it's only been during the last year but I wonder if that's true. I saw an increase in our sexual activity during the last 4-5 years and became very comfortable and contented and thought the increased frequency meant commitment. Wrong! I'm learning now that it was probably a result of his encounters with men or Internet activity. Even though he says he's bisexual, I believe he prefers men. I don't understand desiring both sexes. I've tried and end up feeling angry and inadequate. Don't let sex fool you. You could just be the "release" as my counselor suggests and this is not a happy fulfilling situation.
Faye

* * * * *

The next letter may help those of you who are still having trouble finding out the computer activity. Spy software can

capture all activity going on with your computer from emails to websites.

Bonnie,
Just thought I'd let you know that I caught him! He still denies, but I know. I bought Spectorsoft, a recording program and saw what he was looking at on our computer. He says he was just curious, blah, blah, blah, but I know. Suspicions are confirmed in my eyes. You can mention to your readers that the program, while expensive ($99.00) was well worth it. If it weren't for it, I still wouldn't know.
I appreciate your support and continue to enjoy your newsletters. While I am still in my marriage and house, I won't be for long. It's time to move on…
Thanks!
Sandy

Bonnie endorses the following spyware. To purchase it, put this link into your Internet browser:

http://www.spectorsoft.com/default.asp?affil=1893

✻　✻　✻　✻　✻

Hi Bonnie!
Thanks so much for your recent newsletter. It is so nice to see women that are able to get through this incredibly terrible time in their life. It just kills me when I hear of women that stay in a relationship that you just know is doomed. Don't get me wrong, I don't think that they are a weaker person because of it or that they are wrong or anything. I just can almost feel the heartbreak that they are in for, the constant heartbreak. That's what I knew I was in for if I was to stay with my husband after he told me the news. Every time he answered the phone, every time he was online chatting or every time he met some new guy I knew I was assume the worst. How could I possibly live with that? There is no way.
I know I am very fortunate to have had the man I did for a husband. He came clean and told me right out once he finally came to terms with it himself. He helped me so much with moving out and getting myself established. It has been 1 and 1/2 years now. I still have my bad days, when I feel like my life is hopeless. When I feel

like no one is ever going to want me or love me or cherish me. But most days I am strong. I take care of myself and I exercise and try to eat right (most of the time!). I have finally come to realize that I need to make myself happy and be right with myself before I can get into another serious relationship. And I am definitely getting there!

Your book was like a lifesaver to me. I had searched far and wide for a book about what I was going through that made sense. What I mostly found was a lot of crap! Most of them talked about how many couples created "alternative" lifestyles where they would stay together and have their "flings" on the side. It was insane! All I could think is how the hell do these people think that I could possibly be comfortable in my home while my husband was having sex with a man in the other room! or even just knowing that he was doing that somewhere! Incredible! Your book and your newsletters have been a voice of reason in a sea of insanity. As soon as I started reading it, I was like "Alright! this is what I am talking about! Finally someone telling it to me straight!" (no pun intended!)

Thank you so much Bonnie. You are really an inspiration. I know you have been through a lot of controversy and resistance from all over. Yet you have stayed strong and stuck to your guns! Bravo!

Shelley H.

✳ ✳ ✳ ✳ ✳

Hi Bonnie,

I just wanted to tell you how much help you are being to me at the moment. every time I feel weak and need a bit of strength I read your news letter or the chapters of your book you sent me.

The only difference between our relationship and some of the others I have read is that he was always honest about his sexuality but we both thought love would hold us together but in the end it isn't enough. We were together 12 almost happy years and only got married 2 years ago, as he wanted to. I wonder now if he was mentally leaving me and thought that by getting married it would stop this happening? Sex was never a big part of our relationship but once we got married strangely we only had sex once between then and when he left me. Also he started going out more.

I can't help but wonder why oh why he wanted to get married, our relationship really started to go downhill once we did that. We had no secrets from our friends or relations, they all knew about his sexuality and any one that found it hard to accept at first just got use to it over the years. I feel now that he had a mid life crisis (35) and wanted to get out there and do his thing, life was passing him by so he had to do it. I am also 18 years older than him but he never felt that was a problem and he still said that it wasn't about my age when we parted, but I wonder if just may be it did have something to do with it?

I have attached a letter I sent to my husband last November and as I read it I feel I have moved on a bit, the pain is not quite so bad, I know now that I can't go back, he is gay and needs to do what he needs to do, but it doesn't stop me missing what we had. He stopped talking to me just before Christmas, I don't think he could stand watching my pain, I kept hoping for weeks that he would get in touch and tell me he had made a mistake but reading your information I know how ever much it hurts that it was bound to happen.

Do you think that he will ever realize that just may be what we had was enough.

Barbara

*   *   *   *   *

Dear Bonnie,

I always knew something was missing but I just couldn't put my finger on it. I thought it was because I was overweight and not attractive. Maybe if I lost weight, what if I was prettier. I often asked myself these questions. I knew tgo (the gay one) had effeminate ways, but I kept telling myself the reason for him acting that way was because he grew up without a father in a house with only females. Well let me give you a little advice... if it quacks like a duck, walk like a duck, it's a duck.

Every time I asked him why he wasn't affectionate he replied, "Some men are just not affectionate," and eventually I started believing him, believing that it was normal for him not to kiss me passionately, hold me, desire me. I thought it was normal to go 6 months or more without sex, and for him to never go to bed with me at the same time because he wanted to stay up and watch television. I couldn't understand how television could be more important than me. I would go to bed and cry myself to sleep, because I felt unloved, unwanted, and undesirable. My self esteem was being stripped from me day by day. He never comforted me like I needed to be comforted. He never held me.

One night he left his email opened and my whole life changed.   I read that he had been gay since he was 12.   How the only way he could make love to me was to think of being with a man, that he married me to make his mother happy, and that he had been with 6 men during our marriage. My whole body began to shake. I wanted to scream but nothing would come out.   I wanted to cry but I couldn't cry.   It took me about 3 weeks to confront him, I was terrified. He denied it, even though I told him I read his email. He said he was not gay and I was an evil person and a bad mother and I needed to stop accusing him of being gay and take the blame for the problems in the marriage. Well I thought I should stay married to him for the children. But how could I be a good mother to my children, depending on anti-depressants to help me get through the day.

I was a wreck. I went to counseling.   But the therapist wanted to counsel both of us (she was trying to save the marriage) so I stopped going to her.   The anti-depressants helped a lot, because I was very depressed without them and I could not function.   I began to search the web for anything on being married to a gay man. First I joined this group on yahoo.com and I was happy to find out I was not alone. The group was very helpful to me.   At first I just read and never responded.   But just reading helped me understand things better. Then I found Bonnie's website, and bought her first book.   After reading it I knew that I had to get out of this marriage because I would never be happy.

It was so hard for me to leave. I WAS TERRIFIED. I didn't want to be alone, and was afraid of financial responsibilities.   But I knew I had to GET OUT!!!! On October 15, 2003, I filed for divorce. On October 21, 2003 I was attacked by his family and forced to leave my home and children. My life was threatened if I returned (home was on his family property). I lived with my sister for 6 weeks. The only thing I had was the clothes I had on, and my car.   I only saw my children for 20 minutes maybe twice a week. He even made me meet at the police station to see the boys, like I was a criminal. Any way if I told you the whole story of being married to a gay man it would be a book.

Now 5 months later I have my own home, joint custody of the children and child support. I have met a wonderful straight man who makes me feel like a woman should feel. He is passionate, warm, funny and very, very affectionate. And I cherish every moment that we are together. I look back on this journey and I smile because I did it. I left, I knew I deserved better and I wanted better. Being married to a gay man is one of the most devastating things that can ever happen to you. But there is hope. Bonnie told me I would never regret leaving and I stand proud to say I don't regret it and I never ever will regret getting out of that dysfunctional marriage. I am so happy now even though the divorce is not over (we go to court for the last time 4-15-04) I wake up every day and smile knowing I'm not in that marriage anymore.   Please don't give up, there is a way out. You will have some hard days, but it won't be nothing like what you go through living with a gay husband.

I am still on the road to recovery, and I still struggle with issues, but now I face each day with a smile knowing that I made that step. I have had some difficult situations to deal with, but I just use them as building blocks to help me reach the top. I hope that I have encouraged someone out there who has just started this journey. Please don't give up. There is a pot of gold at the end of the rainbow; you just have to believe.

Connie

* * * * *

Dear Bonnie,

I've spent some time thinking over the past few years of my life lately, and have some things I need to share with you! It's been a long, tough journey. Without the support and love of you, and friends from chat, I am not sure I would have made it through.

I was never able to prove for sure that my husband was gay, although all signs pointed to it. The lack of physical and emotional intimacy from very early in our marriage, perverse and denigrating sexuality, outright attractions to other men, extreme anger at life, pornography, and work addictions, and the list goes on. He lives now with a young man from his church, but more than that I still don't know. What I wanted to share with you though, is that regardless of whether he is Gay or not.....The abuse I went through in the marriage was completely unacceptable, and was grounds enough to leave the marriage regardless of his sexual orientation. It was hard for me to get my brain around that.....I felt if I just had proof he was a gay man......I could shout that to the world, and the Church, and I would be justified in leaving him. That I lived thru 23 years of Psychological, Physical;

Financial and Sexual abuse with an emotionally void man didn't even seem to enter into the picture!

No woman deserves to be shoved around, no woman deserves to be subjected to denigrating or perverted sexuality, no woman deserves to have her finances under the control of another, no woman deserves to be emotionally, or physically beaten, no women deserves to live life with an emotionally void, secretive man. Regardless of whether I was able to confirm my husband was gay, getting me safe on the outside, so that I could heal on the inside, was the most important thing! Once free of the oppression of this man, I was able to start thinking clearly. 3 years later, I am close to being Divorced, completely self sufficient, and in a healthy relationship with a man who treats me with the utmost respect and dignity. I feel whole and complete now, for probably the first time in my life!

Thank you Bonnie for walking with me.....

Much Love,

Grace

* * * * *

Dear, Bonnie,

Thank you for your resent inquiry to see how I was doing. I haven't been in touch with you for a long time. I finally am divorced since April 28th. I knew my husband was gay deep down inside. I too longed for proof to find so I could actually feel at piece over my feelings and pain. My ex did not desire me shortly after our marriage. The only time we would have sex is when he had a lot to drink. The sex was all I knew as far as the way he performed it. Also in time I knew it was only a release or to prove to himself he could do it. Basically it was very cold. In time his reasoning was all my fault. From how I treated him to how I was always busy in other things. Some of his reasons were very heart breaking. I blamed myself and questioned what did I do wrong? I stayed in shape always tried to look attractive and always had many compliments. (not from him) As time progressed our marriage of 19 years fell apart and all the blame was put on me. I still have trouble getting over my depression and the low self-esteem he created for me. I long for a straight man in my life who wants me sexually and loves me for who I am. I tell myself constantly to hang on and know he will come soon into my life. We all deserve a new life and a straight relationship. My point is stay strong continue to tell yourself it wasn't you. No we may never have proof or even a confession but don't wait...it may never come. GET OUT!!! And oh by the way I have experienced sex with a straight man and let me tell you it sure is different than a gay man!!!!! Look forward to it.

BF

*　*　*　*　*

Bonnie,

You are dead on about the abuse aspect of our situation.

I remember during the year and a half I/we were trying to salvage our marriage, I went to confession. During one confessional, I told the priest that my husband was gay, and I wanted him to die. I felt so much hate toward him and I was so hurt. And the first thing he said to me was "God does not want you to be in an abusive relationship."

What???!!! Me??? In an abusive relationship??? WHAT???!!! It took me days to internalize what he said. I couldn't believe that I was participating in an abusive relationship. I was so in shock about it. I mean, I was an educated woman! I was smart! I would NEVER have stayed in a physically abusive relationship. So somehow this had to be different, right?

It completely missed the radar. It was also quite an eye opener. It was hard for me to grasp because it gradually became worse over the years we were together. It started out subtly. By the time I had visited the priest, He had been messing around with men for 5 or so years, and had stopped "messing" with me about 3 years prior.

Now that I am detached from the situation, I look back at those times and realize why it happened this way. I understand why the emotional abuse occurred. I suddenly became the poster child for all he could not be - he could not be straight. If I tried to approach him for affection, he would chide me or use some sort of conversational situation to keep me away. It was easier for him that way. He knew he couldn't "perform", and he also wasn't ready to face the truth or come out to me with honesty. So, he used emotional abuse to keep me away. It worked.

My ex and I maintain a very cordial and friendly relationship. Our marriage failed but our relationship is a success. I also remarried a

straight man a couple of months ago. So, life does go on...
    Regards,
    Jill

✱   ✱   ✱   ✱   ✱

Hi Bonnie:
    I have been getting your newsletter for a few years and I LOVE IT!! I was married to a man for about 12 years who was gay and "fighting" those feelings. Throughout our entire marriage, I had to fight for his attention, his support and his part of the parenting. Finally, I could not take much more and asked for a divorce. Then and only then did he admit to it. That revelation opened the other end of the package for me. Many years I was dealing with ½ of an opened box. Unfortunately, what was to come was not pleasant. It was MY fault that he was Gay. It was NOT the fact that he knew at an early age and suppressed it. Three gorgeous daughters later, this is what I had to crawl through. I begged him not to tell them, a counselor begged him. Our counselor felt that divorce was enough for three children under the age of 7 had to deal with. The time to bring them up to date would eventually follow; just not at this time. However, that was not to be. Their father decided that they needed to know that because I wanted to divorce their father, he has decided to be Gay. As you can imagine I had my work cut out for me.
    Four years later we are doing well. I am proud to say that the things we deal with are somewhat normal, i.e., boys, make-up, shopping!! We do have our moments. In between all of that I was able to reconnect with a very dear friend from 18 years ago. He had a divorce with its own circumstances. However, we are married and in the process of integrated our families.
    As far as my ex-husband is concerned, we are finally on the road to understanding and agreeing to disagree. Of course, I still battle the occasional innuendo from him that implies if I had not asked for the divorce, we would still be together. Sure, we might have, but we would also have been dealing with the ever-growing elephant in the room.
    Suzanne

✱   ✱   ✱   ✱   ✱

Hi Bonnie,

Sometimes I wake up and I can't believe I'm so happy and free.... I look back into last year...I am a totally different person.... it's like I have transformed from a caterpillar to a butterfly...even though I wasted so many years in my mismarriage...and I can't get those 13 years back...but now I am looking forward to many years with my new love.... Bonnie he is so wonderful...when I'm with him I am reminded of Aretha Franklin's song.... He makes me feel like a natural woman...he makes me feel loved, desired, needed, special, beautiful...I could go on and on....I want to help...I want to be support for pain pals...I think I can encourage someone out there who is afraid of leaving and starting their life over....Bonnie everyday and every night I pray to God and thank him for sending you to my life..Because of you I have a bright and wonderful future to look forward to...love you.

Connie

* * * * *

Bonnie,

I want to thank you for your newsletter. Your words and the other peoples, even after 5 years being divorced, make me feel stronger when I read them. It reinforces things for me. It's like my monthly boost of confidence. I say this because I am in an usual situation. I still own a business with my ex. We work together 6 days a week. He did all the usual things, denial, treating me badly, making me feel like things were my fault; we all know the game.....

Anyway by the time I got to my senses and realized I COULD get out, he was in a full blown relationship and basically staying with this man at night and sneaking home in the morning. Before that, he actually had this man stay over OUR house in his bedroom. Imagining finding that when you wake up in the morning. I put my foot down and said not in my house, that's why he was sneaking and staying at the boyfriend's house. Anyway, my stories could fill pages of what went on. When I read what you say, I finally understand why I put up with this. I had always questioned myself. I am a smart business person. What was I thinking?

I had gone to counseling before I confronted and outted him. I still continue to do so every other week. I am still working on my self-esteem and working on understanding to try to start on a new

195

relationship with a heterosexual man. My ex was my one and only boyfriend. We started going out when I was 15. I have been on dates since the divorce. I had a long distance relationship with someone for 4 years after my divorce. That was easy. I think that's why I did that. I am ready for a relationship now and I am having a real hard time trusting. Men say I won't let them in. I have had too many men in my life let me down. I guess I still have unresolved issues there. I feel great; I would just like someone to share my life with. Anyway, I have had 3 different counselors to date. One started to act like my dad, was pushing me to hard. I knew it was time to change. I really don't think the counselors get it. It helps but I don't think the truly understand the depth of what I have been through. It shakes you to your core. It questions everything you have done and everything you are. Since, I was with my ex so long, I really didn't know what I liked, who I was, what I wanted. He controlled so much of my life for the majority of it.

I am 45 now. I was married 20 years. I have been divorced 5. I am feeling great. I have lost a lot of weight, have I more to go. I am like a new person, rediscovering myself. I feel like a teenager. He wasted a good portion of my life with him but I have 2 great kids and I thank God everyday for them. I feel if not for the marriage, I would not have those beautiful children that I love so much. They got me through all this. I was strong for them. They have been the ones hurt the most in all this. I do not think the men think about them. I wanted so much more for my children. I can only hope I did what was right for them.

Your newsletters have answered a lot of my questions. They make me feel like I was not alone in all this. Years ago, when I first found out, I was so ashamed. I only wish I knew about you back then. Thanks again for everything you do.

E.

* * * * *

Dear Bonnie,

I read your newsletter and I hurt for those others that have to go through a thing like me. I have been with my husband 35 years this year and 4 years prior to that dating.

I found out about my husband in 89 and I was in so much disbelief that I blocked it from my mind and he went to counseling for me and I did too. Then in 99 it came up again when I found some gay porn books hidden. I knew then it was still going on. I had a nervous breakdown for the second time in 10 years. I have been in and out of hospitals with suicidal intensions. Now I'm better but I can't get over the fact that my husband has been gay all these years and before our marriage. I feel trapped. I still love and care about him and I am disabled and have limited income and could not make it on my own. Am I to stay in a miserable state just because I see no way out? I can't see leaving him as everyone thinks we are the perfect couple married 35 years and childhood sweethearts. I also can't see staying forever and be heartbroken. I feel like a heavy dark cloud is over me. I'm in deep depression. There is no sex no kisses to speak of and hardly a hug. The only hugs I get are from the grandkids. I don't know what I would do without them.

Signed, Confused in Fl.

* * * * *

Hi Bonnie-

As always - thank you for your newsletter. Though I am one of those lucky women who have moved on... little things still surface and remind me where I came from and your newsletter often does that. This one especially! And to be honest, I don't want to forget because now I can see how much I have grown. Below you stated something that is so very true:

"One of life's great lessons to me is that the most important person to receive love from is YOU. This means that you need to find yourself again or the person you were before you married your gay husband. Most of us lose ourselves in our marriages to our gay husbands because we are trying so hard to be who we are not, just like they are trying to be who they are not."

Just a few weeks ago I was trying to explain to my boyfriend that sometimes I may be hesitant in my decision making process and that it has nothing to do with him....but that I struggle in myself for the balance to *love him freely and to never lose myself again*! Because of my marriage to a gay man (15+ years) I am so programmed to please in order to be loved. I have to be very aware of my own actions and I don't ever want to lose myself again.....it was a very painful process to realize that I gave away my dreams and who

I was to keep the relationship with my former husband. I had not even realized that I had done that until I was out of it. I also now know what it is like to have someone love me for who I am. The good, bad and ugly! :-}

Thank you and I will talk to you later!

Odetta

*　*　*　*　*

Dear Bonnie –

I am so proud to write this letter. I have finally filed for divorce from my Gay husband!

I remember searching the internet after finding Gay porn on our home computer. I came across "Bisexuality" and similar sites. However, the best thing I came across was YOU. That was over two years ago. After discovering your Website and Newsletter I began my quest to find the truth.

I just knew something was not right with my marriage and my husband. We had been married six years and together a total of seven. I am now 37 and he is now 43; however, we never made love and he became increasingly more and more critical of me. I had begun to suspect he was having an affair or that he might be Gay.

I had always been this independent, magnetic, high-energy woman. I knew I was attractive, but always felt my personality and brains were my best features. When I met my husband, I owned my home that was paid for (at age 30…bought it when I was 19). I had money in the Bank, dated constantly and swore, "I'd never get married." When I met my GH, he however, had bad hair, bad credit and lived in a 1 bedroom apartment. However, I still fell for him hook line and sinker. Love truly can be blind. For a while anyway.

I cleaned up his look, his credit and moved him into my home. I rescued him continuously from a failed business and continuous unemployment. I was the steady. I loved his parents and took care of them until they both subsequently passed away. I did everything for him. It started out slow (he was the lost puppy I needed to rescue) and eventually I ended up doing EVERYTHING. And he resented me for it too! When he was down and out, I was the greatest. When he had a job and was earning a decent pay check, he turned into a cold, mean and selfish person. Disconnected is the best way to describe him.

This was the slow tortuous process of manipulation I experienced. It is all a mind game to convince you that YOU are the problem, when your Gay husband knows dam well what the real problem is. I am now convinced my Gay husband was nothing more than a sociopath. Scary.

Your February Newsletter inspired me to write to you. I too am tired of playing "detective." It was consuming me. I was allowing this deceitful and selfish man to steal my self-esteem and my spirit. I broke the pass code and got into his e-mail and found an e-mail proving once and for all that he was in fact GAY! It read exactly like this:

"Thank you for your kind note. I too don't look like, act like, walk like, talk like...nobody ever would think might be eh? **[As if it was a joke that he could fool everyone]**. I am a 36-year-old male with a serious business side; I think you'll like the entire package. I'm looking to hook up with a black male, anything mutual and SAFE."

After I picked myself up off the floor (I'm not kidding), I literally slipped off the chair in my office when I jumped back. Several things in his e-mail immediately struck me. The first was that he was lying about his age. Can you believe it? It's bad enough he is lying to his wife and everyone else, but he could not even be honest in the Gay world. He is 42...not 36. The other thing that struck me is his reference to his "package." Eh um...his "package" is rather small (smirk). The ONLY thing that gave me ANY relief whatsoever is that he capitalized the words SAFE.

Now that I have let this "cat out of the bag" to my friends and family (that took awhile), we have all had a chuckle over his lying e-mail. But please do not think I find this deplorable situation in the least bit funny. This has been one painful journey for me.

I have gone through several stages to get to this point. Here they are:

1. Denial – No way, it can't be so...it must be my fault! I'm not doing enough for him. I'm not a good enough wife.
2. Anger – Why isn't anything I ever do good enough? I'm not pretty enough, thin enough, clever & witty enough. I probably expect too much from him and I am too demanding. The list was endless. However, deep down, the anger was building like a Volcano.

3. Grief – Depression, uncontrollable crying, hopelessness, feeling worthless, unable to climb out of bed. Drained by my knowledge rather than relieved.
4. Acceptance – I have realized it's not me. IT'S HIM! I finally filed for divorce on February10, 2005. After seven years of marriage and TWO wasted years of stages 1 through 3, while playing "detective," I spoiled his Valentine's Day!

I'm now working on my final stage:
5. Gratification. I will become not only the person I was before I married my Gay husband, but even better. I will be stronger, wiser, and hopefully more humbled and compassionate toward other people going through divorce. Gay or not Gay, it is horrible!

I finally got up the courage to contact his ex-wife. (Another reason why your February Newsletter inspired me). Apparently he had 10 jobs in 10 years with her. And he had 5 jobs in 6 years with me. She made me feel better. I wasn't crazy. He was distant and cold to her as well. Her friends tried to tell her he was Gay, but she didn't believe it either.

I take responsibility for my part in all of this. I didn't follow my instincts. I found excuses to stay married because I wanted to believe in the fairytale more than in my life. Thankfully we have no children to burden with this mess. Yes, I am still sad. I wanted children. Five years into the marriage, HE decided we would have a better life without children. I would agree to anything just to please him and gain a few "crumbs" of affection.

He was working on his next victim until a few weeks ago. During my draining work as a "detective" I found out her name, and her roommates cell phone number, so I called the friend and told her to warn her girlfriend about my husband. (I figured it may come easier hearing it from someone other than me). Especially because I heard through the "grapevine" that my husband is playing the poor little abused victim in all this. He has portrayed me as an irresponsible drunk that spent "all his money." (What a joke). He had NOTHING when he met me and would not have a pot to pea in now if it were not for me. See how easily they fool the next woman? Poor, poor me…my ex-wife was just so awful, blah, blah, blah.

Believe me, I'm no Angel. I know there was more than one occasion in the last 2 years that I have drank too much wine, but I was incredulous when I found out the B.S. that was spewing from his mouth.

What the heck, I can't save the world, but he is still MY Gay husband for now, until the papers are final. I'll be dammed if I'm going to allow him to do this to another woman on my watch.

Wow...there are so many great things both you and other women have shared that knocked me in the head like a lightning bolt. Thanks, I needed that.

Please feel free to share my letter if you want to. I would also like to know how to get into your "chat" room. I recall something about it earlier when I looked into your Website.

This is still extremely difficult on me and I could use some continued support. I would also like to offer my support to anyone out there that is still in what I call "Stage 1, 2 or 3."

Thank you so much Bonnie –

Rox

*   *   *   *   *

Hi Bonnie and all the ladies who contributed to the newsletter

Just over four weeks have passed since my spouse of 20 years (husband now seems too intimate a word) emailed me at work to ask my opinion of him spending "an over-nighty with a boy" I have been on an emotional roller coaster. Hate, anger, love, compassion, denial, and loneliness - the whole gambit of human emotions seems to flood your mind, body and soul. The burning question of WHY? Lingers in every thought. Tears come at the most inappropriate times, I am ashamed of my weakness - I know he is the one squarely where the blame lies but I question myself just like so many women in your newsletter. I wanted to thank you for sending me all the back issues of the newsletter. Each morning I would get up just a little bit earlier than necessary and have my coffee while reading about 5 pages. It was the best reinforcement and support I could have asked for and often that is what it takes to get thru another day. I started a journal at the same time so that I could talk to someone - even if that someone was me.

All of the ladies in your newsletter gave me the courage to confront him in a bold manner. I know he is now a "cake and eat it

too" gay man who is using me financially and emotionally. Until I read the newsletter, I never realized how much I missed physical contact even if it was just a hug. I have to beg for even the smallest gesture of affection that he would give so willingly to a stranger for a few moments of lust. I realized how much I have changed my whole demeanor to conform to his ideal of a wife. I am looking for a place that I can afford on my own despite that he wants to stay together - yeah right until the man of his dreams comes along!! We are fortunate not to have any children but we do run a business together in the horse industry and I have the position of Executive Director for the largest horse association in the country while he is a coach and judge. We are known as one of the happiest lucky couples - amazing how easily people are fooled. I will continue to stay in touch and would love to join in on a chat room discussion but the timing has not been right. Thank you so very much to all of the wonderful ladies who survived the ordeal of total rejection.
Vicki

*　*　*　*　*

Dear Bonnie:
I was re-reading your June letter again, had I paid attention to it closely I wouldn't be writing this message. But at stated in your letter, we straight wives always fail because we want to believe that our gay husband will change or can change when in reality that doesn't exist.
Let me tell you how he got me to think again that things could work out, he started to call me again after getting our marriage annulled, and talking nice to me where I felt so comfortable that I bought into his words, he even told me that we didn't even have grounds for being divorce, since neither one has committed adultery. Well, it went on so I started to think it would possible to go back. He even told me about the plants I put in his yard were doing so beautiful that I should go by the house to look at them, to me that was a clear invitation that I felt for.
Well, on Saturday after getting my hair cut, I called him just as we had agreed to. I got there and we saw them, everything went fine, until I hold his hand and started to kiss him to what he refused and say that I was stealing kisses that he would kiss me but if not to steal them. We continue to look at the nice evening view over the mountain, and reminiscing of everything that had happened ever since we

divorced. We had the most beautiful conversation, so I continue to want to kiss him and to sit down. He was resisting it, but he would kiss me here and there. So, then he decided to go in the house, I grabbed him as made him sit with in the sofa, to what he told he didn't want to have sex, I said, who wants to have sex, I just want to hold you close. Then, he said do you know that this could be sexual harassment? I said, I know but I'm not harassing you, you are my husband didn't you tell me that we don't have ground for being divorce? So he said, "Well no, I see the advantage of the relationship, but you know I can't give you what you want." So, I left him alone. To make this story short, everything went smooth after that.

I felt sad again with the realization that nothing had changed since last time. I had the only one mislead again. But anyways he went to my car to say goodbye with a very sweet kiss in my mouse, till then I had no idea of what was coming next. The following week on Monday, July 4, my mother woke me up, saying that I had a phone call from the city he lives in. Picked up the phone, it was from the police department, telling me about a report my ex- had complained about sexual assault, the office told me that nothing to fear, he was not going to arrest me or anything, but he was calling to warm me that he had reported it, and to prevent that I get in trouble because he told them he is gay and he doesn't want it to happen again. I was so shock like never, ever before in my entire life. I was so afraid at that point because I didn't want my mother to hear the conversation I was having with the officer so that she wouldn't worry. It was awful to realize what these undesirable persons are capable of doing. I feel so humiliated, I had to call my lawyer to tell him what had happened, and he couldn't believe he just suggested that I leave him alone for good, which I intend to do. He asked who had initiated this second attempt to reconcile. I said him.

Bonnie I just wish I could erase it from my life, but I know that's not possible. The one thing I hope is that solve the issue with credit cards we have still going on, and to ever never see him again. I don't even want to talk to him, if ever see him I plan not to acknowledge him, he deserves that and more. You don't do to somebody like me that I have been so good to him what he did.

Thank you for being there for us, sharing your experience. I know at the end of the road there is hope for every woman in this same

situation. You are proof of that.
  (Name Withheld)

                    *   *   *   *   *

Bonnie,
  First of all, I have to say "heyyyyyyyyyyyyyyyyyyyyyyyyy." It's been a little while since I emailed you. All is well...I am finally embracing singleness without feeling like a fish out of water. Instead of it being scary to try new things and explore parts of myself that had been "in the closet" with my ex-gay husband, I am now hopeful and inspired to be open and true to myself.
  I just finished reading the June newsletter and had to write you. Oh my God, I could relate to so much that you said. You know my story as I wrote you some years back and you were sooooooooooooooo supportive of me. And I have to agree with you. This thing about being best friends, soul mates and all that with a gay husband, except sex, is preposterous. Oh the things we tell ourselves to help us stay into unsatisfying relationships. I agree. It is ABNORMAL not only to be married to a gay man but to be accepting of it. Marriage, by its on design and definition, is a public celebration of the level of intimacy attained in a female-male relationship. It says to the world that you've picked a person to share your life with and that you trust this person so much as to put yourself in vulnerable reciprocity to them. It is the ultimate definition of unselfishness that deepens over time. I know that may sound lofty in this day and age, but I truly believe that this is what God had in mind. What sets marriage apart from any other relationship? The depth of intimacy. Even in various cultures, sex consummates the marital union. I agree that without sex you don't have a marriage. You have an arrangement but not a marriage.
  I can remember that even when my gay ex and I were "getting along" gingerly, there was always that feeling of lack in the pit of my stomach. There was always that fleeting sadness that got more and more intense as the realization hit that my husband preferred a fun filled platonic relationship and didn't even contemplate, think about, desire, ponder sex with me. It was like he was showing me a "better way." Like saying "See, we don't need sex to be happy." Ain't that an absolute CROCK.
  And I've had friends to say that no situation is any different and my feelings are no different than the ones they felt when their

"straight" husbands cheated on them with other women. I beg to differ. You've said it in your own words. How can it be the same when your very wiring, your very plumbing, your very feminine essence makes him want to puke. I remember that when I simply wanted to plant a wet, juicy, sensual kiss on my gay ex's lips, he would jump in horror like I was molesting him or something. He would be startled and almost fight me off. That is not friendship!!!

A friend does not withhold good things from another, KNOWING he is denying you something that you should be getting whenever the mood hits you. It's like your very loving, feminine, sensual essence is being drained and you don't know why the very life is being stolen from you yet he knows why. A friend doesn't do that to another friend. You don't pretend that everything is hunky dory and you are stealing from me. You are benefiting from everything about me at my expense. That is soooooooooo cruel. And I feel sorry for women who have set their standards so low for whatever reason.

I don't plan on being alone and I am convinced that I don't have to be; but if I had the choice between being lonely with a gay man and being lonely with myself, I'd prefer myself. At least it's real. At least, I'm not dissin' me. At least, I know why I am lonely. And at least, there is room for some other straight man who is just waiting for me to show up so he can swoop me up!!!!! Hey!!!!! I don't want to be the go-to girl for when his other relationships don't go right. I want to be NUMBER ONE, not number two, three, four, five, six......one hundred. If he isn't available for me, then why in the world am I keeping the porch light on for him. He isn't doing enough to deserve that kind of loyalty. And I'm happy to report that this is not only true when it comes to gay men, but straight men who think they should be given special attention just because they exist. I believe that men only respect what they have to work for. And someone said "you teach people how to treat you." And the longer I live and experience life, the truer that saying is for me.

So, thanks Bonnie. Keep telling us the truth. Might not be right now with every woman, but the day will come that the smoke will clear and reveal what substandard lives we have lived. And we'll pull out our newsletters and be sooooooooooo relieved that there is support and life outside the closet.

Suzette

*   *   *   *   *

205

Dear Bonnie,

Remember me, Lynn in Florida. I'm 53 and still with my Gay/Bi husband. I found out 10 years ago and I have been on an emotional roller coaster the last 35 years trying to figure out what was going on. I had learned to put aside the Gay and tried to except my husband as my best friend, companion, to stay married because I loved him, and I'm disabled on an $800 a month income. I am trapped. I read in your newsletter and felt like you were talking to me. Wow! Best friends don't lie to you or try to deceive you. Companions want to spend time with you not just when it's their interest. I go to car shows and get together with his friends. He won't even sit at the table with me to eat. He is so interested in TV that I cannot talk to him about anything. At night it's "Too late to talk." Some companion. I feel so lonely and beat down emotionally that I believe almost everything he tells me.

I asked him if the doors were locked yesterday and he said why? No one would want you. He laughed and I thought about what he said and became angry. That was a put down. He said it was just a tease, but I believe it. No one would ever want me if I were to separate. I'm too fat, poor health and depressed all coming about after I found out the truth. When he told me that he had been with many men throughout our marriage, I just thought that if he really loved me he would have taken precautions in and out of the marriage. They were all casual sex. Many he just met on the prowl. Maybe he has a sexual addiction to men. Thank you for being there for all of us. May God bless you. So many of us are hurting and feel stuck with the nice guys. Everyone thinks we are the perfect couple. If they only knew

Lynn

✳ ✳ ✳ ✳ ✳

Dear Bonnie:

Thank you for the July newsletter. I especially felt akin to the letter from Suzette. She is strong and true in her definition of this dysfunctional and wasted-life marriage between gay men and straight women. She addressed the matter so well and it struck many similar cords in my life's current situation. It helps to see the written word to help sort out what really is happening in my life. I am so sad to hear this happens in so many other marriages.

This marriage set-up is still so foreign to me, yet I have been living it for 10+ years, but unable to define and diagnose what has caused my marital sadness. (So much has come to light for me recently, in the last couple of months.) Also, and especially, since reading your book, as well as your newsletters, I have been helped immeasurably, tremendously.

To realize the cause of my misery and sadness helps me feel understood, and at least like I am not the only one and that I should not feel guilty anymore for my suspicions of this man. He is one of those who thinks that though he had several relations with gay men as he grew up and even into early adulthood (which he just confessed based on information revealed by his ex-wife), but he states that he then made a choice that he preferred women and left all that past history behind once he met a woman he wanted to be with (his first wife who says it was the "marriage from hell"). My marital experience has been: this cold, verbally-abusive, sometimes-here-and-there-fleeting-sexual-moments, sometimes-fun-and-friendship-here-and-there-moments, hate-filled, laughter-and-jokes, threatening, selfish, frightening, and insult-throwing, sometimes-soft-and gentle, sometimes-rage-filled-and-tantrum-throwing marriage-partner kept me confused, took me down from a soft, loving, confident woman, to someone I hardly know anymore...I don't recognize myself. I have lost who I am in this marriage; this is a form of cruel torture to be in this type of marriage. I just wish he would be truthful and admit what he tries so hard to hide, even from himself, perhaps. But, I am fairly certain he never will admit. He is the example of the gay man who is in denial and will probably always be. I am sure that once this marriage ends, he will find another woman to fill my role in his life (poor unsuspecting person, whoever she might be). He is so handsome and so masculine appearing, that no one would believe this about him. He is also so narcissistic, as well as admitting that he is quite taken by a fine male body (he finds no problem with saying that because he is so self-body conscious and once was a body-builder). Yet he never makes usual male type comments or gives long (or even short) looks towards a lovely woman (though this would make for jealousy, it is still common for a man to show some appreciation for a good-looking woman now and then, but this doesn't happen with him).

He told me when we met and first married that he did not have a huge sex-drive. After 7 years of being single and having to deal with men who only wanted sex on dates, it seemed refreshing and even respectful that he wasn't out for just sex. Thus began the snow job on me and I blame myself too for not seeing this as a potential problem. I really believed that the marriage vows would release the passion in him. He "performed" as a somewhat believable passionate husband for awhile early in the marriage, but it just never reached close to the height of passion I have always felt, nor was it the great experience a woman has with a man who is straight (it was something in between that I just could not identify, did not want to face, and learned to accept as "his way", yet it was so unfulfilling for me). He was quite clever at making me feel like I was not the adequate one (not sure how he did this, but I began to feel shaken and believed I was losing it as a sexual partner, and felt more and more undesirable).

I was not educated at all about gay men, never thought I had to be because who would have thought that a gay man would have any interest in a woman. He even called me his best friend so often, but I just thought this was another good thing...you and your husband should be best friends. Recently, he told me that when we married, he committed to a good friendship with me. I was shocked! I said I committed to a loving husband/wife relationship with him. I realized more and more that this was never going to be the deep, meaningful, close, intimate, passionate relationship that I had dreamed of. I felt sick. I was so confused about what it really was though. Now, I see and have been almost physically ill over it whenever I think of what it is and has been. I cry inside for the death of what I had hoped it would be). Now, I just want to be me again and not to be distrusting or cold myself. Lacking intimacy has made me force myself to not want it. Yet, I want it so much. It is horrible, because I am a very sensual, sexual, loving person. I have given up so much, missed out on so much. I want him to go to where and whom he needs. I want to reclaim myself.

Reading your book, as well as your newsletters, has helped immeasurably, tremendously. I feel hope and see a light at the end of my tunnel. Thank God! All I am waiting for at this place in time is to find a good-paying job so that I can take care of myself and get on with my life. I know there will be other obstacles in getting out of this marriage, but at least I have finally found the strength within myself to make the change that needs to be made. I don't hate my husband. I feel deceived. I know he will get along just fine because he is a true survivor, so I do not worry about him. I am numb and still indifferent about him, but I don't wish him any misery. I just need to focus on myself now (all this time in this marriage I have given love and focus to him); it's my turn.

Well, Bonnie, thank you for listening. I feel blessed and fortunate to have you there to talk and listen to in this huge painful matter in my life. I know you truly feel and empathize with this problem (a problem I share with so many, each with our own situation). I agree with your direct approach. A gay man has no business being married to a straight woman. It is not a healthy marital relationship. If gay and straight have a friendship, that's fine. But it should not ever be a marriage. They can never fulfill each other in a way that marriage requires.

Barbara

*   *   *   *   *

Bonnie,

I love reading your newsletters, but wanted to remind others out there not all gay spouses are uninterested in sex. I am married to a perfectionist, overly critical to others yet hypersensitive to even the most innocent criticism toward him. He always has to be the best at everything - he was raised to think this is the way the world works and you have to care what others think about you... he has to have the best house, the best car, the best career - and he thrives at almost all he does. He is an executive at a prestigious company and plays that role well. Having a wife and kids helps maintain that 'image' of the perfect guy. He does initiate sex (I do not want it) -- he refers to me as 'his wife' and says a husband is supposed to make love to his wife...he gets upset if we do not have sex. He has no idea it is not his right or obligation! Is he not gay? Of course he is gay... the signs were all there. From his anger lashing out over silly unimportant thing, especially women (he has a deep seated disrespect of women) and acting giddy around the guys, to the internet gay porn , to the ridiculous excuses for coming home late and the frequency of it, to the eventual discovery of gay chat and email propositions to other men from him for a 'round of golf and BJ at the turn'... though he denies, denies, denies - and makes every excuse he can to justify things - deep in my heart I know he is gay. Deep in my heart I realize he does not love me the way I need or deserve to be or be my full partner because he does not have the ability to fully partner with me - a woman... I am planning my exit -- though my plan encompasses a number of years (small kids and money reasons are keeping me here - for now)... I do enjoy my weekly therapy sessions and the knowledge of knowing this is not going to be the relationship my children see as 'normal' for the rest of their lives...

To all other readers, keep in mind lack of interest in sex is only one sign...but not a telltale sign...

Belinda

*　*　*　*　*

Dear Bonnie,

I wrote you a few months ago, just before your surgery. I had found out that my husband was downloading child porn off the internet (when the police arrived with a search warrant) and after being confronted he also admitted to being gay. The letter from 'B' was dead on. Her description of her marriage was mine. Her feelings of not knowing who she is any more is me. It is so freeing to read what I have been unable to express. My marriage will officially be over by the time you read this letter. Would I have ever had the courage to do it if he hadn't been found with internet child porn? Who knows, it doesn't matter anymore. The truth has set me free and I am free indeed!

To all you ladies who are wondering if you can make it on your own, or whether it's worth the risk--it's worth it! I have not had a single night since changing the locks that I had to deal with a temper tantrum over the dinner I had slaved to cook, no hissy fits about the laundry not be folded 'just so', no rage and anger strikes over the simplest of things--I have peace! I come home to a sanctuary! It is worth it for your sanity and that of your children! Have I had sleepless nights? Yes, but I had them before as I lay awake in fear of what would set him off the next day so I can handle it. Have I laid in bed and cried? But I cried before, silent tears of pain after being rejected in bed again or from overwhelming, aching loneliness and pent of passion, these tears are good ones that release the pain and bring healing so I can handle it. Do I worry about finances? Yes, but I worried before too only now I am learning to ask God to direct me and take care of my needs and He is doing it so I can handle it.

God will protect you and provide if you trust Him! I had no car to drive to work. I prayed to God and told him I needed a car and reminded him that I had no money and that I was trusting Him to provide a car. WITHIN 1 1/2 WEEKS I RECEIVED A PHONE CALL-- OUT OF THE BLUE--FROM SOMEONE WHO HAD DECIDED TO BUY A NEW CAR AND WOULD I WANT THEIR OLD ONE!!!!!! GOD WILL TAKE CARE OF YOU!

To the gal who wrote that the therapist says he has a sexual addiction problem. Be careful. My soon-to-be-ex's counselor is saying he has a sexual addiction problem too. BUT HE ISN'T INTERESTED IN SEX WITH WOMEN--don't let them label it nicely and send him back home. He MAY have an addiction problem BUT IT'S WITH MEN! My ex tried to worm his way back into our home using this label. An alcoholic is an addict so I will use this as my example: I told him an alcoholic drinks everything at home FIRST, then goes out looking for more. Since he never 'drank' at home I wasn't buying the counselors theory! Sex Addiction is just a pretty label to package him up and make him look legitimate again!

Well, anyway, glad I was able to get that off my chest. Honestly, ladies, just get out. Don't wait, don't plan, just get out. The peace and tranquility and immediate health you will begin to experience are far better than the hell you are living in. Feeling you are unloved and being unloved is like depriving flowers of water and watching them wither and die a slow and painful death. Your life has value and meaning and purpose and you are worth so much more than an existence of nothingness. Spread your wings, dare to dream, dare to fly. You can do it.

Patti

*   *   *   *   *

Dear Bonnie

Thank you for the awesome newsletter for August! WOW!!!

I sat here reading and reading and reading, and a couple of times I caught myself wanting to scream out, "THAT'S ME THEY ARE TALKING ABOUT"!!!!! How do they know this about my life??? I have goose bumps running up and down my spine, my arms, and my legs!! I cannot tell you how many of the letters I related to because I think a part of each one has a part of my life in it! I have been going over this for months and months and months now, trying to find my way out of this marriage and back into sanity!

Bonnie, I feel like a private investigator most days. My husband cannot speak without my subconscious telling me he is laying. Over the last few months, I have grown colder and more distant from him, finding more and more proof of his love for other men. Also Bonnie my husband has a huge boot fetish. He belongs to so many boot groups through yahoo and MSN and some I am sure I have not found out about yet, that all revert to gay/bi men who love their boots.

They all take pictures of themselves with nothing on but their boots! I have seen so many pictures of penises in the last 6 months it would make your head spin. These men get sexually aroused over boots. I do not understand this fetish. I have tried to justify it, but I cannot. My husband has over one hundred pair of cowboy boots, he tells me it's because he collects them. OHHHH bull!! I have found pictures of him having sex with the boots and then posting these pictures to the gay websites!! I told him I found them, he said it is all in fun, it means nothing; he says it gives the other guys pleasure and perhaps that is the only pleasure they get that day. He acts like he is doing them a service, when in reality he is finding his sexual outlet without physically cheating on me! At least right now anyway.

I am sitting here wanting to scream, wanting to cry, wanting to run, I can't explain everything I am feeling, I am so hurt, so mad, so downright pissed off at him! I pray that God helps me and I pray for all the women out there that have been hurt and deceived by these men.

I have tried to assure myself that if my husband was gay, he would not be turned on by me...he always initiates sex, always tells me I'm beautiful, his compliments are very sincere. I have told myself this same thing over and over and over. How can he be gay if he loves me??

I skate around here from day to day not knowing what kind of mood he will be in. One day he is funny and joking and loving, and all of us have a great day, the next day something as small as the newspaper flying off the table due to the ceiling fan ticks him off that he doesn't speak to me for a week! One minute happy, the next minute he is so hateful I could punch his lights out. He always tries to make me believe that I am crazy, tells me that I'm nuts, he doesn't act like this; I imagine it, that no one else has ever told him that he is mean or cruel. It's always me that is negative about him. I have finally realized that I'm not mean or cruel to him, but he has so many bottled up issues that I feel he snaps. Maybe when he realizes he is enjoying his family that all of a sudden his gay guilt causes his attitude to plummet and takes it out on us. I don't know.

I have read so many newsletters over the last several months and so many of your responses from your other readers, I could take a piece from every one of their stories and it would make up my life completely.

I do not know where I will be in another 6 months, I do not know if I will be here or if I will have finally gotten the nerve to do what has to be done. But all I know right now is that I feel so much better knowing that I am not in this mess alone, and to thank you for helping so many women rally together. If you would like to post my email please feel free to do so and if you want to put my email address with it that is fine also, as I would love to talk to some of these other women also.

Thank you Bonnie from the bottom of my heart, I know this email is a little babbled but I was just typing as fast as my mind was racing.

Anita

＊　＊　＊　＊　＊

Dear Bonnie,

Another of my passions is trying to help other women who are going through or have gone through "the gay thing" with their "husbands" - - for lack of a better term!!! Another long story shortened - - at age 29 (I am now 53) I married a man I had known for 10 years and been engaged to for 2 years! I really don't think I could have ever known anyone any better! Sam was a wonderful Southern gentleman, very well-educated and well-read, genius IQ, same values as I (so I was led to believe), gourmet cook, loved antiques - - my perfect man - - so I thought!

In short, I was married for 18 years to my (at one time) lover, best friend, and (I thought) "soul mate." I stuck by him through thick and thin, good and bad, several of his threatened suicides (though in hindsight, they may have just been ploys to get my sympathy), but he was never able to be trustworthy for long and could never be counted on to provide steadily for his family. I was the rock, the steady one. I finally grew tired of all of his deceit [thinking and even being told by psychiatrists that he was depressed ("that is why he has no interest in sex with you"), had had overly demanding parents as a child, and was passive-aggressive]. After all those years, and with a 7-year-old

213

daughter by him, I decided I could not take any more of his deceit and the lack of security I felt with him. (The lack of sex was there too, but it was just a small reason - - I could have lived without the sex, but I really did miss it so much! It had been wonderful in the beginning . . . .) Anyway, I did not want my daughter growing up in a household where we never knew whether Daddy would be coming home with a paycheck or not, or even where Daddy was on many occasions! (Offers to go to the grocery store for milk late at night and being gone for an hour, etc. - - and this was before cell phones!)

So I threw him out in 1998 and the divorce was final a year later. I started the new millennium as a free woman, but a woman who still felt very guilty for walking out on her marriage, and a woman really still in love with her husband, though unwilling to put up with his ways. (I took my marriage vows VERY seriously, having been raised in a strict Presbyterian household with wonderful strong parents and grandparents and no divorces in the family!)

Yes, looking back there were MANY clues over the years (read between the lines above!), but I really did not see them, though my father even asked me before the wedding if I was sure that Sam was not gay - - even my own father picked up the vibes all those years ago!! Anyway, I continued in denial, and continued to feel guilty for abandoning my husband, though I never even considered taking him back (nor did he ask, once the divorce was final). Finally, 3 years after our divorce (summer of 2002), I found out the truth and it hit me like the proverbial ton of bricks!!! An old high school friend of mine who had finally come out of the closet told me that Sam had approached him over the Internet through a gay website. I was devastated, but finally all of the pieces of the puzzle fit!!! Much trauma and gnashing of the teeth, crying, total agony that I had lived with this all those years, testing for AIDS and other STDs (even though it had been about 8 years since Sam and I had had sex!!) at the Health Department the next day after learning the truth (I thank God that I am disease-free). But I really don't think I could have handled this knowledge at the time of the divorce - - that would have been too much overload!! God knows what He is doing! Thanks (?) to network TV ("Will & Grace") and other media, my daughter had started asking me 2 years earlier if Sam was gay - - at age 9 she had figured out that all of his friends were gay (they were becoming more flamboyant as their parents were dying off and she had picked up on this on her weekends with Sam - - of course, I was no longer seeing his friends). Anyway, about 2 weeks after I found out about Sam, I finally got him to face our then 11-year-old daughter and tell her the truth (she had been asking me for 2 weeks why I was so upset and crying all of the time and I thought she needed to hear this with both of us present). She took it well, but fell apart a couple of hours later when the reality hit her. I still have her working with a therapist, though much of that work now centers around normal teenage girl issues, thank goodness, instead of her gay father issues - - though they do crop up from time to time and she is very afraid that her friends (both girls and boys) will find out about him. Sam now has a "man-panion" and that upsets her greatly - - she has not met "the lover" and does not want to, of course. As she says: "Gross out!!!"

Anyway, I had been overweight - - a "fatty" - - all of my life with the small exception of a few years in college when I was a little smaller than the size I am now. I'm sure that my lack of self esteem from weight issues played into Sam's hands when he chose me to marry - - I'm a classic example of the theories about women unknowingly married to gay men. But when I found out about Sam and began working through my anger and feelings all around that issue, it was like a light went off!! I finally gave myself permission to pay attention to myself! Within 3 months of learning about Sam, I was considering RNY surgery and within another 3 months I had found Dr. Rutledge and the MGB. I had my surgery at the end of June 2003. The truth really does set you free!!! God is good!! It has been amazing to me how all of this has tied together.

I've had a couple of dates in the last few months, but nothing of any interest or promise. I do hope that God has a good man picked out somewhere for me, but in the meantime, I am very happy with my life. I have a beautiful 14-year-old daughter that would not be here if God had not put me with Sam for all those years - - she is worth every bit of the anguish and pain that I have had. I feel great, I have NO medical problems, and I think I look pretty good, though no men ever "hit" on me. But then, men never have really "hit" on me - - must be my defective personality!! LOL!!!

Well, I'm sure that this is WAY more than you ever wanted to know about me. I do find that the thing that seems to help us the most as wives, ex-wives, and someday-to-be-ex-wives of gay men, is talking and sharing with each other. No one can really grasp or appreciate our special pain but another spouse who has been in our shoes. The pain is indescribable. I have found it very helpful to read everything I have been able to find on the subject (Bonnie's books are great!) and to listen as well as share with anyone who wants to share or vent.

Carol C.

* * * * *

Hi Bonnie,

My name is Kathy and I appreciate your newsletters and support. I don't feel nearly so isolated and alone now as I have felt being in this confusing and cruel marriage for the last 15 years. As I read the info you sent, I couldn't get over how similar the stories are. So very many things that I have struggled to understand during our marriage and that just never made sense no matter what spin I put on them, now are crystal clear. Smoke and mirrors. That's what we live with. Nothing is real, just an illusion created to keep our husbands secret.

If someone would have told me years ago that I would allow myself or my children for that matter to be subjected to a life like this I would have been incensed! I would never allow that to happen! After all I was an intelligent and articulate woman. And yet, here I am looking back, and thankfully now looking forward, realizing that none of us can blame ourselves. We were not living within a valid and true relationship. Love can't exist where it isn't reciprocated. These men are not available to love us. So many of the women I read about talk about having lost themselves in the marriage. To say I can relate is an understatement. Empty. That's what I was for so many years and that is how they are able to persuade us that all the problems are our fault. No healthy woman would buy that explanation.

Life is less confusing, less painful, and less overwhelming since I found out my husband is gay. We tried a "family vacation" shortly after I "talked" to you the first time. While there were some lousy times, we also had some good times. The lesson I took from the experience was to remove the word "Until" from my vocabulary. I have spent the entire time we have been married rationalizing and wishing away my today's. Telling myself "until we have_____, or until he isn't working so hard, or until I am _____." I cannot spend any more energy on that way of thinking. I am focused on my two children and building a new, happier, healthier life for all three of us.

My guess is that my husband will just go back to burying his head in the sand (i.e. work) and find excuses not to deal with anything he needs to deal with. His choice. For me it is onward and upward.

Thanks to you and all of the women who bravely shared their feelings and bared their souls. It is a tremendous support to know that someone else wouldn't think you were crazy if you told them what life "really" was like. Not only wouldn't they think I was crazy, but for the first time in years I felt total relief. I have had one after another "light bulb moments" where things made sense. I'm beginning to see the woman I used to be. She shows up in my actions and my thoughts and it's like finding an old friend. That is the greatest cruelty- the taking of someone else's soul and self for the purpose of keeping a gay husband's secret. It seems as if they do it without thought, notice or remorse. How very sad.

All the years I've heard my husband say "I love you" and always felt something was lacking. No real emotion or passion; they were just words. Someday I hope to hear someone say "I love you" and be able to hear those words with an unburdened heart. For now it is enough to know that he is incapable of loving anyone right now. His first step will have to be learning to like himself. I am taking steps to protect my kids and myself and to begin to build anew.

Take care of yourself. You are a lifeline. We appreciate you and all you do, Bonnie.

Warmly,

Kathy

✳   ✳   ✳   ✳   ✳

Dear Bonnie,

Thank you so much. I am just getting to my e mails. I am on the computer all day at work, so it is the last thing I want to do at home. But I have this new internet...

I starting reading your newsletters last evening at 11 pm and still was not finished around 3 am. All that, and I have to get up at 6 am to go to work. My 14 year old son said both alarms on the clock radios went off. I slept right through them, and didn't get up until I heard him rushing out to the school bus. All this because I could not stop reading about much of what has been similar to my life story for the past 10 or so years, since my now ex-husband met "Joe". Many of the things I have wondered about over the years were in your newsletter, and it has made me come to a greater understanding of the situation, and the incredible emotional pain I have suffered, and the post traumatic stress I currently experience.

I have been divorced for 2 years now (was married for 22 years). I did not suspect he had a lover until 14 years into the marriage, and did not realize it was most likely a gay lover, his "best friend" (who had also been married with 2 children, and divorced) until I found IOU's to the tune of $6,000 over a 6 month period to this person, in addition to daily calls to this person from his cell phone. I resented this as I was leaving my home and children every day to go to work, and he was "loaning" his boyfriend approx $1,000 per month. The boyfriend is 9 plus years younger than the ex-husband. When I found the IOU's (copied them, and put them away for evidence and safekeeping) and confronted him, he threw one of my nice ceramic lamps on the floor, then jumped on it and smashed it. This was 2 and 1/2 years ago-the last straw- and the very next day I filed for divorce. I could write a book, and probably should, but I am still trying to survive, financially and emotionally.

My recommendation to those who contemplate leaving their gay spouses, is to get a safe deposit box and put cash in it, so that you never go hungry or go without gas for your car, etc, etc. I also recommend getting a PO BOX for your mail so that he doesn't get into your business. I got a separate checking account when the financial abuse and control started-etc about 11 years ago.

Also, get the best lawyer you can. Not necessarily the best family law attorney, but one who is ethical, honest, with a good reputation in the community-i.e. not one to just keep things churning to make the price go up. I got a recommendation from a mother of my son's friend who is an attorney. My attorney happened to be a former elected state attorney. I actually interviewed 3 and was especially comfortable with the one I chose.

I hope this helps.

D.

✳   ✳   ✳   ✳   ✳

Hi Bonnie,

I'm another one from an extremely dysfunctional but small family. My father is a pedophile. He swears he has never acted on it and only fantasizes (Yuch!) But he did try, for a period of time, to act on it when I was a budding adolescent. He later went on to tell me he could have nothing to do with me and my daughter when she was a budding adolescent because he was having fantasies about her. Wasn't that nice of him to share that with me?

When he started to try to get close to me I had thought that he finally loved me as his daughter. I was 13 and 14 and it was the early sixties and I was naïve, naïve but not without intuition.

He rejected me when I was a baby, toddler and in my childhood up until I started to bloom. So, when he started to want to talk to me warmly, I thought he was finally caring about me. However, it FELT creepy. That was the clue, how I felt. He was an alcoholic and when he was sober, a very backward person. He would come into my room at night after being out in a tavern all night and lean over me and talk with a creepy smile on his face. I didn't like it but I thought what if the creepy feeling is wrong and he really just cares about me? So, I let it go on. He didn't touch me or proposition me for quite a while. Later, he did and the very next day I told my mother I was moving to my grandmother's. She begged me to stay and that she would do something. Well, I had to be alone with him in the house every school day for three hours until she came home from work and it was a small house we lived in. I hated having to be alone with him. He never tried anything again, but it was awful having to be around him. Finally my mother divorced him and when he was gone it was like we just let out a giant sigh of such relief.

My mother, grandmother and my aunt have told me so many things he did to neglect and to hurt me. He slapped me when I was 2 and a half and made my eye bleed so badly it was squirting out blood.

My mother left me alone with him when I was very little when she went to church. Well, my father was in bed sleeping off his drunk from the night before and didn't bother with me at all; I had newspapers spread all over the apartment and every gas jet on the stove up full force. The house and he and I could have died.

Once I fell in the toilet, while my rather stupid mother left me with him, and he would not get out of bed to fish me out, my aunt had heard me from downstairs and came up and got me out.

When I was a baby my mother left me with him when she went to church and when she arrived home she said I was screaming at the top of my lungs and my crib and me were just sopping wet. She also so there was a big mess on the floor and the wall. I guess he tried to give me a bottle and I didn't want it so he just threw the glass bottle crashing against the wall and left me to scream and soak.

And he used to take me for car rides to a little lake near our home and sometimes to a forest preserve and we would just sit there. He never talked to me. Now, I wonder whether he was thinking of how he could maybe kill me or just leave me behind.

My mother was so wrapped up in her own misery alternated with her escaping the situation that I think she forgot that this might not be the best thing for me to have to live with my father. And this was the day and age of worrying about what the neighbors, family and the church would think, so she wanted to keep up "appearances", Oh God, I am so glad those days are gone.

The bottom line is since my father was sadistically rejecting and neglectful of me I worked at not having men rejected me all of my life until I married my gay husband. I was depressed when he bounded into my life and my home and maybe by that time by subconscious just told me I didn't deserve anything more than to marry a man who couldn't give me the love I needed.

My father also left the area right before my gay husband made way into my life. No one knew where my father went to. That to me was the ultimate rejection. Why? Because now I had been an adult for quite a while, he had gotten sober and was in AA for at least two decades and we were good conversation friends. (My father is also very intellectual, and aside from his mental illnesses, a very interesting person) So, now I took that as I was still a big nothing, he didn't even bother to tell me he was leaving and where he was going.

There are so many other things, but this is where I will end. You've gotten the picture by now.

I actively staved off being with a man of terrific dysfunction, but there were too many things that occurred within the same time frame that set me up to allow Jim to come into my life and just take it over for his own use.

My mother still doesn't understand, but by now I know she has herself wrapped in many layers of denial so that she won't experience any guilt...it would be just too traumatic for her, I suppose...she herself was molested repeated by her own alcoholic father before she was ten years old! And she never told a soul until she told me when she was in her mid forties! Her father and her silence and maybe a displaced sense of guilt as a child really screwed her up....this all really messed with her mind because she doesn't face realities the way most people do...she always pretties things up...and this just creates a fiction of the truth. She isn't a liar...she just changes nasty realities into niceties. Because she raised me...I used to do the same thing and didn't really realize this until I was in counseling in my early twenties. My cousin and I were like joined at the hip since I was born 8 months after her and she would make fun of me and my all-too-sunny outlook that was a clone of my mother's.

Life is a hell of a lot of work, isn't it Bonnie? I hope this helps.

Take care, and love to you and your readers,

Lynda

Bonnie,

In response to Di, the reader who wanted to know how and what to tell her children about her impending divorce...

I don't remember the names of the books I found, but there are plenty out there on how to tell children in an age appropriate manner. (Our children were 7, 6 and 3 years of age when we told them about the divorce.) Having found some of those books at the library, we used what we read and told them that we had been unhappy for a long time, we tried all we could to make it better, but it just wasn't going to work so we were going to divorce and daddy was moving out. We also reinforced that it had nothing to do with them and there was nothing they did or could do to change the situation. We also told them we still loved them and we would both be involved in their lives.

It was very confusing to them because we weren't arguing. They had no outward sign that there was a problem. (We got along pretty well, actually. But toward the end, we were walking on pins and needles around each other.) They didn't have many questions at all, other than 'why?' To that we repeated the same information and that seemed to appease them... for a while. They took the news pretty well. I think the truth of the moment was harder for us than it was for them because they didn't really understand what was happening. The oldest said "Yeah! We get a new dad!" (Which of course he didn't mean, but he was nervous) The middle child cried, but not for long. The youngest was clueless.

As with anything, this took years of reinforcement because it would pop up time and again. We had to continue to repeat the

52cbHB6mn

vague reasons we made the decision to divorce. When the older two were around 10 and 9, I began dating again. This caused them to kick up the volume about our divorce, and had them stretching to find a way to blame one of us (i.e. Me). I COULDN'T HAVE THAT. I couldn't have their incorrect assumptions damage their opinion of me as a mother, so I had to tell them the truth (because their dad wouldn't do it). By that time I felt they were ready for the truth. And, again, it was in an age-appropriate manner. Such as... Dad wants a boyfriend, not a girlfriend/wife. I won't share my husband with anyone else, etc. I never brought up the subject of sex or intimacy, and they never asked. Which is just as well, because the sex aspect or lack thereof was just a symptom of the problem anyway, and not the deal breaker.

Best of luck to Di and all others facing this situation.
Jill

✻   ✻   ✻   ✻   ✻

Dear Bonnie's Readers (and my personal sisters for life)

I want to share my story with all of you. Here I sit, one year after I discovered my 7 year marriage was over. I discovered my husband was Gay. He moved to Florida (in order to set up "our" new life) when in reality he was running from it. We bought a beautiful home on the Gulf, while I stayed behind (as usual) to "do" everything because I could.

I'm not sure if I was angry at finding out he was Gay, or the fact that he had no compassion for the hell he had created in my life (left behind). I had taken care of all of his needs during our entire relationship. That's what women do. We nurture, we enable (with a positive approach, not negative). I have no children, but I know what it feels like to be worried sick, sacrifice my own happiness and accommodate the needs of someone else, because I could and I wanted to.

Without going into the obvious (disbelief, anger, confusion, anguish, grief, acceptance and finally not giving two Shi***ts) I want you to know that I did come out of the most devastating period of my life. And anyone who is reading this should please believe that you can to. (I never did, while it was happening to me).

I left my business 24 months ago. For the first time, dependent on him! He couldn't just leave. He had to "take me down" with him. I never could understand that. Now I understand that it is because Gay men prey on anyone they think they can manipulate. Your misery is their pleasure. It "justifies" them somehow. ("Look at her…so pathetic and weak, she <u>deserves</u> this). Trust me their manipulation knows no bounds. If I sound harsh…replace yourself with your own daughter and re-think what I just said.

Gay men that steal straight woman from successful hetero relationships have no compassion. No acknowledgement. They will never admit that they wronged you because they are living a lie.

One year ago, I was living off my credit cards and crying my eyes out in a bottle of wine every night. Today, I am closing $2.5 million in business and the top "dog" in my Company. Today is my best day ever. Not because of the money…but because his "problem" didn't take me down with him. I would never have made this difficult journey were it not for discovering Bonnie. She doesn't even know me and she saved me. Reach out without shame and let your fears and suspicions become real. We can't hide the boogie-man. But we sure as heck can expose the liar without shame. Question: If your child came to you and said "Mommy, I'm afraid of this man because he doesn't make me feel happy or good about myself." Would you tell her to "hush" be a good girl?

Girlfriends (chicks) I send my love to each and every one of you. You must believe that you deserve more. It is not your fault. Take back your power and <u>know </u>that you will get past this nightmare. Anyone that doesn't believe you or support you…get rid of them! (And make it snappy). One day you will recognize (each in your own time) that YOU DIDN"T DO ANYTHING WRONG.

Kisses & Hugs, Roxanne

* * * * *

Hi Bonnie,

I just read the November newsletter and felt compelled to write. I am one of the fortunate ones. I did not grow up in a dysfunctional family. I grew up with both parents loving each other as God intended. They've been married 55 years now! My brothers and I knew our limits as kids and were loved unconditionally.

I did not know my ex was gay until we had been married 26 years. We, too, had a happy marriage with two beautiful children we reared in a Christian home. In reading Linda's letter from New Zealand, I know we each have to make our own choice about staying in the marriage based on our Christian convictions and walk with God. I am praying for the love she now shares with her new husband--how wonderful for her! One of the most hurtful things my ex said to me after we had been divorced and he was with his partner was "Now I know what true love is--now I know what I was REALLY supposed to feel when I was with you." It's been three years since my divorce--I too know the Lord has someone special planned for me!

Thanks for all you do--I only wish I had known this was there four years ago!

Lynn

✳   ✳   ✳   ✳   ✳

Dear Bonnie,

I don't know why I didn't reply to you last month, but here I am a month late!

It made me sad to see that if I were to place myself in any of the categories that gay man offered, I'd be in No. 2 - the not very attractive, practical earth mother type. (I've grown a lot over the years since, and am not just that person now, however)

In contrast to most of the other respondents, my family life was close to perfect. I had loving parents, who loved each other dearly all their lives (dying exactly a month apart), and who loved my 2 brothers and me, supporting us, though they struggled financially, in any endeavor we tried. I was blessed.

My husband, however, had an alcoholic father who was abusive to his wife and was often absent from the home because he was stuck in a pub somewhere. He also told my husband when he was quite young that he, my husband, was the greatest disappointment in his life because he didn't play football and cricket. As my husband grew older, he was often sent into pubs to get his father to come home, so until he was 19, he hated strong drink. (Unfortunately, he got to know and love it too well because he's now an alcoholic, too, though he's not violently abusive, as his father was. Sometimes, though, he can be very cutting and hurtful with his tongue as he is intellectual and clever with words.) His mother, behaved quite strangely too. She taught him to knit when he was 4 and used to sit him near the front gate so all the neighborhood women who passed by would see him and stop and say how cute and clever he was. As he grew older, she also taught him the things women usually teach only their daughters, like cooking and ironing - for which I'm very grateful, but at the time, it was unusual. She also had affairs with other men, which my husband, even very young, knew. There was lots of unhappiness in his life growing up!

I'm certain that he didn't know he was gay when we married. He discovered that (after a drunken encounter that apparently disgusted him at the time, but later became very appealing!) after 23 years of marriage. I realized that something had happened - and he told me that he was impotent, so I tried to believe and accept that, but was always suspicious. And as years went on and I'd try and confront him with my suspicions, he'd always deny that he was gay, so I kept trying to believe that. I guess I wanted to because the alternative was terrible for my self esteem. Anyway, he outed himself 35 years into the marriage and pleaded with me to stay with him because he had always loved me and still did. He said that the only reason he stopped having sex with me was that he felt so guilty, but he still felt desire for me.

Well, I stayed, believing in miracles - and because of family reasons - elderly parents who adored him and me etc.etc. but I don't need to say more. I've read so many letters from all those women in your newsletters and the experience was the same - the honeymoon period eventually faded!

I'm still in the marriage, but wonder what would happen if I won the lottery! Stupid thing is I do love him and I know he loves me, but as you know, not the way married couples should love each other - in every way, emotionally and physically!

Anyway, this was a long letter. I didn't mean to tell so much of my story, but thought that the context of both of our families might be of interest to you.

Thank you for being there for us all.

Joan

*   *   *   *   *

Dear Bonnie,

I received your newsletter today and enjoy reading it and finding out I'm not the only one out there that has suffered. However, you may have heard different stories like mine, but I think the reason I was so confused about my gay marriage if that my gay husband did not fit the description of the most common facts. There are certainly similarities, but I see my case more confusing. My husband will NEVER admit to his gayety, and I will never have closure.

I just thought it might be helpful to describe my circumstances that differ. I don't see my family life as being abusive at all. I had two wonderful parents and a life that was fairly normal with no physical or verbal abuse. I met my husband in college and he was a member of a
popular fraternity and really showed no obvious characteristics of being gay. I had no idea.

We married and had a wonderful 7 years. We have two daughters. Although I was the instigator of sex most of the time, my husband was very determined that I enjoy sex and always did what was satisfying to me. Of course, now I realize that his sex drive wasn't up to mine at all, but he was very caring and considerate.

He was an excellent daddy to the girls and they loved him dearly. It wasn't until my second daughter was born that I realized he wasn't affectionate at all anymore. He blamed it on me taking care of the baby and he was busy taking care of our older daughter. For years after that I cried not understanding what was wrong with our marriage. He was getting more and unhappy with his job and I knew he had a terrible new boss and things were bad. I blamed our problems on his unhappiness and the fact that he was so depressed.

He transferred to a large city and told me later that he hated the city and so would I and that it would be better to live separate and keep the girls in a nice size city with good schools. I was stupid and lived like this for over 15 years.

I cried for about 4 years wanting my family back until I realized that I could get a divorce or deal with it. Neither one of us wanted a divorce. I got to the point I didn't care if he came home on weekends or not. He would only come ever 3-4 weeks or so. I guess I became numb and dealt with it. I had my own life with my kids. I had a house, yard, full time job, and two kids to raise and no time to think about anything.

I found out quite by accident that the man he was living with was gay and that he knew him before he moved away. We were never allowed to go see him (he wanted to come home and do yard work etc.) But this was still so confusing because when a job here came along, he applied for it and kept trying to get back home....or so I thought.

Then, he retired from his job and remained in the big city with his FRIENDS. I have been divorced over two years and I am happy. I really don't feel like dating and am happy with things they way they are. I guess maybe I have been alone for so long, that I prefer it. I do feel for him and what he went through, but at the same time I blame him for many things. I dislike him for getting married and doing this to his children. My daughters have suffered so much and I wasn't even aware of it.

I hope this isn't too long, but I was fooled for many years and as I said before, he does not want to discuss anything and he will never admit to being gay.

Sally

✳   ✳   ✳   ✳   ✳

I would like to end this book with a letter I received from a new support group member, Estelle, in August 2008. Her letter articulates the emotions that so many of us feel while living in this state of confusion. Please read her heart-felt words:

Dear Bonnie and Support Network Members,

I was married to a homosexual man, who I divorced 20 years ago. At the time that I divorced him, I was doing so after feeling *suffocated* for years in the relationship. Also during this time, and for years afterwards, I was so "coated" over by the lies of this man, that in my mind, I did not think he was homosexual. And even though, my body, my *instinct*, knew that something was "off" in the area of sex with this man, my mind was "convinced" that the problem just had to do with him being "different." I know now that he wanted so badly to be "normal" that he did a pretty good job at "convincing" himself as well, and using me as his "wife," was the ultimate "proof" that he so desperately desired. It wasn't until after having sex with straight men that I instinctually realized, that this man, who I had "mismarried" was indeed **homosexual**. I never had any proof of this, since proof was no longer possible. I was already divorced, and hadn't seen him in years. So as a result, even though my "gut" knew the truth, for many years, my mind has struggled with doubt about it. This is the story of the battle between my mind and my instinct, and how my instinct won.

I met, my homosexual ex-"husband" Kai in college, when I was 21 years old and he was 22. I use quotes around the word '*husband*', because he never *felt* like that to me. I had him in several of my Spanish classes, and he stood out to me, because he was outwardly very intelligent, charming, physically attractive, and also spoke Spanish extremely well, for a "white boy!" My background is Mexican-American, so this was very "impressive*"* at the time. In any case, we both noticed one another, and starting studying together.

I remember we once asked each other what it was that first attracted us to each other. I told him, being the healthy, heterosexual woman that I was, that it was his "chest," because he used to wear these very tight, low-cut shirts. He told me that it was the "sincerity of my eyes." Now while at the time, I did appreciate the "depth" of this answer, looking back on it now, I see it as the first of many "red flags" to come.

After a few of these study sessions, Kai asked me out on a date. This date led to a whirlwind "romance", where he bought me all sorts of **too** expensive gifts, and was even so "inspired" by his "love" for me, that he wrote me poetry. And by the way, all of the gifts were paid for by his **mother**/parents. He was an only child, and had *carte blanche* privileges on their credit cards. Now, I had come from a Latin-Catholic background, and had led a pretty sheltered life up until this point. So while I was flattered by all of this attention, there was also a part of me that was uncomfortable with it. And what felt uncomfortable to me, even back then, was that he seemed a bit *too eager* to "win" me over. Just the same, because I was flattered by it all, I overlooked this *discomfort.*

It wasn't until years later that I realized, what was behind all of this *eagerness* to "win" me over. As I would find out with time, Kai was an extremely controlling, manipulative person, who needed to dominate and control every aspect of me, for reasons that would come to "light" years later. And so it was this need to *dominate* me that led to him working so hard to "reel me in", so to speak. I remember the first time that "I" told him that "I loved him". I did it **not** because it flowed out of my **own** heart, but because **he** had told me that he "loved" me, and pressured me to do the same. He did this by telling me, that if I could not, it was the sign of some "inadequacy" on my part. And since I already had such low self-esteem, and didn't want to be "more inadequate", I fell for it.

So we went on to become a "couple". And even though Kai had pressured me into telling him that I loved him, later on, I truly did feel that I did. Because at the time, I had never met any man with the type of "sensitivity" that I saw in him . . . a sensitivity that matched my own. This made me feel, "safe," because now, I not only had a "boyfriend", but **more importantly** a "best friend," as well. I realized years ago, that I was also very much **hiding** from life, although not for the **same** reasons.

As I said before, I had led a very sheltered life up to this point. So when I met him, I was still a virgin. So for the first six months of our courtship, we only kissed and had oral sex, which Kai didn't seem to mind in the least. In any case, it was during this 6-month period, that I first witnessed a very abusive side to him. I had noticed it before, but in a more general and *subtle* way, in the very arrogant, pompous and condescending way Kai would deal with me, and with the world in general, whenever he felt it didn't meet up to his "expectations." This was very different, though, because it was during one of our "petting" sessions when out of nowhere, it seemed he became completely **enraged** at me. This happened because apparently I wasn't giving him oral sex in precisely the way he needed it in order to feel satisfied. He became so enraged that he actually got up from the bed and slammed his fist into a mirror, shattering the mirror to pieces. I remember being so confused and scared by this. But even in this confusion, I knew in my "gut" that there was something "very wrong with this picture." Something so wrong, that a voice inside me said, "Get the hell out of here now," meaning out of the relationship.

But I was just so confused, that I became kind of "paralyzed" and didn't listen to that *inner voice*. And so I ended up staying instead. After awhile he ended up calming down. But he never apologized for the outburst. Instead, he justified it, making me think that it was somehow my "fault." Still I never quite understood what I had done "wrong." I know now, that I had done **nothing** wrong. Just that I was the **wrong sex**.

Even though my gay ex-"husband", Kai, never physically hit me, ever since the outburst, I was always intimidated by his potential for violent anger. So the abuse continued, strictly in the psychological, emotional sense, with him always finding a way to make me feel his "superiority" and my "inadequacy." Still, what kept me in the relationship was the fact that when he was not being emotionally and psychologically abusive, he was, if you can believe it, a very "fun-loving" and "playful" person. Also, I still considered him to be my "best friend." And so it was that all of these "positive" factors were enough of a *distraction* to keep me in the relationship. So this is what I focused on and not so much the abuse, because of the **low self-esteem** that I had. At the age of 52, I am still working on this, but I am much better!

After being in the relationship with "Gay Kai" for 6 months, I had actual sexual intercourse with him. I remember being in bed together, lying side-by-side, and straight as mummies. I was completely naked, but he was not. He didn't have on *underpants*, but insisted on keeping on his *tee shirt* and *socks*. (Real "sexy", right? A "red-flag" for sure!) In any case, what made me even more nervous than I already was, was that even though he was not a virgin, he seemed more anxious than I was. He was not making any moves, and because I didn't know what moves to make, I didn't either. Finally, after an extended silence, he turns to me and asks, in this *whiney*, *little-boy* voice, "*Do you want to have sex with me?*" And by the way, this same *little-boy* voice was the way he would initiate sex, the few times that he did, in the future. Of course, I did not realize this at the time, but I know now, that he was so insecure about himself and his sexuality, and the fact that he was really **not** "that into me," that he felt the need to *manipulate* his way in. And it was this manipulation, intended to provoke *sympathy* that served as a *distraction* from the **real** problem.

So I felt "sorry" for him and told him that I did. Also, I did not want to *anger* him. I thought at the time besides wanting to "appease" him that I really did want to have sex with him. But I realize now that it wasn't so much that I wanted to have sex with *him*--it was just that I wanted to experience sex. Still, my body *sensed*, even back then, the complete **absence** of male/female *chemistry* in him.

So we had sex. And as one might imagine, it was truly, one of the most boring and **enervating** experiences I have ever had. And this **never** changed over time. During sex, and pardon my explicitness here, I always felt like I was just a "trash can" for him to ejaculate into. And after sex, I always felt like a washcloth, that had been completely used, wrung out and left out to dry. I had absolutely no energy left in my body, and could have stayed in bed, to "sleep it off" for days, had I not had a job to go to.   This was in vast comparison to the limitless energy I would feel after having sex with a truly heterosexual man!

Another thing that I noticed is that when it came to Kai having an orgasm, it always seemed so *laborious* for him. Again this was in vast comparison to the straight lovers that I would later have where the *labor* came from **prolonging** the time it took to have an orgasm and not from **trying** to have one. Also with my homosexual ex, there was **never** any foreplay, kissing, or caressing during sex.   Still, since he was my first, I never knew any of these things to be physically **missing**.   Just the same, I know now, that I instinctually knew that something was missing. Because I remembered how as a little girl, I always had these "fantasies" about the **beauty** and **passion** of sexual union between a man and a woman.   Just the same, after the "physical proof" of sex with him, I convinced myself, that these were indeed **only** the "fantasies" of a little girl.

It was not long after this first sexual experience, that I got one of the biggest **clues** I would ever get as to Kai's **true** sexual orientation. And it was this **clue** that would later help me put the "pieces of the puzzle" together regarding the **true** problem with this **mis**marriage. One day, when we had just finished having "sex", he turned around and asked me, "Do *you* think *I* am **homosexual**?"   Needless to say, I was *taken for a loop* with this question.   After all, he was my first sexual experience, and I didn't exactly have anything else to compare him to.   In any case, and justifiably so, I was very confused and scared by this new "turn of events".   So I just answered that I didn't think he was, and that he was just "different", due to his "sensitivity" blah, blah, blah.

Okay, I knew something was wrong, but I didn't want to believe it was that he was homosexual. After all, I had given my virginity to this guy. And at the time, I had definite stereotypes of what homosexual men were like. I was very *uninformed*. So when I answered him, I really did believe my answer, because I had to, because I needed to.

Now, although one might "applaud" him at this point for his attempt at honesty, I have come to realize that it was really not so much an attempt at honesty on his part. But more to the fact that on some level, he *knew*, that because of my lack of experience and "malleability", I would not be able to give him an accurate answer. And so it was this "answer", that provided even more of a "security blanket" for him to hide behind, along with having me in his life. And this still "pisses" me off, more than I can say.

So after receiving the answer that he *knew* on some level he would get, he was of course, "heartened", and said to me, "Yeah, I couldn't have done what I just did, if I was . . .", meaning he had been able to have an orgasm. It's pretty funny to me now! But at the time, I believed it . . . sort of. So we went on as a "couple", and not long after this, we became engaged. And by the way, his **mother**/parents **also** paid for the engagement/wedding rings. And of course, because according to him, "it wasn't *fair* that *just the woman* should get an engagement ring," he also ended up getting **his own** engagement ring. In any case, I knew even back then, that it wasn't so much a matter of "fairness" for him, but more a feeling of "*safety,*" "*protection,*" and *acceptance* that he so desperately craved from the world. But because I was as deep in the closet as he was, I accepted his reasoning, wanting to be as "open-minded" as possible.

Over the period of our engagement, which was a total of 4 years, the sex started to become more and more infrequent, almost to the point of non-existent. And it was also during this time that he decided he wanted to go into therapy. Not because of the infrequency of the sex, but just to "learn more about himself." He "suggested" that I do the same. At some point, during this time, I remember mentioning to Kai that our sex seemed "too infrequent." Even though I was bored with it, I never admitted this to myself at the time. Just the same, I *sensed* that its infrequency was a *sign* of something being *off.*

When I mentioned this to him, he registered complete "non-concern" about it. Instead, he rationalized that it was "my problem," having to do with "unrealistic expectations" that I had, based on "stereotypes." He was pompously "intellectual," and could use the "talents of his tongue" to talk anybody "into a corner." Also, he *fancied* himself as being very "unconventional" and "open-minded." He couldn't have been farther from the truth.

Later, when the male therapist, that incidentally, Kai picked out for the both of us, "confirmed" Kai's theory about my "unrealistic expectations," I thought that they were both right, and I was the one that was "off", yet again. So basically, I just gave up any "expectations" about the frequency of sex. Also, I remember learning quite early on, that I could never be the one to suggest sex, because whenever I did, he would never want to do it. It was only when he happened to get an erection--that seemed to make him a little bit "too happy"-- that we ever did it. And when we did have sex, Kai had to **control** every aspect of it--what position, when, and how we would move, etc. I also learned to **never try suggesting** anything **myself** during sex, because the one time that I did, he again became totally **enraged** at me. Enraged like the last time, only this time he didn't break anything . . . just my "spirit."

I remember how scared and vulnerable I felt, with him "inside" me, and this rage, penetrating me like some poison. Anyway, needless to say, I never wanted to go there again. And so I didn't. I didn't ever ask for sex, nor did I *suggest*. I just gave up on it. And so the sex became practically non-existent. And this was all in the five years *before* we were "married", with us still only in our 20's.

During the course of my relationship with Kai, another thing that I noticed was that he had very few male friends. And with the few male friends that he did have (I could count them on one hand literally), two of them being very sweet, openly gay men. I would always notice a certain *giddiness* and excitement that would come over him whenever they would call or he would socialize with them. I remember feeling it as the "*excitement* of a young girl," wanting to be called or spend time with a boy that she "liked"; an excitement that felt like a *physical attraction*. This felt *foreign* to me, because I knew that this feeling never existed in our relationship.

He **never** took **any** *notice* of me physically. Except for the time he actually began a *heated* discussion with me at a Burger King about the fact that he was "physically *prettier*" than I was . . . and he was actually being *serious*. And the time that he told me that I had legs that looked like "tree trunks." Again, he was *serious* here, but also thought he was being "cute." Still, for me, it was *anything but*. In any case, I remember quite distinctly *noticing* his *giddiness* with men, but like everything else, I ended up *pushing it back* "into the closet."

I know I have been painting a pretty bad picture of Kai, and with good reason. But as with everything, he did also have a "good" side. He did have *some* "sensitivity" in his heart; otherwise, there would have been nothing for me to be inwardly attracted to initially. In any case, about a year after we got married, he had the opportunity to join an *ashram*. It was not a "live-in ashram"; it was one in which you attended weekly seminars. So he joined up, and soon after, so did I, as I had always been the "spiritual type".

It was soon after this that the sex pretty much ended altogether because now he had the *excuse* of his "self-discovery" where celibacy is encouraged at different periods of time. And since I never liked sex with him anyway, this was fine with me. I didn't realize it back then, but I see now, how much he used his "spirituality" as another place to hide behind, in order not to have to deal with, his lack of interest, in sex with women. It was just another very convenient "cover" like I was for him not to have to think about his true **preference** for **men**. Still, because I was so happy in the ashram, and being "let off the hook" from the draining sex with him, I went along with it.

So now, we could both be "happy" in being **only** "best friends," and now "spiritual buddies." I remember thinking once, during a meditation session, how much fun meditation was, and "who needed sex anyway." Well, I found out later, just how **important** sex is, especially in the course of self-discovery.

After 6 years of "marriage", 5 of those in the ashram, I finally got up the courage to leave the relationship, tired of feeling *suffocated*. I didn't realize it at the time, but now, years later, I realize that it was the *core* of my being, my **femininity**, that was being *suffocated*. And even though I consider myself to be a very compassionate person, the suppression of this most **precious** part of me, my **femininity**, is something that I will **never** be able to **forgive** or **forget** . . . especially, when there is no recognition on Kai's end for what he did.

In any case, I ended up initiating the divorce, and because we were still "best friends," it was amicable enough. Even so, when I did mention divorce, I will never forget how he *"wimpishly"* protested, saying, "I don't know how you can just throw your *'husband'* out like the *trash."* This made me laugh inside, intuitively thinking, "*Husband* . . . you were **never** that to me." But I was kind to him because of course, we were still "friends," and so I felt the need to "appease" him. Soon after, I *alone* completed the process of our divorce. And because I was still **so deeply in the closet with him**, I thought that I was just divorcing him because I needed to end a "suffocating" friendship with a man who was just "different" and more "spiritually" inclined than most.

Interestingly enough, even though I was not able to see the "obvious" back then, others could. When I told my father about the divorce, he came right out and asked me if it was because Kai was *homosexual*. And of course, because of the closet that I was in, I thought my father's question "ridiculous." I remember even telling my gay "friend" Kai about this and *chuckling* about it *together.* That is how "linked" we were together "in the closet." I wish now, that I could apologize to my father for this, but I cannot, since he passed away one year ago.

Years later, after opening my eyes to the truth, other family members and friends, told me that they too, had always sensed that he was homosexual, though they dared not say anything, because they knew I would have to figure it out for myself. And I know they were right.

It was not until 7 years after my divorce that I had my first **real** sexual experience with a **truly** heterosexual man. It was so **beautiful** and **ecstatic**! Never in my life, had I ever experienced anything so powerful! And it was so much like the "fantasies" I had as a little girl! And by the way, it was with another man *from the ashram*, so the "theory" of my homosexual ex-husband, just being "more spiritually inclined" than other men, really flew out the window! As you might expect, it was during my affair with this man that I started to suspect that my ex, Kai, had been homosexual. And as the years progressed, and I had other affairs with straight men, I became more and more convinced because now, I had something to compare him to. At one point, I got extremely angry. And by the way, even 20 years later, I am **still** extremely **angry**.

So I decided to confront him with my anger, by writing him a letter. And over the years, I wrote him two more letters, detailing all of my realizations, **holding nothing back**. And even though, he never replied to any of them, I always *felt* his "replies" intuitively, which were always filled with **much** anxiety, and at times, anger. Whenever I would feel him angry, I would also feel him justifying it all by the "fact" that I was now "just a very *off and* aging woman." Just the same, I wanted closure to it all, but realized that he was **still** so deeply "in the closet," especially with himself, that I would probably never get the closure from *him* that I so desperately desired.

So after all of this, even though I knew in my heart that Kai was/is **homosexual**, my mind still continued to play "tricks" on me, making me doubt what I instinctually knew. I have realized since then, that this was due to the fact that he had done an extremely good number on me, *psychologically* "closeting" me just as deeply as he was. And since I never had any *proof*, and was probably never going to get any

(20 years since my divorce and seeing him), I realized that I was going to have to get out of this *psychological* "closet" for myself. In any case, after reading all of the stories, and seeing all of the similarities that I had to all of the beautiful women in Bonnie's network, I realized that I needed to "spill" my story and my doubts, in order to see the fallacy of them, and get myself out of this ***psychological closet***.

So here are those doubts, and the reasons why I now know them to be complete fallacies. The first doubt had to do oral sex. I thought because he could perform oral sex on me, the **few** times that he did, without getting "grossed out," it *might* mean that he was *heterosexual*. I realize now though that a homosexual man can **learn to do anything** in the way of sex if he wants to hide his preference for the male sex badly enough. Because it matters not what the gay man is doing outwardly; what matters, is where he *travels* to in the *privacy* of *his own mind*.

The second and last doubt, had to do with the fact that during the "peak" of our "sex" lives, he needed to watch "hetero porn" in order to get excited enough to have sex with me. Again, I used to think, that because it was "hetero" porn, he "*might* be heterosexual". But I realize now that I always *sensed* that he was not excited by, nor was he focusing on the women when we watched it (because he needed me to watch it with him). He was excited by the men and their penises. I know, because I *felt* it at the time, though, again, I *shoved* it away "in the closet." I have also realized that he needed to watch "hetero porn" with me because he could not bring himself to participate in the *foreplay* necessary, to get me "in the mood." "Hetero" porn was *his* foreplay with the men in the video and also mine. And if all of this wasn't enough . . . Phew!

Then again, I have had 20 years to think about it! I realized that he was "excited" by the *subjugation* and *denigration* of women, because he deeply resented them for not being able to excite him the way that they were "supposed" to. He had so **much hostility** for women, due to this fact, that their *subjugation* "excited" him. This **sickens** me to no end, and at times, I feel "shame" for not having seen this sooner.

In any case, as long as I am writing about "porn" and dispelling all doubt about **Kai's homosexuality**, I feel the need to mention that once while watching "hetero porn" with him, he just "happened to mention" that we might rent some "gay porn just for the hoot of it." But I told him that I was not interested. I know now, that his mentioning this was **no** coincidence. I also remember that it was **not** a coincidence about the time that he took me to check out a gay beach "just for the hoot of it." Nor were all of the times a "coincidence" that he just *had to* take me along for his clothes shopping to exclusively gay men clothing stores where he did the **majority** of his shopping, for fear of the gay men "trying to pick up on him." Funny, but for a guy so *fearful* of being "picked up," he was sure *giddy*, "chatting it up" with all of the gay men sales personnel.

I know now, that with me by his side, acting as his "security blanket" he now, had no reason to *"fear"* Glad to be of "service"--NOT.

In conclusion, because it has been so many years since my divorce, and I never had any concrete *proof* of Kai's homosexuality, it has been my battle to learn to **trust** my intuition. I can now see though, with more clarity than ever, that this intuition is truly a **gift**, a **power**, that we all have as women; a power that we **must all learn to use** to its' fullest potential, in order for us to **free ourselves** and learn to love ourselves, in the ways that we truly deserve. My meditation teacher once told me, "Where there is *light*, there is *truth*." And so I know that with the *light* of my intuition, I will learn to live in *truth*.

It is with this knowledge that I am also learning to accept more and more that I will **never** have the physical "proof" I still so strongly desire. Just the same, since reading all of the stories from the beautiful women of Bonnie's network, I realize, that my *feminine* **instinct** is the **greatest**, and most blessed "proof" I will ever need.

With sincere gratitude and love, I extend my heartfelt thanks to Bonnie, and **all** the **truly beautiful** women of the support group. You will **always** have my true love and support,

Estelle

About the Author

Bonnie Kaye, M. Ed., author of *Bonnie Kaye's Straight Talk*, is internationally recognized as a counseling expert in the field of straight/gay marriages. Since 1984, she has counseled over 35,000 women who discovered their husbands are gay. She has also worked with hundreds of gay men helping them to come out to their wives.

Kaye began her counseling after the demise of her own painful marriage to a gay man in 1982. Her books, support groups, and monthly newsletters have helped these women understand the dynamics of marriage to a gay man. Kaye's website at **www.Gayhusbands.com** offers information to get people connected.

Kaye received her Masters Degree in Counseling from Antioch University in 1986. She has appeared on international, national, and local television and radio to explain how this phenomenon happens and the damage it does to a marriage. She also consults for major national television talk shows and news shows about this subject. Kaye runs an online support group three times weekly to lend support to women during and after their marriages.

Kaye's other books include: *Doomed Grooms: Gay Husbands of Straight Wives; ManReaders: A Woman's Guide to Dysfunctional Men; Straight Wives: Shattered Lives;* and *How I Made My Husband Gay: Myths About Straight Wives.* **The Gay Husband Checklist for Women Who Wonder** is an updated version of her first book previously titled *Is He Straight? A Checklist for Women Who Wonder.*

Bonnie Kaye can be reached at **Bonkaye@aol.com**. She is available for private counseling sessions by telephone or email.